TEENAGE MUTANT NINJA TURTLES

LEATHERHEAD

VOLUME 15

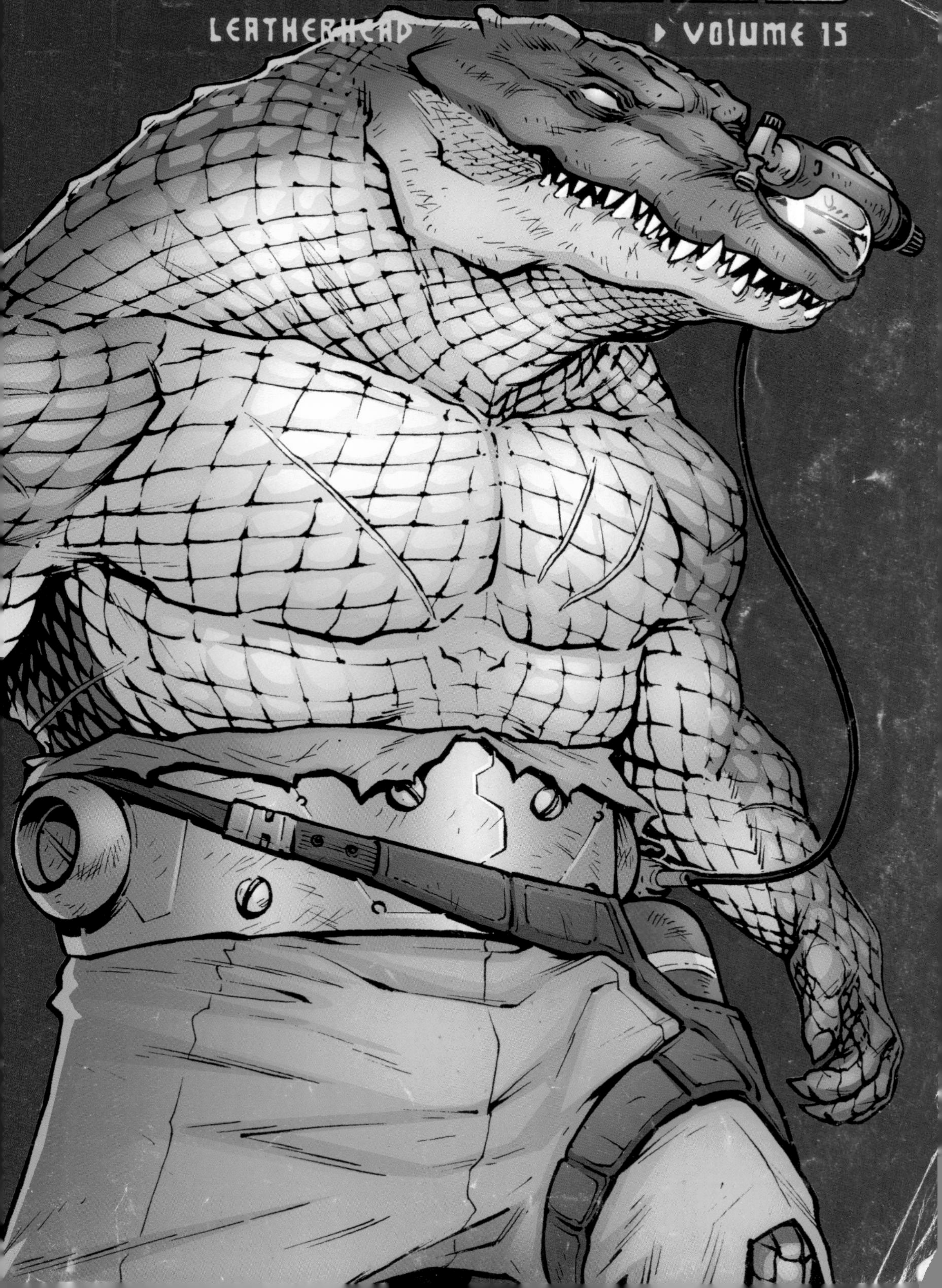

Special thanks to Joan Hilty and Linda Lee for their invaluable assistance.

For international rights, contact **licensing@idwpublishing.com**

ISBN: 978-1-63140-746-8

19 18 17 16   1 2 3 4

Ted Adams, CEO & Publisher
Greg Goldstein, President & COO
Robbie Robbins, EVP/Sr. Graphic Artist
Chris Ryall, Chief Creative Officer/Editor-in-Chief
Laurie Windrow, Senior Vice President of Sales & Marketing
Matthew Ruzicka, CPA, Chief Financial Officer
Dirk Wood, VP of Marketing
Lorelei Bunjes, VP of Digital Services
Jeff Webber, VP of Licensing, Digital and Subsidiary Rights
Jerry Bennington, VP of New Product Development

www.IDWPUBLISHING.com

Facebook: **facebook.com/idwpublishing**
Twitter: **@idwpublishing**
YouTube: **youtube.com/idwpublishing**
Tumblr: **tumblr.idwpublishing.com**
Instagram: **instagram.com/idwpublishing**

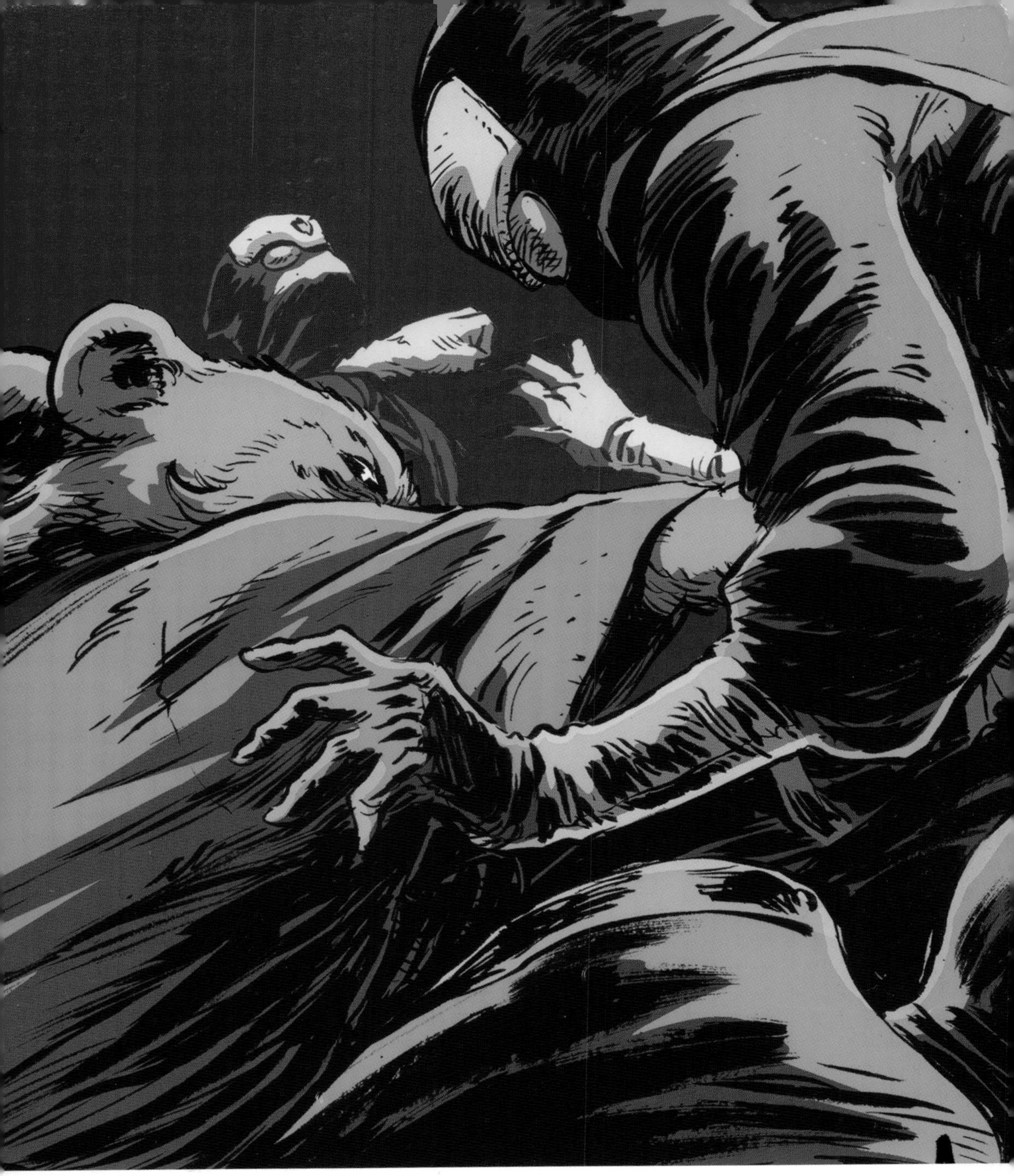

Story by Kevin Eastman, Bobby Curnow, and Tom Waltz

Script by Tom Waltz Art by Mateus Santolouco and Dave Wachter

Colors by Ronda Pattison Letters by Shawn Lee Series Edits by Bobby Curnow

Cover by Mateus Santolouco

Collection Edits by Justin Eisinger & Alonzo Simon

Production by Gilberto Lazcano

Publisher Ted Adams

Based on characters created by Peter Laird and Kevin Eastman

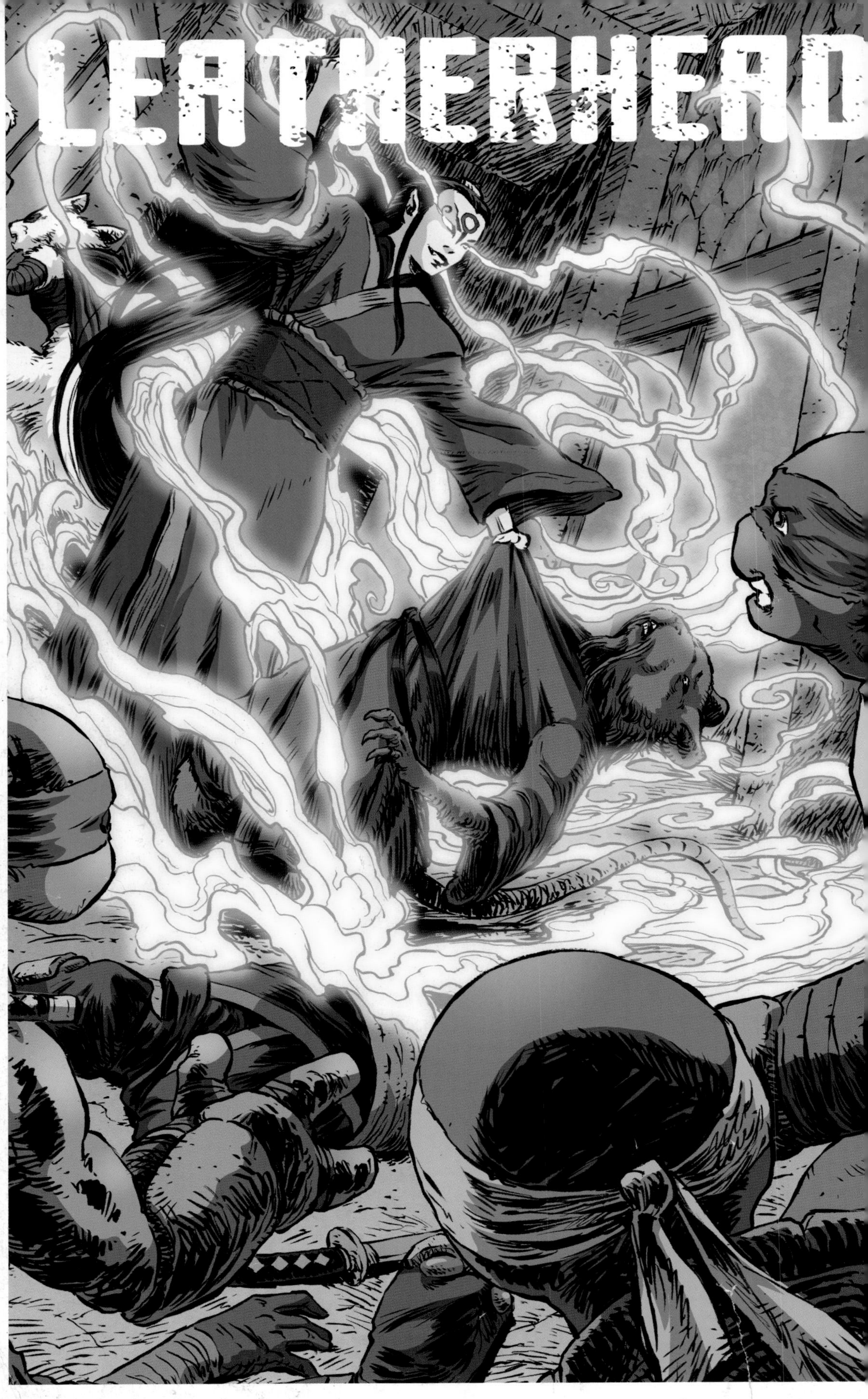
LEATHERHEAD

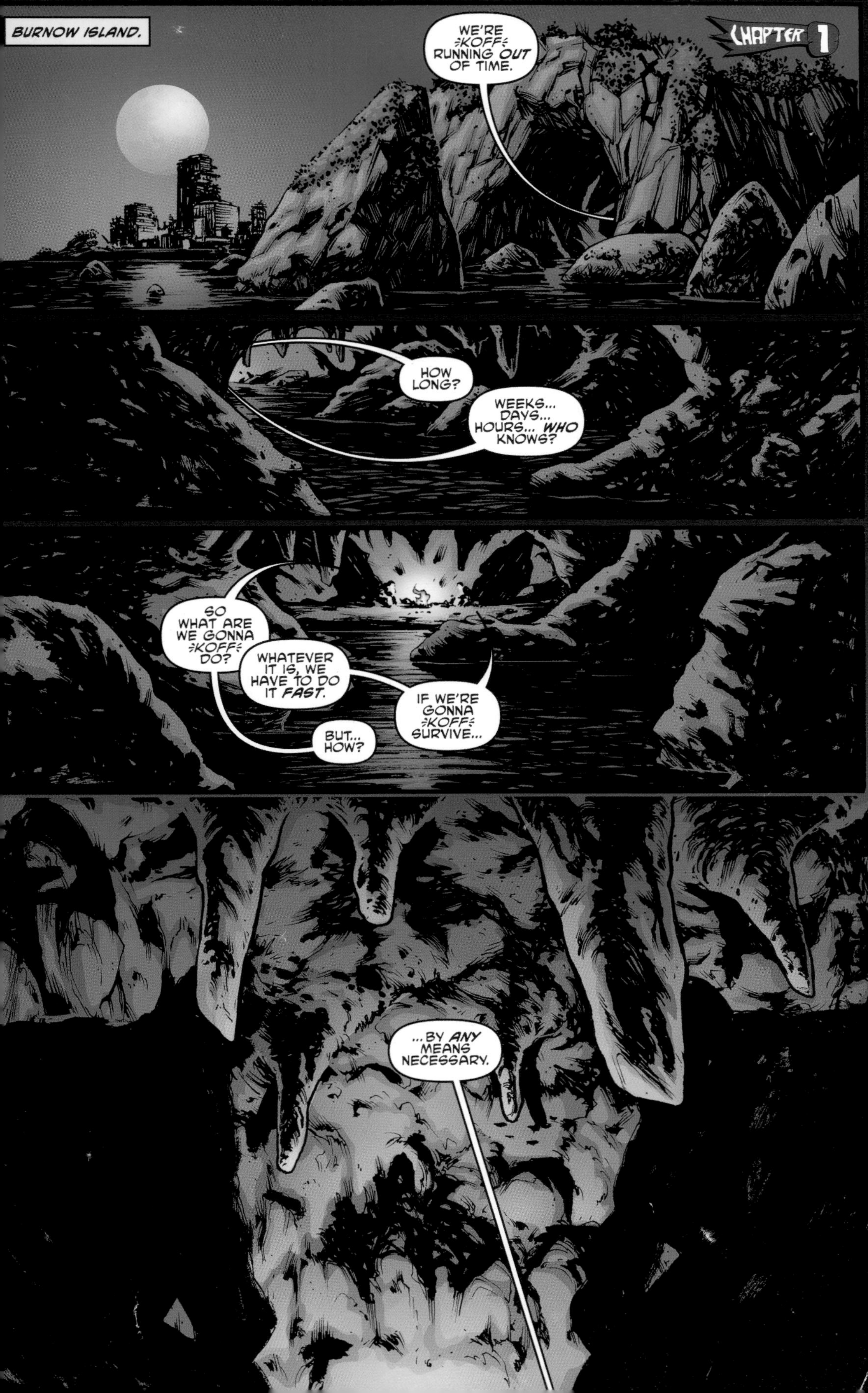
BURNOW ISLAND.
CHAPTER 1
WE'RE *KOFF* RUNNING OUT OF TIME.
HOW LONG?
WEEKS... DAYS... HOURS... WHO KNOWS?
SO WHAT ARE WE GONNA *KOFF* DO?
WHATEVER IT IS, WE HAVE TO DO IT FAST.
IF WE'RE GONNA *KOFF* SURVIVE...
BUT... HOW?
...BY ANY MEANS NECESSARY.

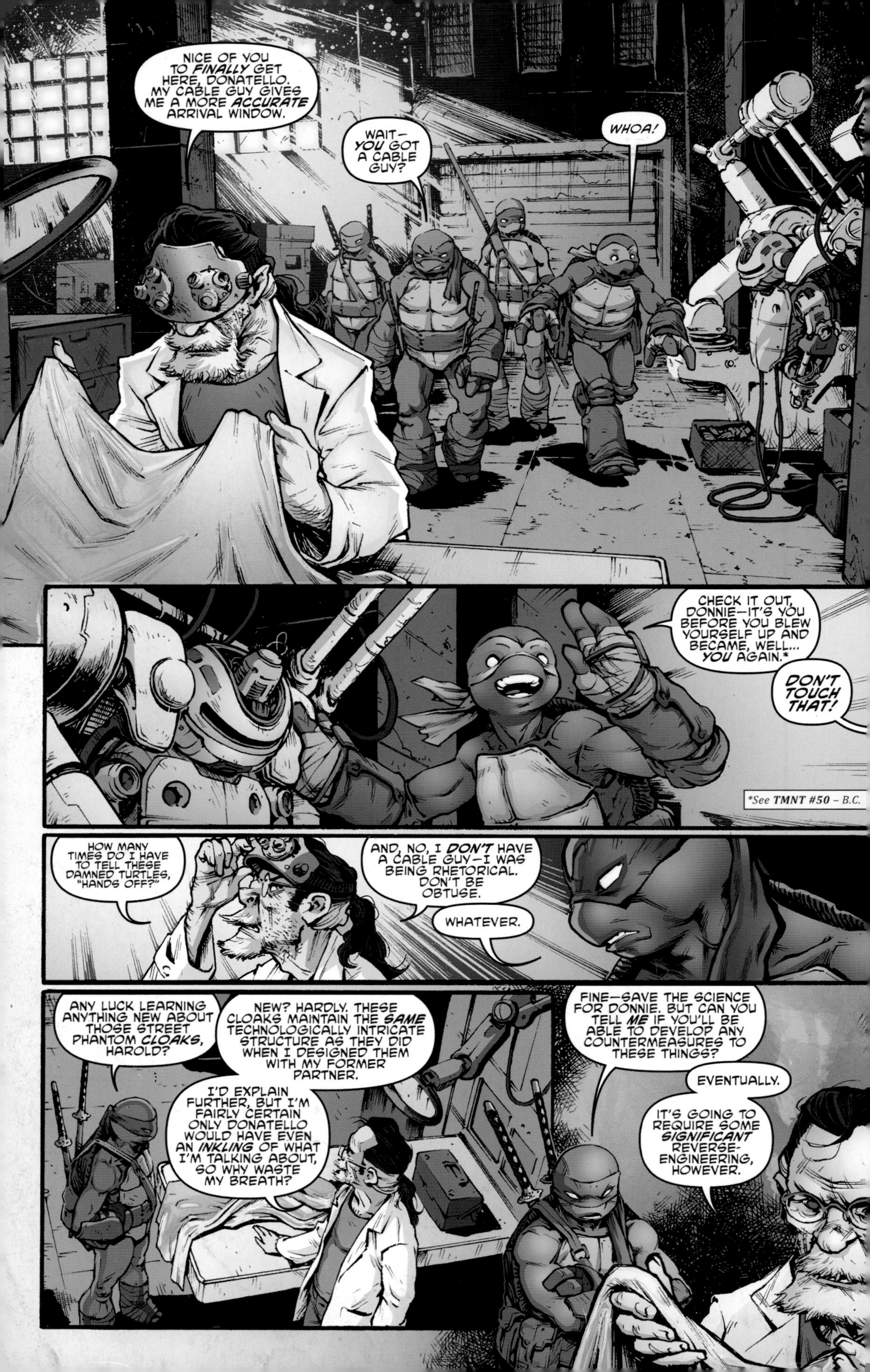
NICE OF YOU TO FINALLY GET HERE, DONATELLO. MY CABLE GUY GIVES ME A MORE ACCURATE ARRIVAL WINDOW.
WAIT— YOU GOT A CABLE GUY?
WHOA!
CHECK IT OUT, DONNIE—IT'S YOU BEFORE YOU BLEW YOURSELF UP AND BECAME, WELL... YOU AGAIN.*
DON'T TOUCH THAT!
*See TMNT #50 – B.C.
HOW MANY TIMES DO I HAVE TO TELL THESE DAMNED TURTLES, "HANDS OFF?"
AND, NO, I DON'T HAVE A CABLE GUY—I WAS BEING RHETORICAL. DON'T BE OBTUSE.
WHATEVER.
ANY LUCK LEARNING ANYTHING NEW ABOUT THOSE STREET PHANTOM CLOAKS, HAROLD?
NEW? HARDLY. THESE CLOAKS MAINTAIN THE SAME TECHNOLOGICALLY INTRICATE STRUCTURE AS THEY DID WHEN I DESIGNED THEM WITH MY FORMER PARTNER.
I'D EXPLAIN FURTHER, BUT I'M FAIRLY CERTAIN ONLY DONATELLO WOULD HAVE EVEN AN INKLING OF WHAT I'M TALKING ABOUT, SO WHY WASTE MY BREATH?
FINE—SAVE THE SCIENCE FOR DONNIE. BUT CAN YOU TELL ME IF YOU'LL BE ABLE TO DEVELOP ANY COUNTERMEASURES TO THESE THINGS?
EVENTUALLY.
IT'S GOING TO REQUIRE SOME SIGNIFICANT REVERSE-ENGINEERING, HOWEVER.

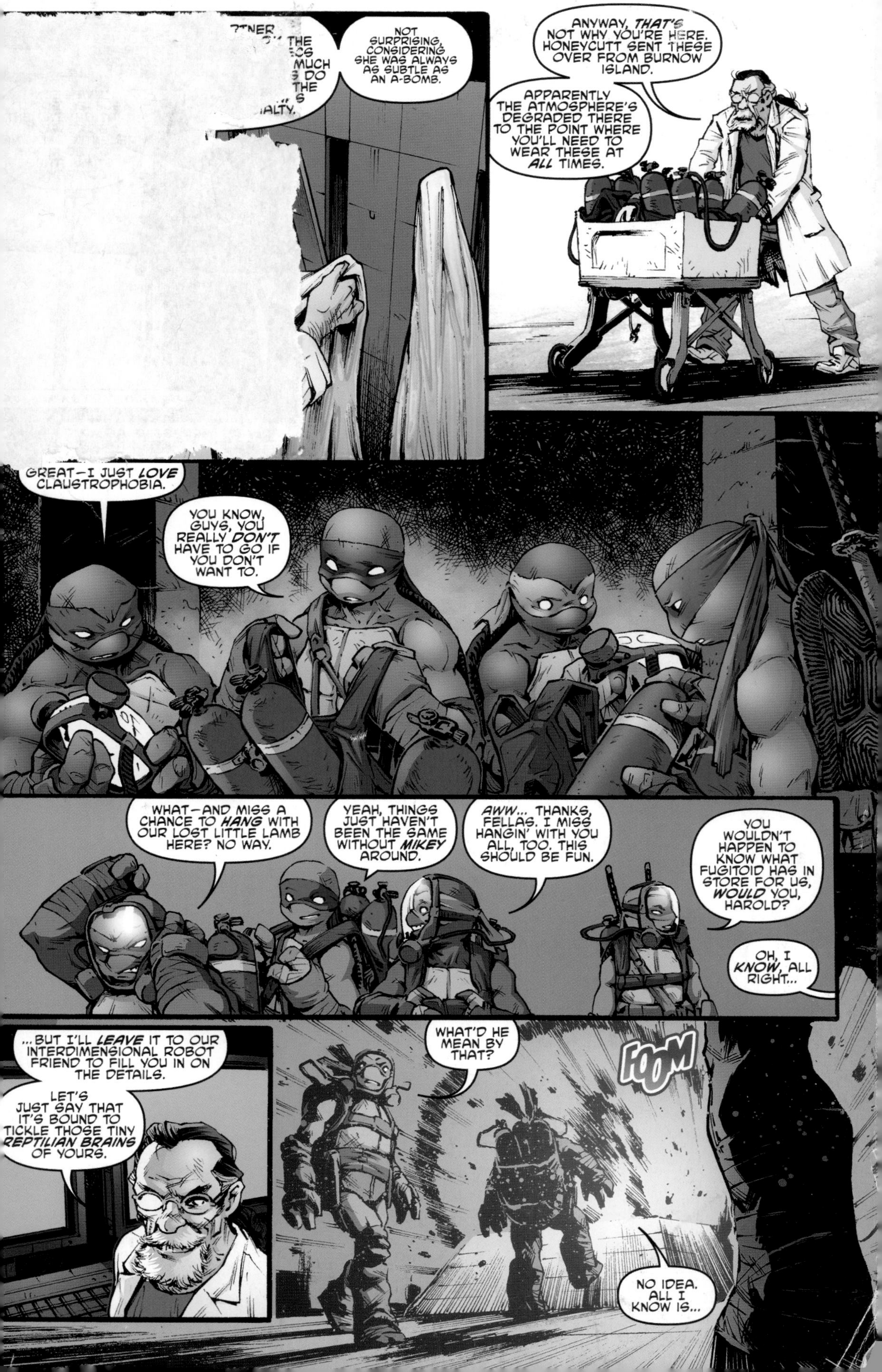
NOT SURPRISING, CONSIDERING SHE WAS ALWAYS AS SUBTLE AS AN A-BOMB.
ANYWAY, THAT'S NOT WHY YOU'RE HERE. HONEYCUTT SENT THESE OVER FROM BURNOW ISLAND.
APPARENTLY THE ATMOSPHERE'S DEGRADED THERE TO THE POINT WHERE YOU'LL NEED TO WEAR THESE AT ALL TIMES.
GREAT—I JUST LOVE CLAUSTROPHOBIA.
YOU KNOW, GUYS, YOU REALLY DON'T HAVE TO GO IF YOU DON'T WANT TO.
WHAT—AND MISS A CHANCE TO HANG WITH OUR LOST LITTLE LAMB HERE? NO WAY.
YEAH, THINGS JUST HAVEN'T BEEN THE SAME WITHOUT MIKEY AROUND.
AWW... THANKS, FELLAS. I MISS HANGIN' WITH YOU ALL, TOO. THIS SHOULD BE FUN.
YOU WOULDN'T HAPPEN TO KNOW WHAT FUGITOID HAS IN STORE FOR US, WOULD YOU, HAROLD?
OH, I KNOW, ALL RIGHT...
...BUT I'LL LEAVE IT TO OUR INTERDIMENSIONAL ROBOT FRIEND TO FILL YOU IN ON THE DETAILS.
LET'S JUST SAY THAT IT'S BOUND TO TICKLE THOSE TINY REPTILIAN BRAINS OF YOURS.
WHAT'D HE MEAN BY THAT?
FOOM
NO IDEA. ALL I KNOW IS...

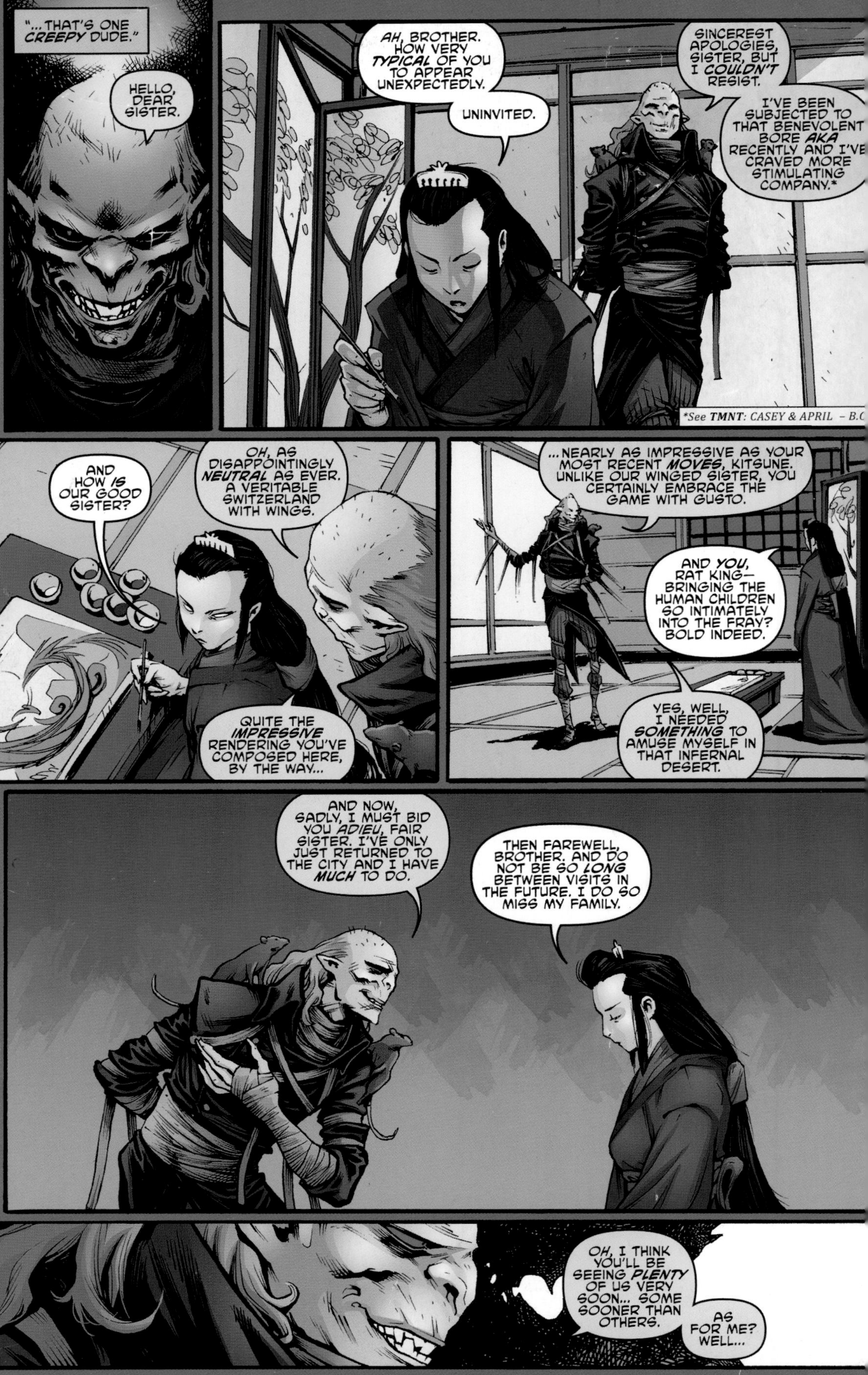
"...THAT'S ONE CREEPY DUDE."
HELLO, DEAR SISTER.
AH, BROTHER. HOW VERY TYPICAL OF YOU TO APPEAR UNEXPECTEDLY.
UNINVITED.
SINCEREST APOLOGIES, SISTER, BUT I COULDN'T RESIST.
I'VE BEEN SUBJECTED TO THAT BENEVOLENT BORE AKA RECENTLY AND I'VE CRAVED MORE STIMULATING COMPANY.*
*See TMNT: CASEY & APRIL – B.C.
AND HOW IS OUR GOOD SISTER?
OH, AS DISAPPOINTINGLY NEUTRAL AS EVER. A VERITABLE SWITZERLAND WITH WINGS.
QUITE THE IMPRESSIVE RENDERING YOU'VE COMPOSED HERE, BY THE WAY...
...NEARLY AS IMPRESSIVE AS YOUR MOST RECENT MOVES, KITSUNE. UNLIKE OUR WINGED SISTER, YOU CERTAINLY EMBRACE THE GAME WITH GUSTO.
AND YOU, RAT KING—BRINGING THE HUMAN CHILDREN SO INTIMATELY INTO THE FRAY? BOLD INDEED.
YES, WELL, I NEEDED SOMETHING TO AMUSE MYSELF IN THAT INFERNAL DESERT.
AND NOW, SADLY, I MUST BID YOU ADIEU, FAIR SISTER. I'VE ONLY JUST RETURNED TO THE CITY AND I HAVE MUCH TO DO.
THEN FAREWELL, BROTHER. AND DO NOT BE SO LONG BETWEEN VISITS IN THE FUTURE. I DO SO MISS MY FAMILY.
OH, I THINK YOU'LL BE SEEING PLENTY OF US VERY SOON... SOME SOONER THAN OTHERS.
AS FOR ME? WELL...

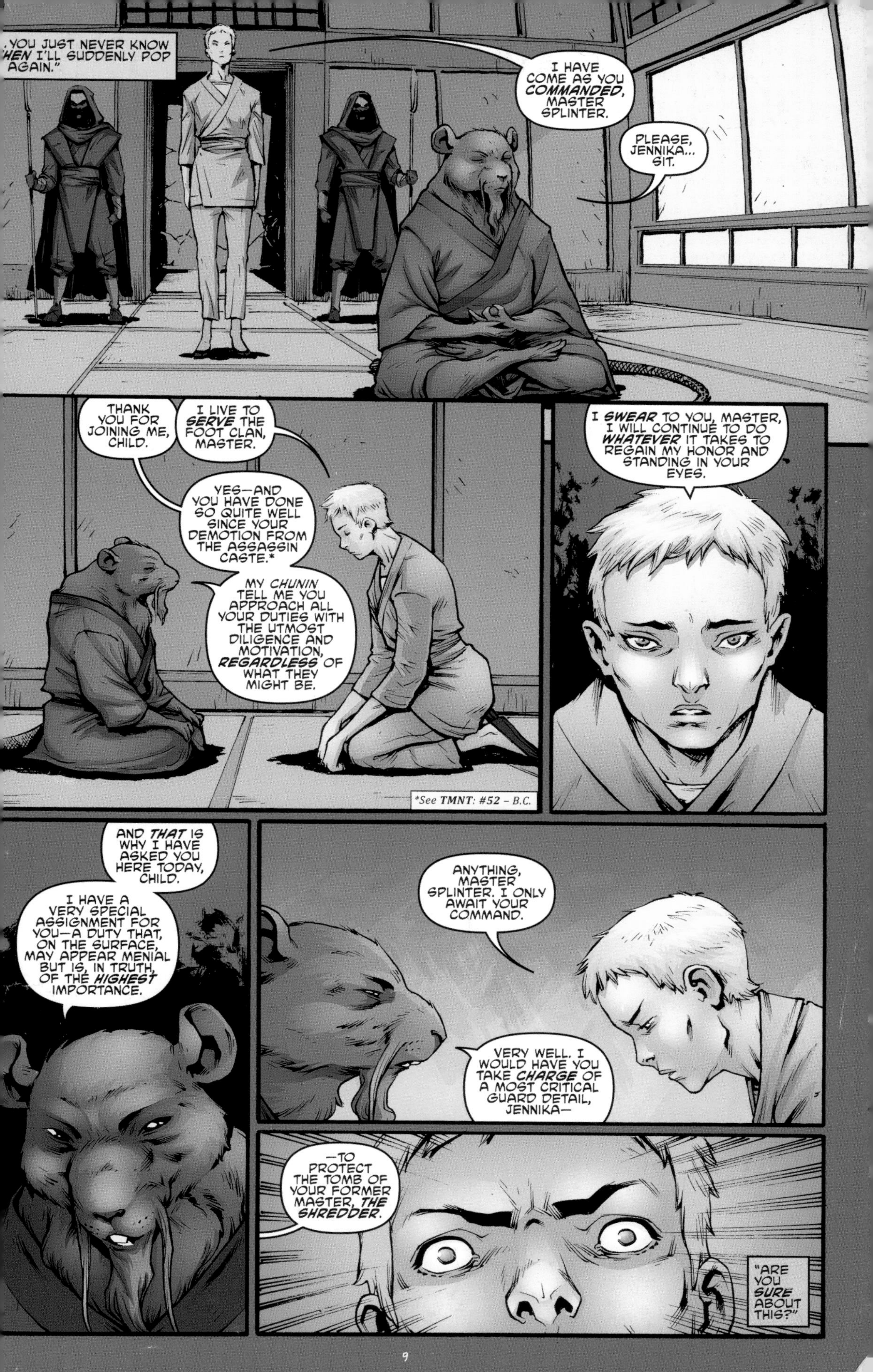

.YOU JUST NEVER KNOW HEN I'LL SUDDENLY POP AGAIN."
I HAVE COME AS YOU COMMANDED, MASTER SPLINTER.
PLEASE, JENNIKA... SIT.
THANK YOU FOR JOINING ME, CHILD.
I LIVE TO SERVE THE FOOT CLAN, MASTER.
YES—AND YOU HAVE DONE SO QUITE WELL SINCE YOUR DEMOTION FROM THE ASSASSIN CASTE.*
MY CHUNIN TELL ME YOU APPROACH ALL YOUR DUTIES WITH THE UTMOST DILIGENCE AND MOTIVATION, REGARDLESS OF WHAT THEY MIGHT BE.
*See TMNT: #52 – B.C.
I SWEAR TO YOU, MASTER, I WILL CONTINUE TO DO WHATEVER IT TAKES TO REGAIN MY HONOR AND STANDING IN YOUR EYES.
AND THAT IS WHY I HAVE ASKED YOU HERE TODAY, CHILD.
I HAVE A VERY SPECIAL ASSIGNMENT FOR YOU—A DUTY THAT, ON THE SURFACE, MAY APPEAR MENIAL BUT IS, IN TRUTH, OF THE HIGHEST IMPORTANCE.
ANYTHING, MASTER SPLINTER. I ONLY AWAIT YOUR COMMAND.
VERY WELL. I WOULD HAVE YOU TAKE CHARGE OF A MOST CRITICAL GUARD DETAIL, JENNIKA—
—TO PROTECT THE TOMB OF YOUR FORMER MASTER, THE SHREDDER.
"ARE YOU SURE ABOUT THIS?"

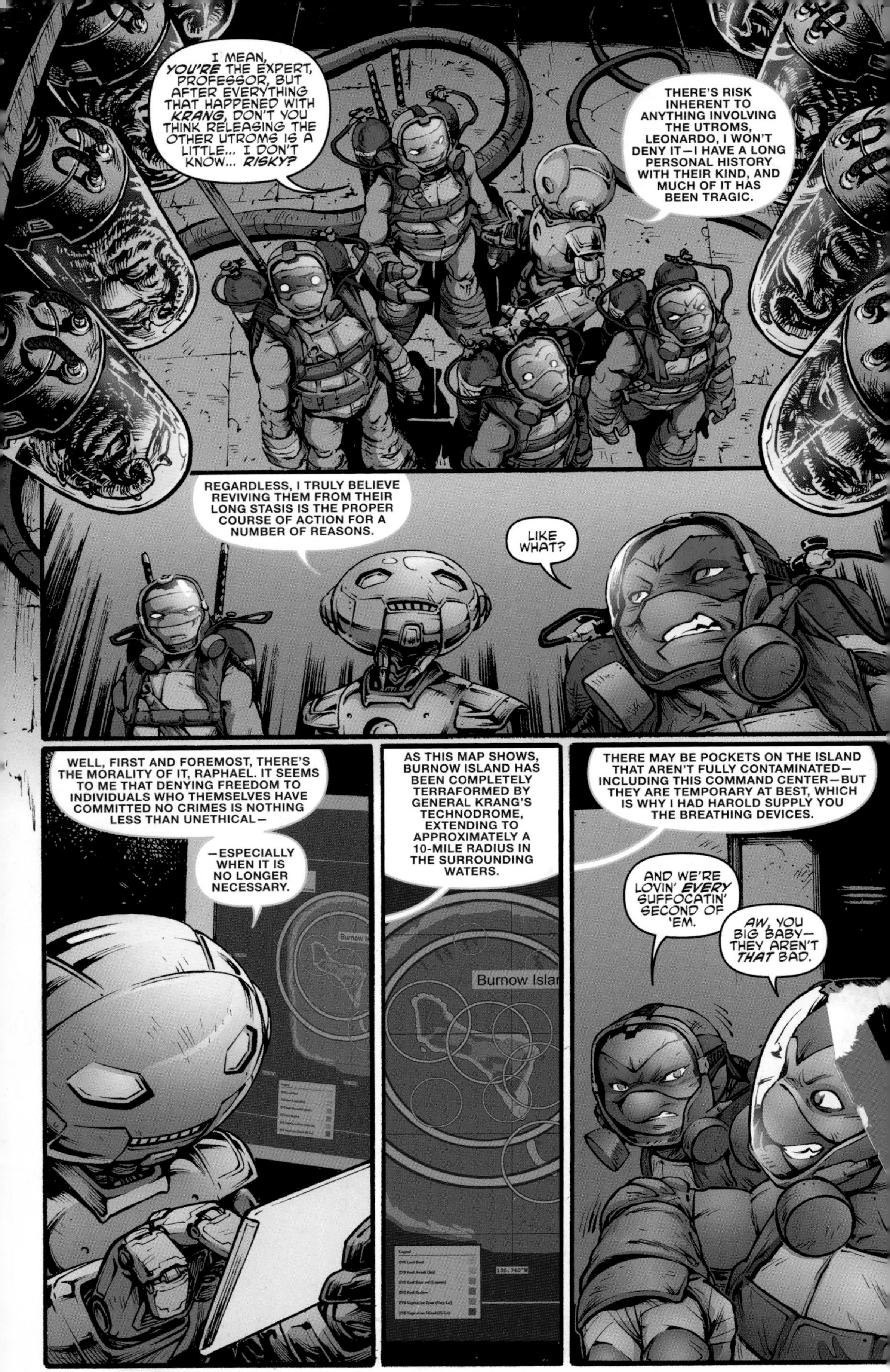
I MEAN, YOU'RE THE EXPERT, PROFESSOR, BUT AFTER EVERYTHING THAT HAPPENED WITH KRANG, DON'T YOU THINK RELEASING THE OTHER UTROMS IS A LITTLE... I DON'T KNOW... RISKY?
THERE'S RISK INHERENT TO ANYTHING INVOLVING THE UTROMS, LEONARDO, I WON'T DENY IT—I HAVE A LONG PERSONAL HISTORY WITH THEIR KIND, AND MUCH OF IT HAS BEEN TRAGIC.
REGARDLESS, I TRULY BELIEVE REVIVING THEM FROM THEIR LONG STASIS IS THE PROPER COURSE OF ACTION FOR A NUMBER OF REASONS.
LIKE WHAT?
WELL, FIRST AND FOREMOST, THERE'S THE MORALITY OF IT, RAPHAEL. IT SEEMS TO ME THAT DENYING FREEDOM TO INDIVIDUALS WHO THEMSELVES HAVE COMMITTED NO CRIMES IS NOTHING LESS THAN UNETHICAL—
—ESPECIALLY WHEN IT IS NO LONGER NECESSARY.
AS THIS MAP SHOWS, BURNOW ISLAND HAS BEEN COMPLETELY TERRAFORMED BY GENERAL KRANG'S TECHNODROME, EXTENDING TO APPROXIMATELY A 10-MILE RADIUS IN THE SURROUNDING WATERS.
Burnow Islan
130.740°W
THERE MAY BE POCKETS ON THE ISLAND THAT AREN'T FULLY CONTAMINATED—INCLUDING THIS COMMAND CENTER—BUT THEY ARE TEMPORARY AT BEST, WHICH IS WHY I HAD HAROLD SUPPLY YOU THE BREATHING DEVICES.
AND WE'RE LOVIN' EVERY SUFFOCATIN' SECOND OF 'EM.
AW, YOU BIG BABY—THEY AREN'T THAT BAD.

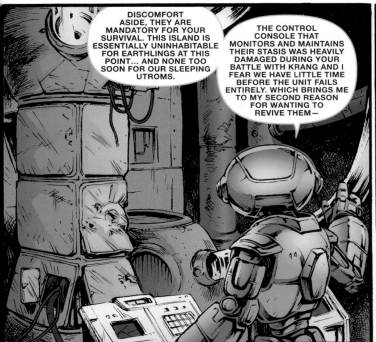

DISCOMFORT ASIDE, THEY ARE MANDATORY FOR YOUR SURVIVAL. THIS ISLAND IS ESSENTIALLY UNINHABITABLE FOR EARTHLINGS AT THIS POINT... AND NONE TOO SOON FOR OUR SLEEPING UTROMS.

THE CONTROL CONSOLE THAT MONITORS AND MAINTAINS THEIR STASIS WAS HEAVILY DAMAGED DURING YOUR BATTLE WITH KRANG AND I FEAR WE HAVE LITTLE TIME BEFORE THE UNIT FAILS ENTIRELY. WHICH BRINGS ME TO MY SECOND REASON FOR WANTING TO REVIVE THEM—

—THEY WILL PERISH IF WE DO NOT.

WELL, IF *THAT'S* WHY YOU CALLED US HERE, PROFESSOR, THEN YOU CAN COUNT ON US TO HELP OUT, *RIGHT*, GUYS?

YEAH. WHATEVER CONCERNS WE HAVE, NONE OF US WANTS TO SEE *INNOCENTS* DIE, *ESPECIALLY* IF WE CAN DO SOMETHING ABOUT IT.

I KNEW YOU WOULD AGREE IT IS THE RIGHT THING TO DO. I'VE BEEN PREPARING THE STASIS TUBES FOR THE REVIVAL PROCESS AND EVERYTHING IS READY TO GO, EXCEPT...

...EXCEPT FOR THE OTHER REASON I ASKED YOU TO THE ISLAND TODAY.

HELLO...

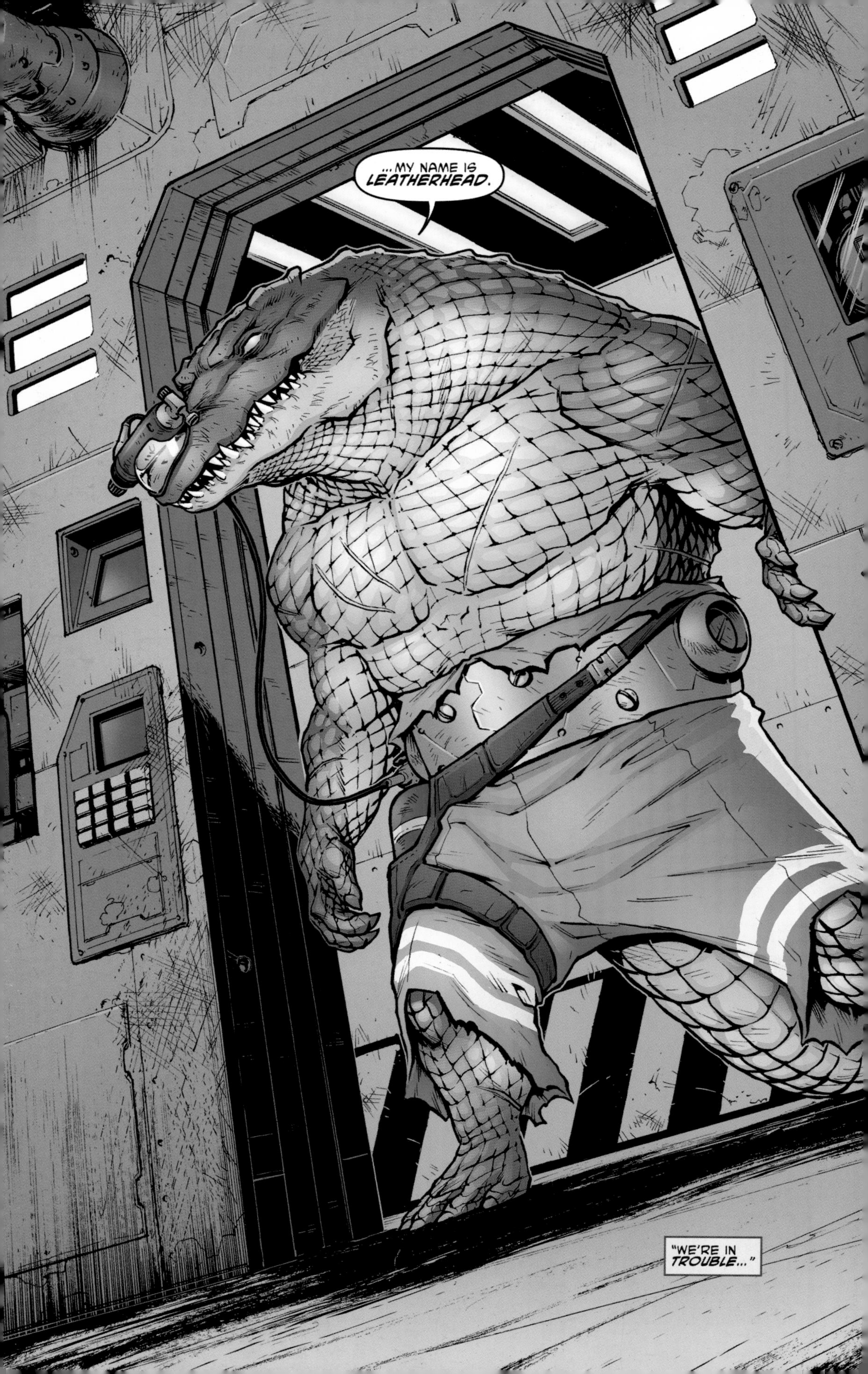
...MY NAME IS LEATHERHEAD.
"WE'RE IN TROUBLE..."

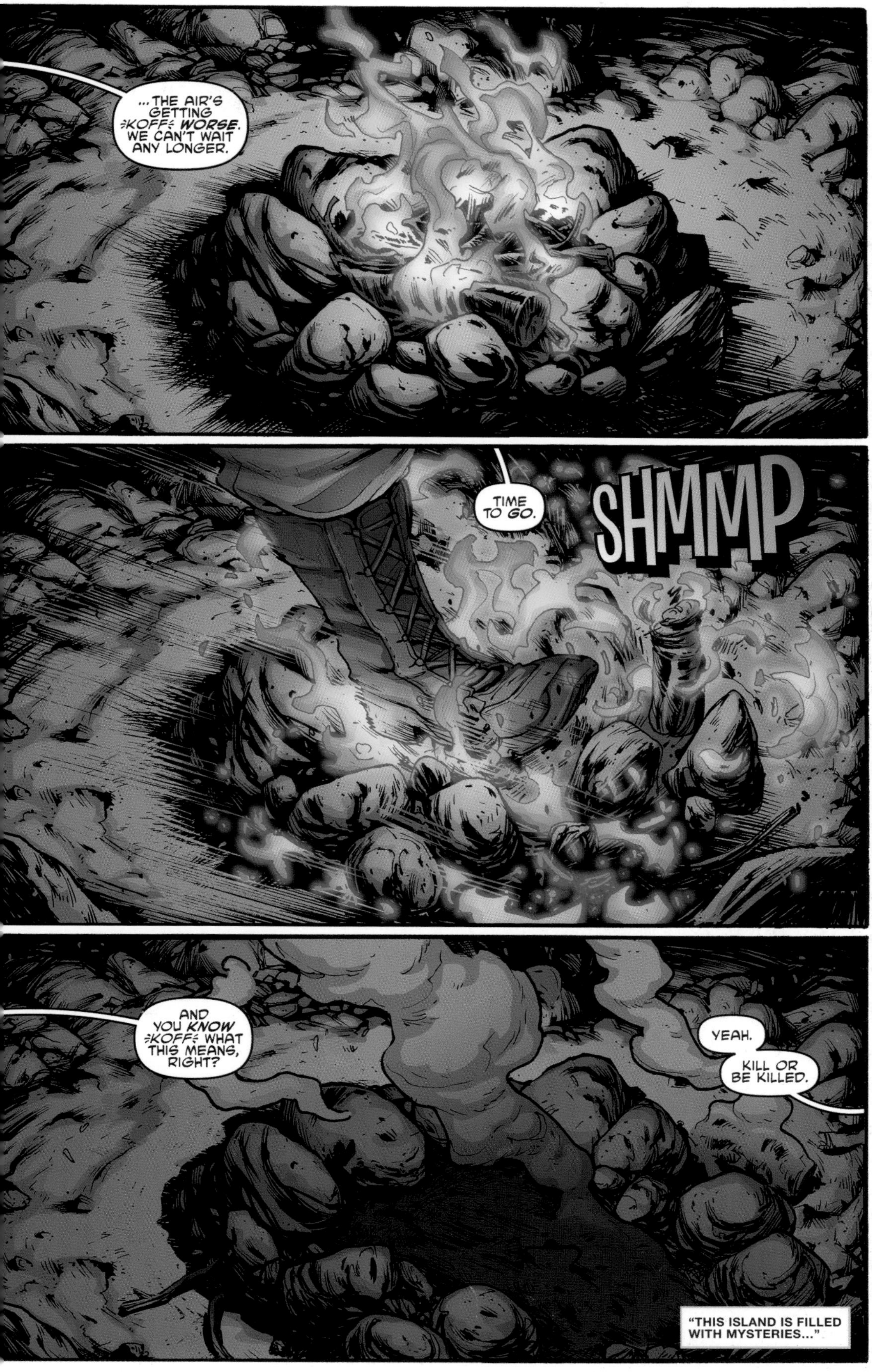
...THE AIR'S GETTING =KOFF= WORSE. WE CAN'T WAIT ANY LONGER.
TIME TO GO.
SHMMP
AND YOU KNOW =KOFF= WHAT THIS MEANS, RIGHT?
YEAH.
KILL OR BE KILLED.
"THIS ISLAND IS FILLED WITH MYSTERIES..."

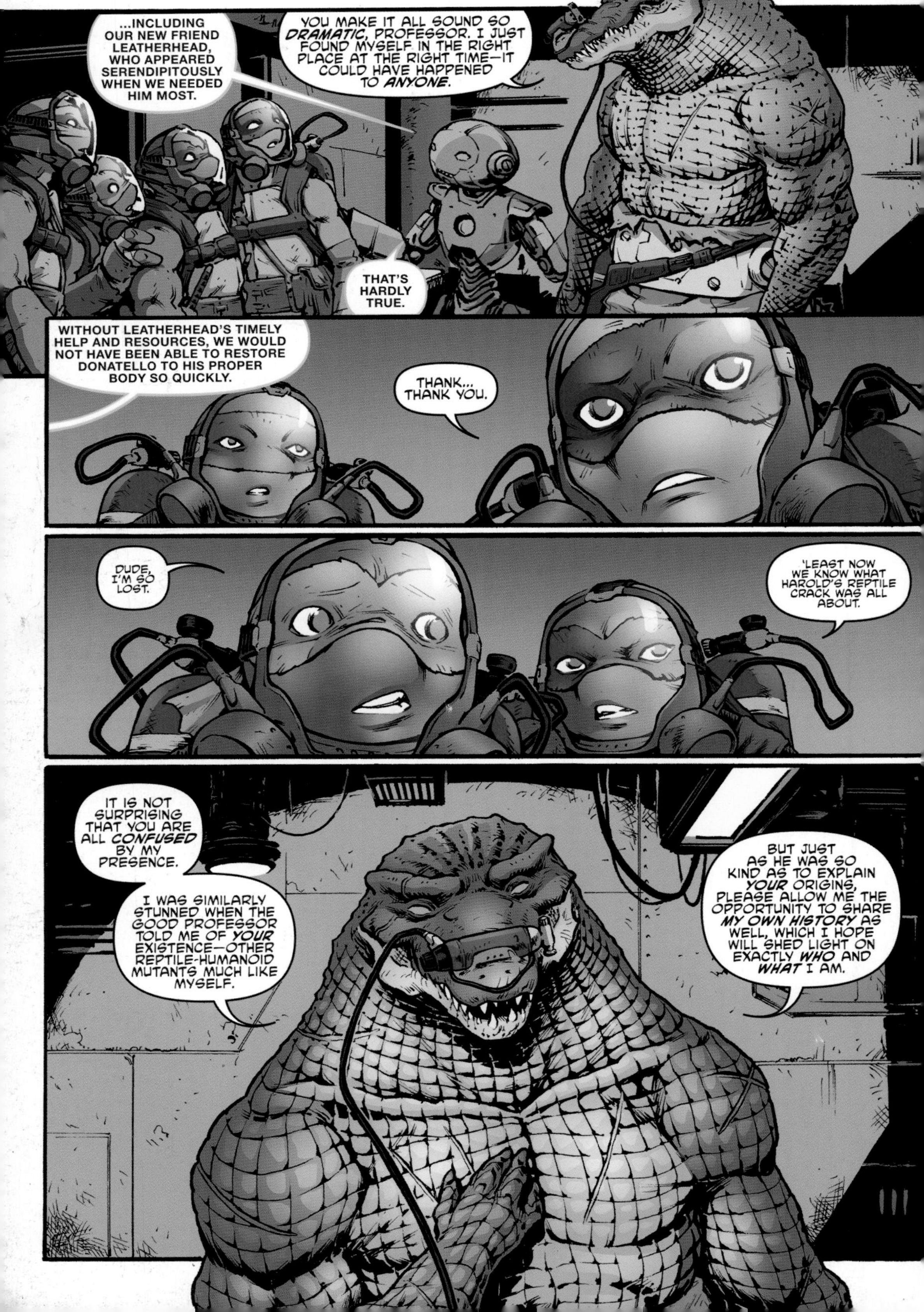
...INCLUDING OUR NEW FRIEND LEATHERHEAD, WHO APPEARED SERENDIPITOUSLY WHEN WE NEEDED HIM MOST.
YOU MAKE IT ALL SOUND SO DRAMATIC, PROFESSOR. I JUST FOUND MYSELF IN THE RIGHT PLACE AT THE RIGHT TIME—IT COULD HAVE HAPPENED TO ANYONE.
THAT'S HARDLY TRUE.
WITHOUT LEATHERHEAD'S TIMELY HELP AND RESOURCES, WE WOULD NOT HAVE BEEN ABLE TO RESTORE DONATELLO TO HIS PROPER BODY SO QUICKLY.
THANK... THANK YOU.
DUDE, I'M SO LOST.
'LEAST NOW WE KNOW WHAT HAROLD'S REPTILE CRACK WAS ALL ABOUT.
IT IS NOT SURPRISING THAT YOU ARE ALL CONFUSED BY MY PRESENCE.
I WAS SIMILARLY STUNNED WHEN THE GOOD PROFESSOR TOLD ME OF YOUR EXISTENCE—OTHER REPTILE-HUMANOID MUTANTS MUCH LIKE MYSELF.
BUT JUST AS HE WAS SO KIND AS TO EXPLAIN YOUR ORIGINS, PLEASE ALLOW ME THE OPPORTUNITY TO SHARE MY OWN HISTORY AS WELL, WHICH I HOPE WILL SHED LIGHT ON EXACTLY WHO AND WHAT I AM.

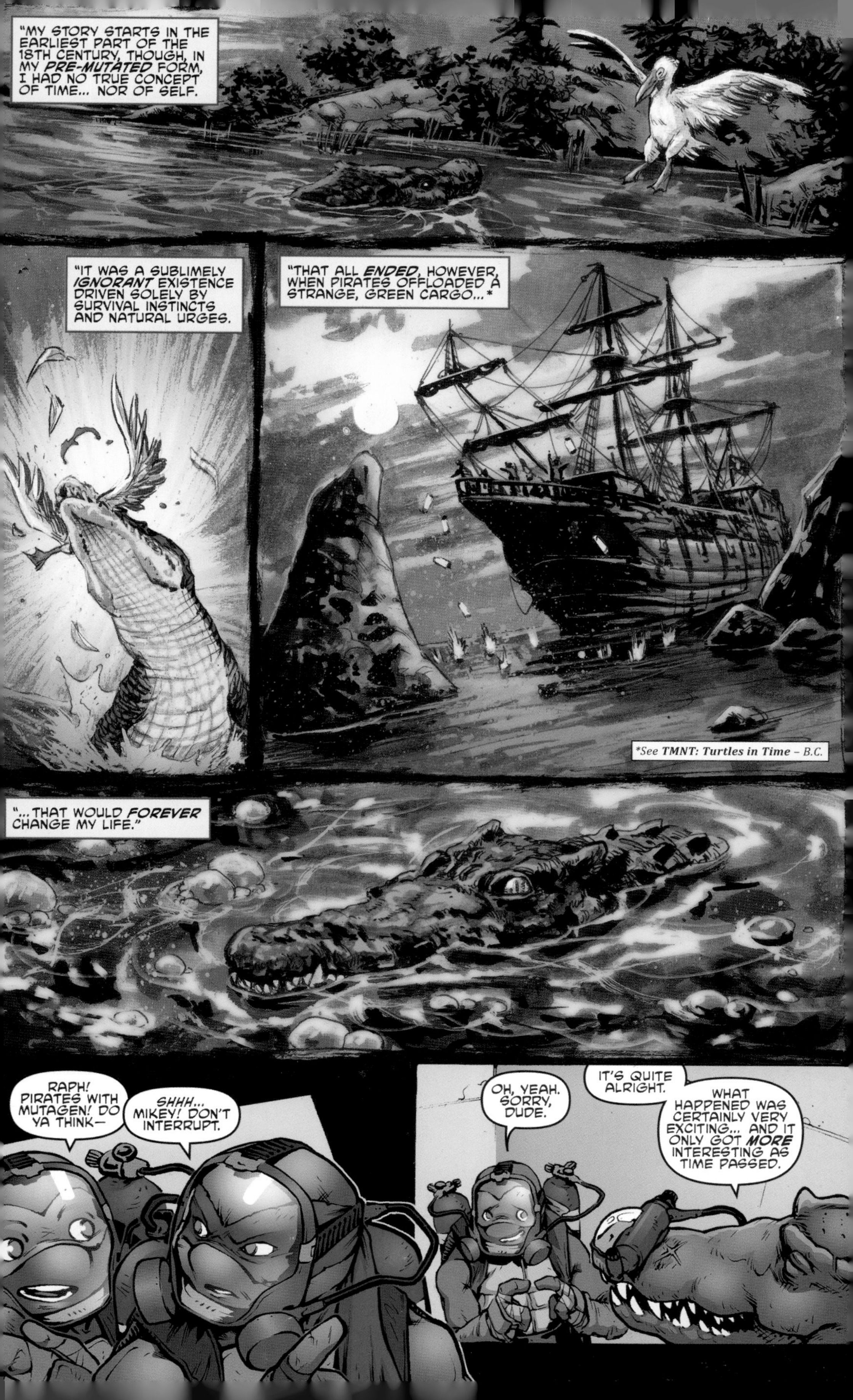
"MY STORY STARTS IN THE EARLIEST PART OF THE 18TH CENTURY, THOUGH, IN MY PRE-MUTATED FORM, I HAD NO TRUE CONCEPT OF TIME... NOR OF SELF.
"IT WAS A SUBLIMELY IGNORANT EXISTENCE DRIVEN SOLELY BY SURVIVAL INSTINCTS AND NATURAL URGES.
"THAT ALL ENDED, HOWEVER, WHEN PIRATES OFFLOADED A STRANGE, GREEN CARGO...*
*See TMNT: Turtles in Time – B.C.
"...THAT WOULD FOREVER CHANGE MY LIFE."
RAPH! PIRATES WITH MUTAGEN! DO YA THINK—
SHHH... MIKEY! DON'T INTERRUPT.
OH, YEAH. SORRY, DUDE.
IT'S QUITE ALRIGHT.
WHAT HAPPENED WAS CERTAINLY VERY EXCITING... AND IT ONLY GOT MORE INTERESTING AS TIME PASSED.

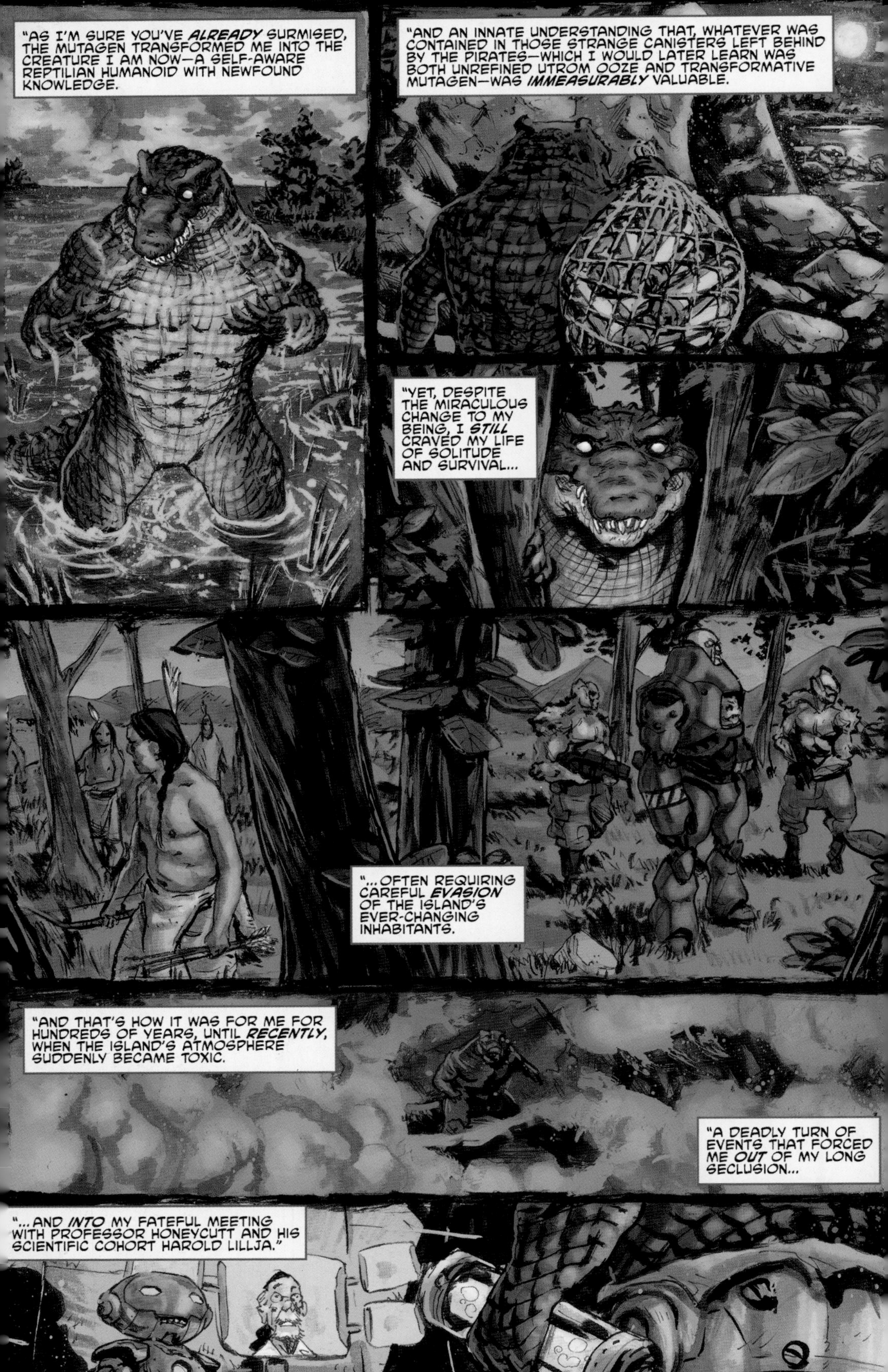
"AS I'M SURE YOU'VE ALREADY SURMISED, THE MUTAGEN TRANSFORMED ME INTO THE CREATURE I AM NOW—A SELF-AWARE REPTILIAN HUMANOID WITH NEWFOUND KNOWLEDGE.
"AND AN INNATE UNDERSTANDING THAT, WHATEVER WAS CONTAINED IN THOSE STRANGE CANISTERS LEFT BEHIND BY THE PIRATES—WHICH I WOULD LATER LEARN WAS BOTH UNREFINED UTROM OOZE AND TRANSFORMATIVE MUTAGEN—WAS IMMEASURABLY VALUABLE.
"YET, DESPITE THE MIRACULOUS CHANGE TO MY BEING, I STILL CRAVED MY LIFE OF SOLITUDE AND SURVIVAL...
"...OFTEN REQUIRING CAREFUL EVASION OF THE ISLAND'S EVER-CHANGING INHABITANTS.
"AND THAT'S HOW IT WAS FOR ME FOR HUNDREDS OF YEARS, UNTIL RECENTLY, WHEN THE ISLAND'S ATMOSPHERE SUDDENLY BECAME TOXIC.
"A DEADLY TURN OF EVENTS THAT FORCED ME OUT OF MY LONG SECLUSION...
"...AND INTO MY FATEFUL MEETING WITH PROFESSOR HONEYCUTT AND HIS SCIENTIFIC COHORT HAROLD LILLJA."

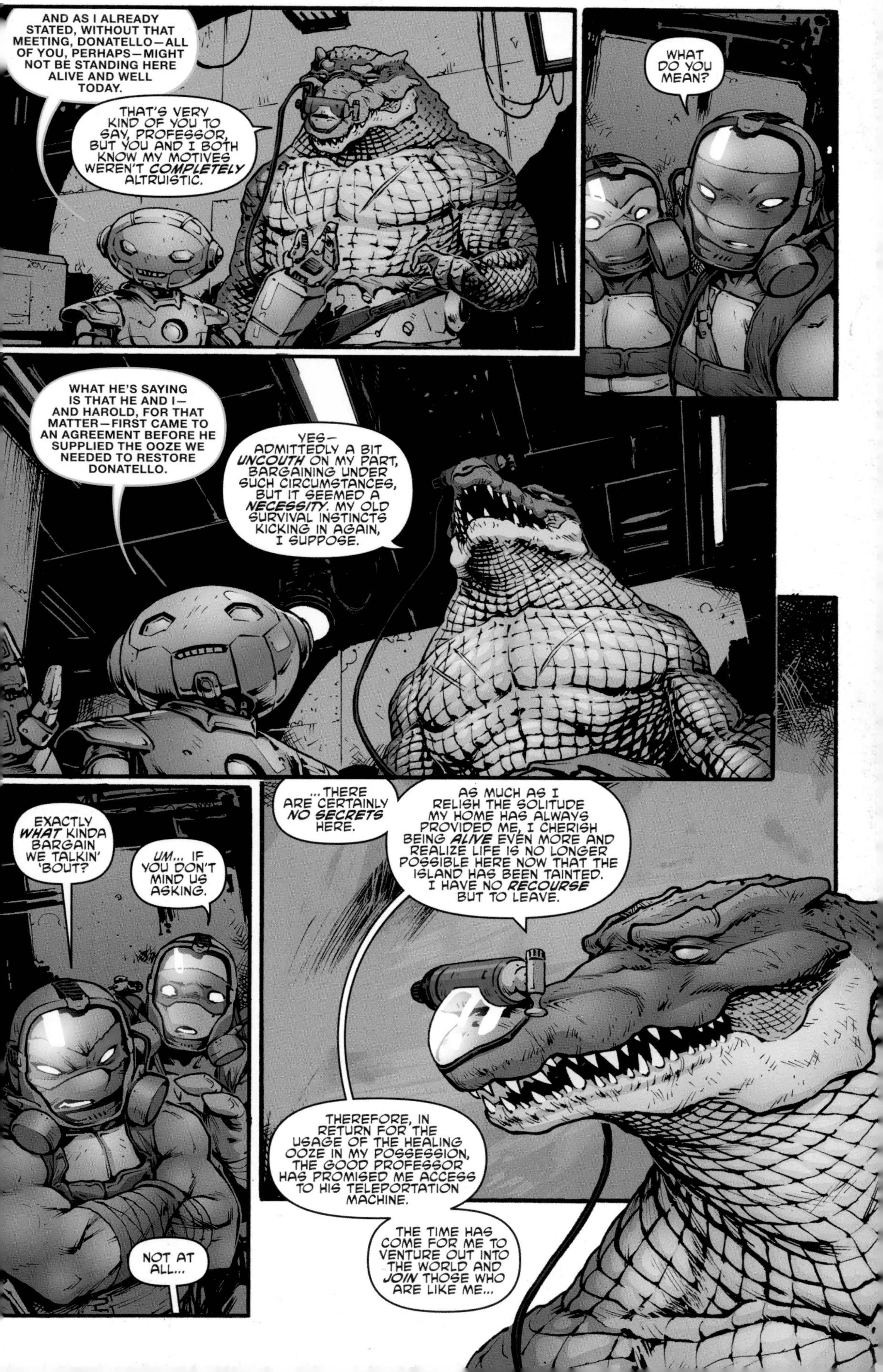
AND AS I ALREADY STATED, WITHOUT THAT MEETING, DONATELLO—ALL OF YOU, PERHAPS—MIGHT NOT BE STANDING HERE ALIVE AND WELL TODAY.
THAT'S VERY KIND OF YOU TO SAY, PROFESSOR, BUT YOU AND I BOTH KNOW MY MOTIVES WEREN'T COMPLETELY ALTRUISTIC.
WHAT DO YOU MEAN?
WHAT HE'S SAYING IS THAT HE AND I—AND HAROLD, FOR THAT MATTER—FIRST CAME TO AN AGREEMENT BEFORE HE SUPPLIED THE OOZE WE NEEDED TO RESTORE DONATELLO.
YES—ADMITTEDLY A BIT UNCOUTH ON MY PART, BARGAINING UNDER SUCH CIRCUMSTANCES, BUT IT SEEMED A NECESSITY. MY OLD SURVIVAL INSTINCTS KICKING IN AGAIN, I SUPPOSE.
EXACTLY WHAT KINDA BARGAIN WE TALKIN' 'BOUT?
UM... IF YOU DON'T MIND US ASKING.
NOT AT ALL...
...THERE ARE CERTAINLY NO SECRETS HERE.
AS MUCH AS I RELISH THE SOLITUDE MY HOME HAS ALWAYS PROVIDED ME, I CHERISH BEING ALIVE EVEN MORE AND REALIZE LIFE IS NO LONGER POSSIBLE HERE NOW THAT THE ISLAND HAS BEEN TAINTED. I HAVE NO RECOURSE BUT TO LEAVE.
THEREFORE, IN RETURN FOR THE USAGE OF THE HEALING OOZE IN MY POSSESSION, THE GOOD PROFESSOR HAS PROMISED ME ACCESS TO HIS TELEPORTATION MACHINE.
THE TIME HAS COME FOR ME TO VENTURE OUT INTO THE WORLD AND JOIN THOSE WHO ARE LIKE ME...

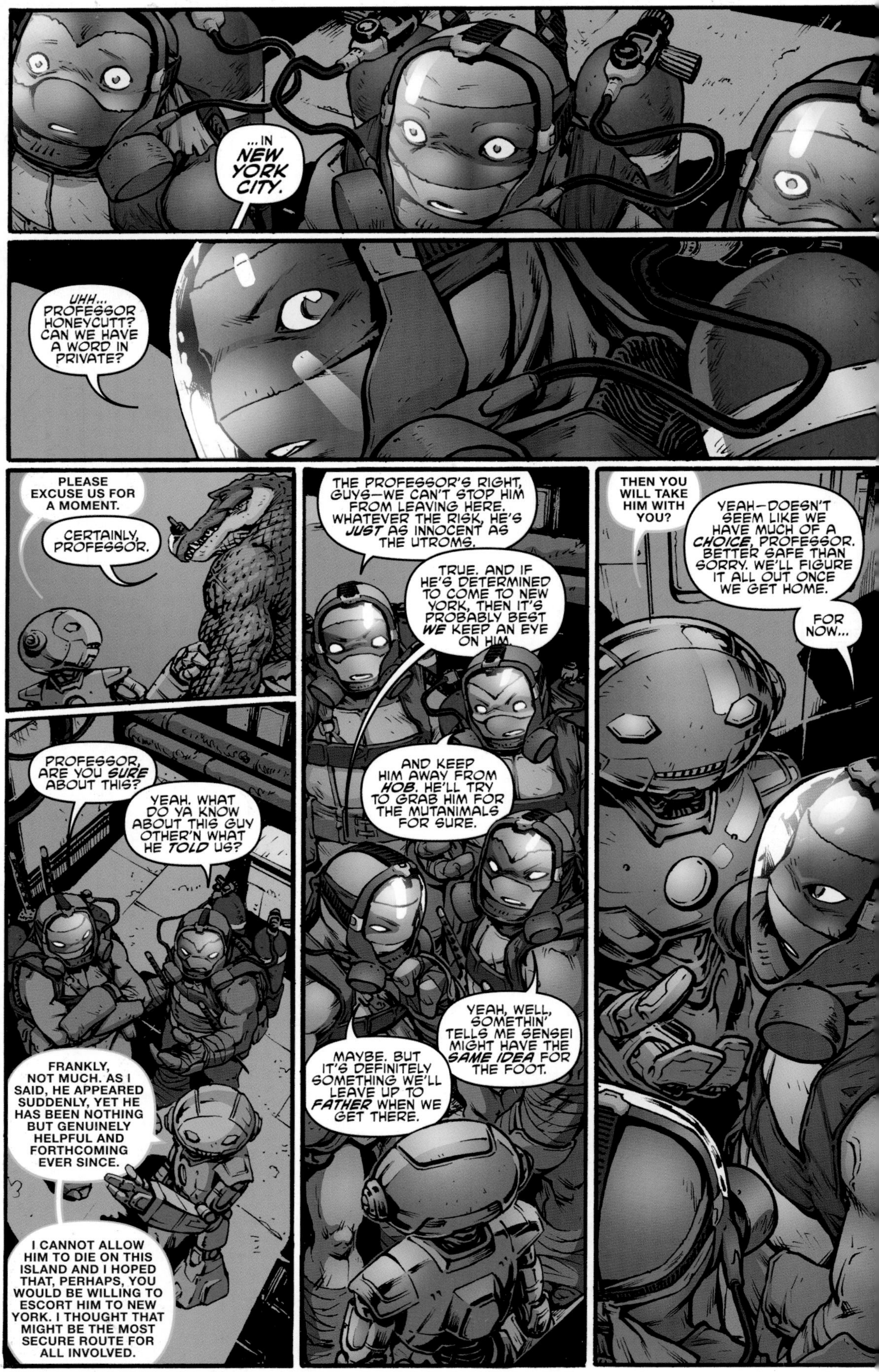
...IN NEW YORK CITY.
UHH... PROFESSOR HONEYCUTT? CAN WE HAVE A WORD IN PRIVATE?
PLEASE EXCUSE US FOR A MOMENT.
CERTAINLY, PROFESSOR.
PROFESSOR, ARE YOU SURE ABOUT THIS?
YEAH. WHAT DO YA KNOW ABOUT THIS GUY OTHER'N WHAT HE TOLD US?
FRANKLY, NOT MUCH. AS I SAID, HE APPEARED SUDDENLY, YET HE HAS BEEN NOTHING BUT GENUINELY HELPFUL AND FORTHCOMING EVER SINCE.
I CANNOT ALLOW HIM TO DIE ON THIS ISLAND AND I HOPED THAT, PERHAPS, YOU WOULD BE WILLING TO ESCORT HIM TO NEW YORK. I THOUGHT THAT MIGHT BE THE MOST SECURE ROUTE FOR ALL INVOLVED.
THE PROFESSOR'S RIGHT, GUYS—WE CAN'T STOP HIM FROM LEAVING HERE. WHATEVER THE RISK, HE'S JUST AS INNOCENT AS THE UTROMS.
TRUE. AND IF HE'S DETERMINED TO COME TO NEW YORK, THEN IT'S PROBABLY BEST WE KEEP AN EYE ON HIM.
AND KEEP HIM AWAY FROM HOB. HE'LL TRY TO GRAB HIM FOR THE MUTANIMALS FOR SURE.
YEAH, WELL, SOMETHIN' TELLS ME SENSEI MIGHT HAVE THE SAME IDEA FOR THE FOOT.
MAYBE. BUT IT'S DEFINITELY SOMETHING WE'LL LEAVE UP TO FATHER WHEN WE GET THERE.
THEN YOU WILL TAKE HIM WITH YOU?
YEAH—DOESN'T SEEM LIKE WE HAVE MUCH OF A CHOICE, PROFESSOR. BETTER SAFE THAN SORRY. WE'LL FIGURE IT ALL OUT ONCE WE GET HOME.
FOR NOW...

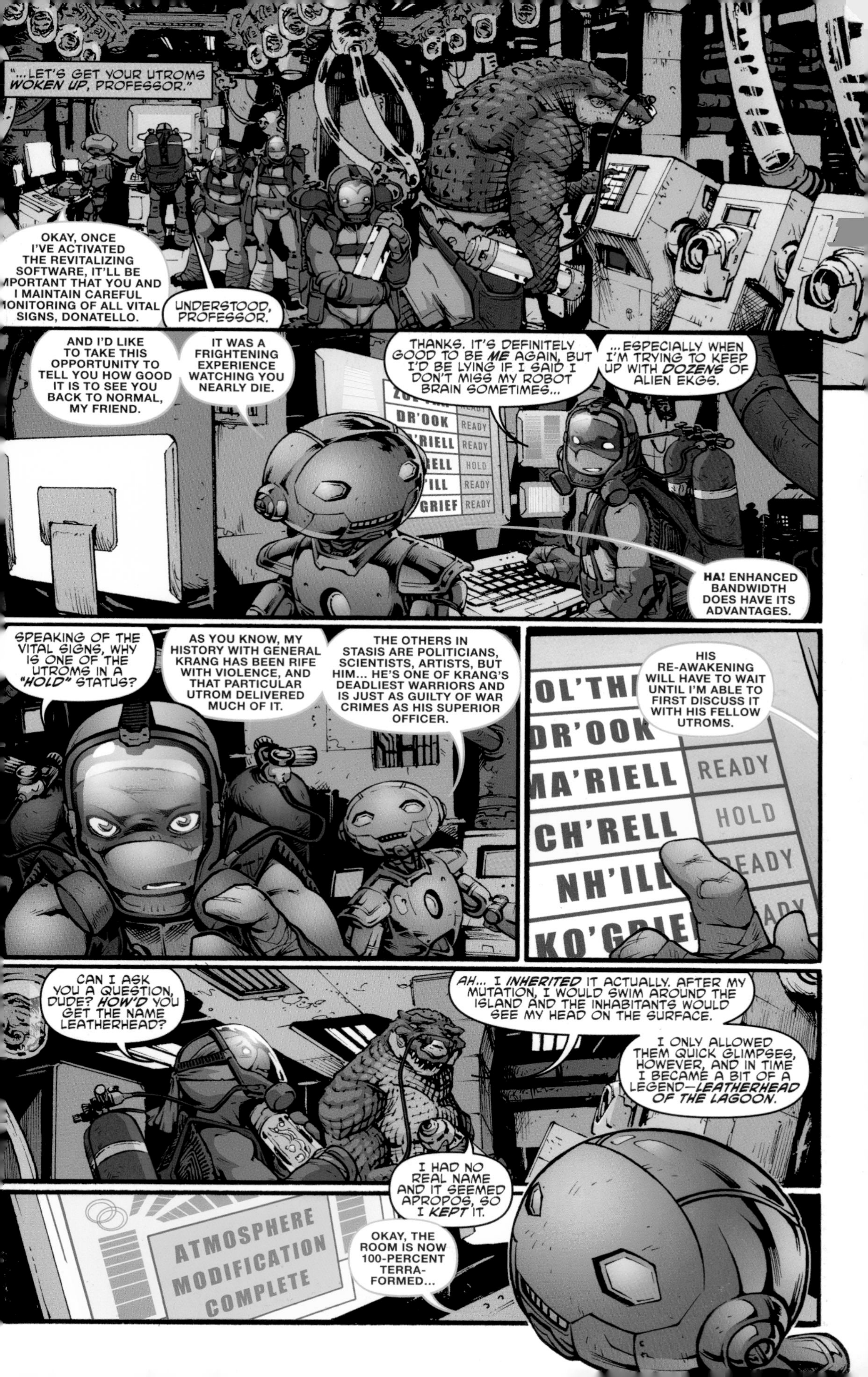
"...LET'S GET YOUR UTROMS WOKEN UP, PROFESSOR."
OKAY, ONCE I'VE ACTIVATED THE REVITALIZING SOFTWARE, IT'LL BE IMPORTANT THAT YOU AND I MAINTAIN CAREFUL MONITORING OF ALL VITAL SIGNS, DONATELLO.
UNDERSTOOD, PROFESSOR.
AND I'D LIKE TO TAKE THIS OPPORTUNITY TO TELL YOU HOW GOOD IT IS TO SEE YOU BACK TO NORMAL, MY FRIEND.
IT WAS A FRIGHTENING EXPERIENCE WATCHING YOU NEARLY DIE.
THANKS. IT'S DEFINITELY GOOD TO BE ME AGAIN, BUT I'D BE LYING IF I SAID I DON'T MISS MY ROBOT BRAIN SOMETIMES...
...ESPECIALLY WHEN I'M TRYING TO KEEP UP WITH DOZENS OF ALIEN EKGS.
DR'OOK READY
READY
HOLD
READY
GRIEF READY
HA! ENHANCED BANDWIDTH DOES HAVE ITS ADVANTAGES.
SPEAKING OF THE VITAL SIGNS, WHY IS ONE OF THE UTROMS IN A "HOLD" STATUS?
AS YOU KNOW, MY HISTORY WITH GENERAL KRANG HAS BEEN RIFE WITH VIOLENCE, AND THAT PARTICULAR UTROM DELIVERED MUCH OF IT.
THE OTHERS IN STASIS ARE POLITICIANS, SCIENTISTS, ARTISTS, BUT HIM... HE'S ONE OF KRANG'S DEADLIEST WARRIORS AND IS JUST AS GUILTY OF WAR CRIMES AS HIS SUPERIOR OFFICER.
HIS RE-AWAKENING WILL HAVE TO WAIT UNTIL I'M ABLE TO FIRST DISCUSS IT WITH HIS FELLOW UTROMS.
DR'OOK
MA'RIELL READY
CH'RELL HOLD
CAN I ASK YOU A QUESTION, DUDE? HOW'D YOU GET THE NAME LEATHERHEAD?
AH... I INHERITED IT ACTUALLY. AFTER MY MUTATION, I WOULD SWIM AROUND THE ISLAND AND THE INHABITANTS WOULD SEE MY HEAD ON THE SURFACE.
I ONLY ALLOWED THEM QUICK GLIMPSES, HOWEVER, AND IN TIME I BECAME A BIT OF A LEGEND—LEATHERHEAD OF THE LAGOON.
I HAD NO REAL NAME AND IT SEEMED APROPOS, SO I KEPT IT.
ATMOSPHERE MODIFICATION COMPLETE
OKAY, THE ROOM IS NOW 100-PERCENT TERRA-FORMED...

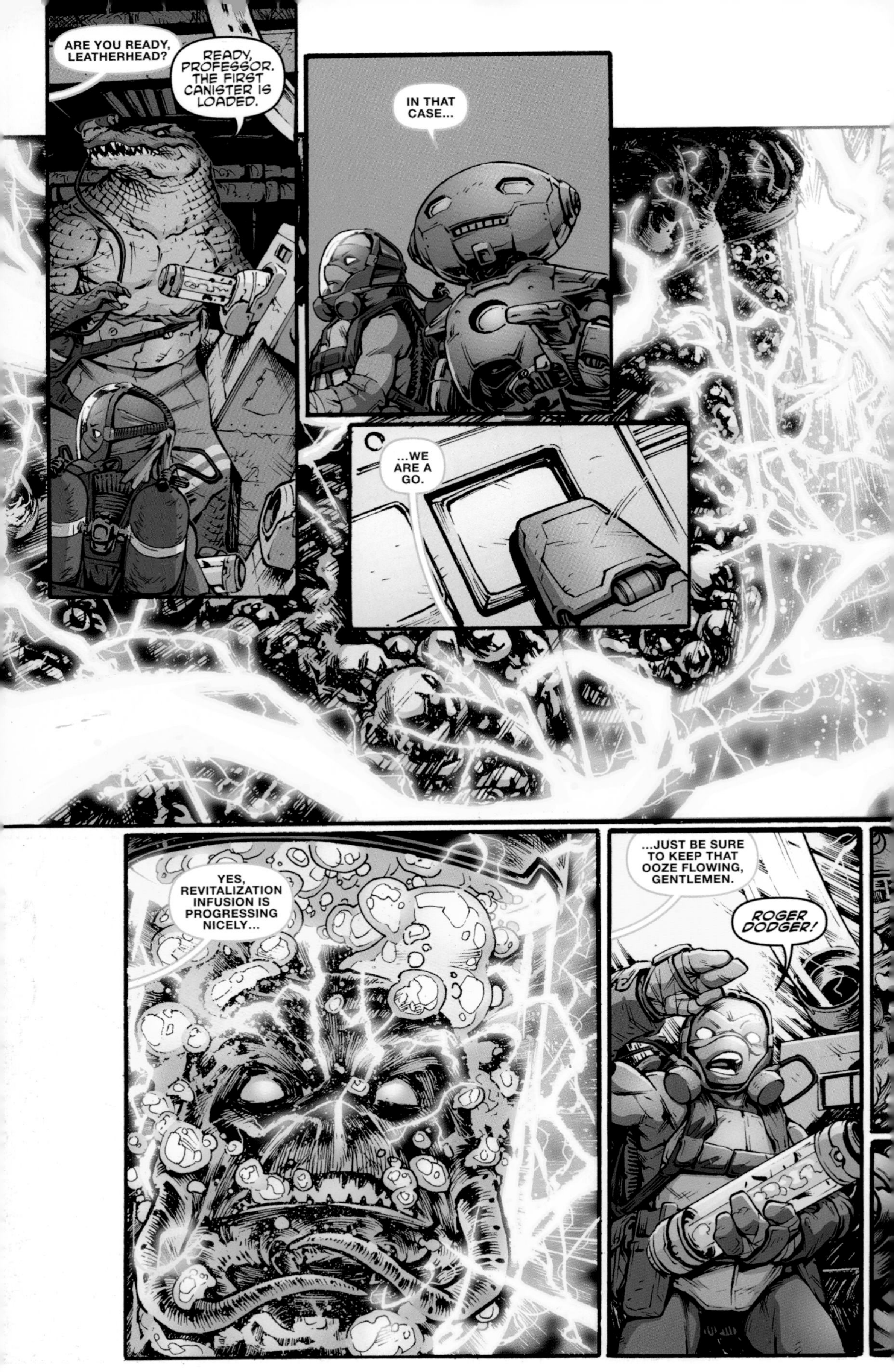
ARE YOU READY, LEATHERHEAD?
READY, PROFESSOR. THE FIRST CANISTER IS LOADED.
IN THAT CASE...
...WE ARE A GO.
YES, REVITALIZATION INFUSION IS PROGRESSING NICELY...
...JUST BE SURE TO KEEP THAT OOZE FLOWING, GENTLEMEN.
ROGER DODGER!

VITAL SIGNS *STABLE,* PROFESSOR.

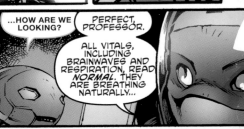

...HOW ARE WE LOOKING?

PERFECT, PROFESSOR.

ALL VITALS, INCLUDING BRAINWAVES AND RESPIRATION, READ *NORMAL.* THEY ARE BREATHING NATURALLY...

DRAINAGE COMPLETE...

INFUSION COMPLETE. COMMENCING TUBE DRAINAGE...

...HOW ARE THOSE VITALS, DONATELLO?

A-OKAY ACROSS THE BOARD.

...AND ARE *FULLY* REJUVENATED.

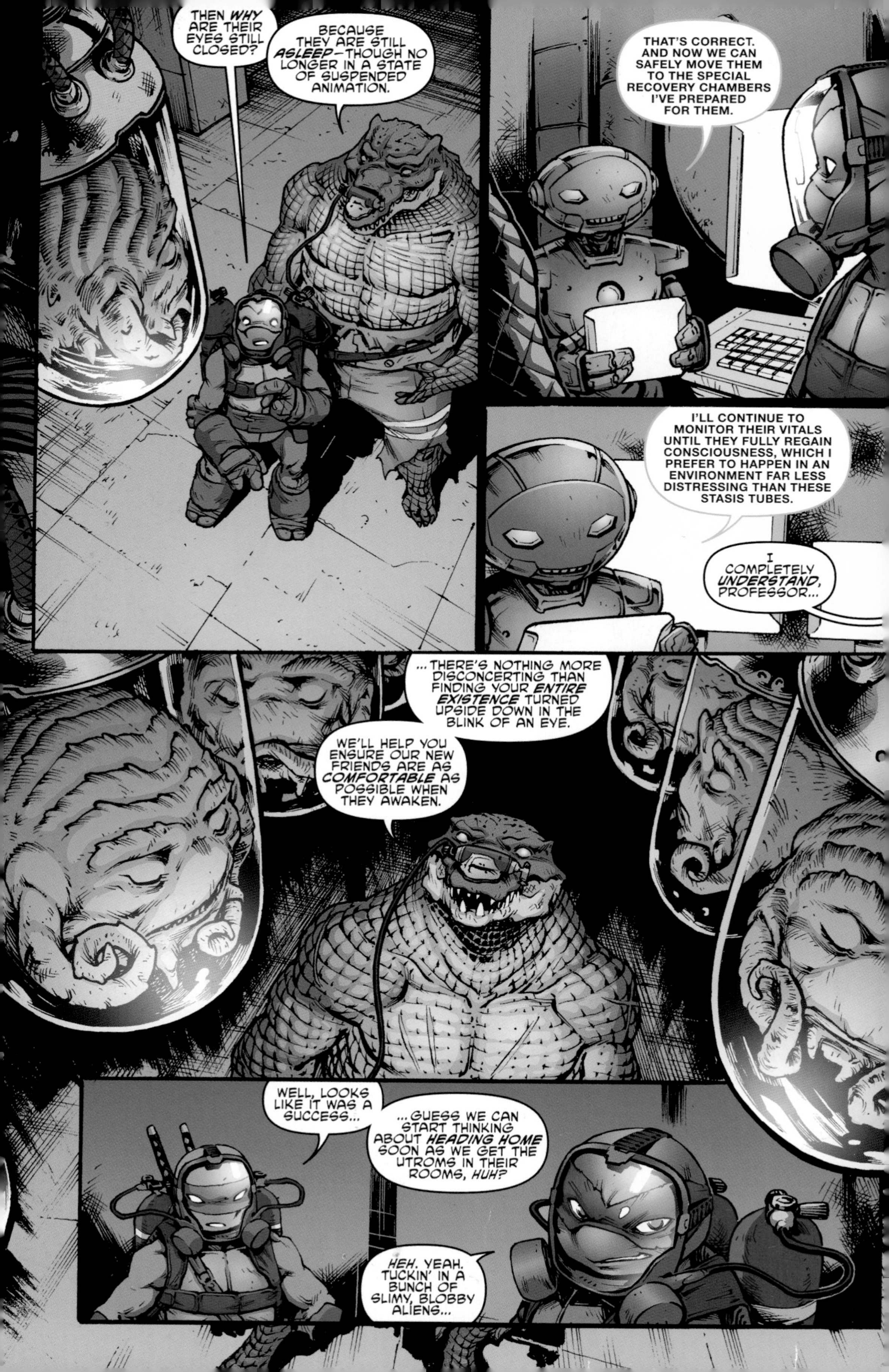
THEN WHY ARE THEIR EYES STILL CLOSED?
BECAUSE THEY ARE STILL ASLEEP—THOUGH NO LONGER IN A STATE OF SUSPENDED ANIMATION.
THAT'S CORRECT. AND NOW WE CAN SAFELY MOVE THEM TO THE SPECIAL RECOVERY CHAMBERS I'VE PREPARED FOR THEM.
I'LL CONTINUE TO MONITOR THEIR VITALS UNTIL THEY FULLY REGAIN CONSCIOUSNESS, WHICH I PREFER TO HAPPEN IN AN ENVIRONMENT FAR LESS DISTRESSING THAN THESE STASIS TUBES.
I COMPLETELY UNDERSTAND, PROFESSOR...
...THERE'S NOTHING MORE DISCONCERTING THAN FINDING YOUR ENTIRE EXISTENCE TURNED UPSIDE DOWN IN THE BLINK OF AN EYE.
WE'LL HELP YOU ENSURE OUR NEW FRIENDS ARE AS COMFORTABLE AS POSSIBLE WHEN THEY AWAKEN.
WELL, LOOKS LIKE IT WAS A SUCCESS...
...GUESS WE CAN START THINKING ABOUT HEADING HOME SOON AS WE GET THE UTROMS IN THEIR ROOMS, HUH?
HEH. YEAH. TUCKIN' IN A BUNCH OF SLIMY, BLOBBY ALIENS...

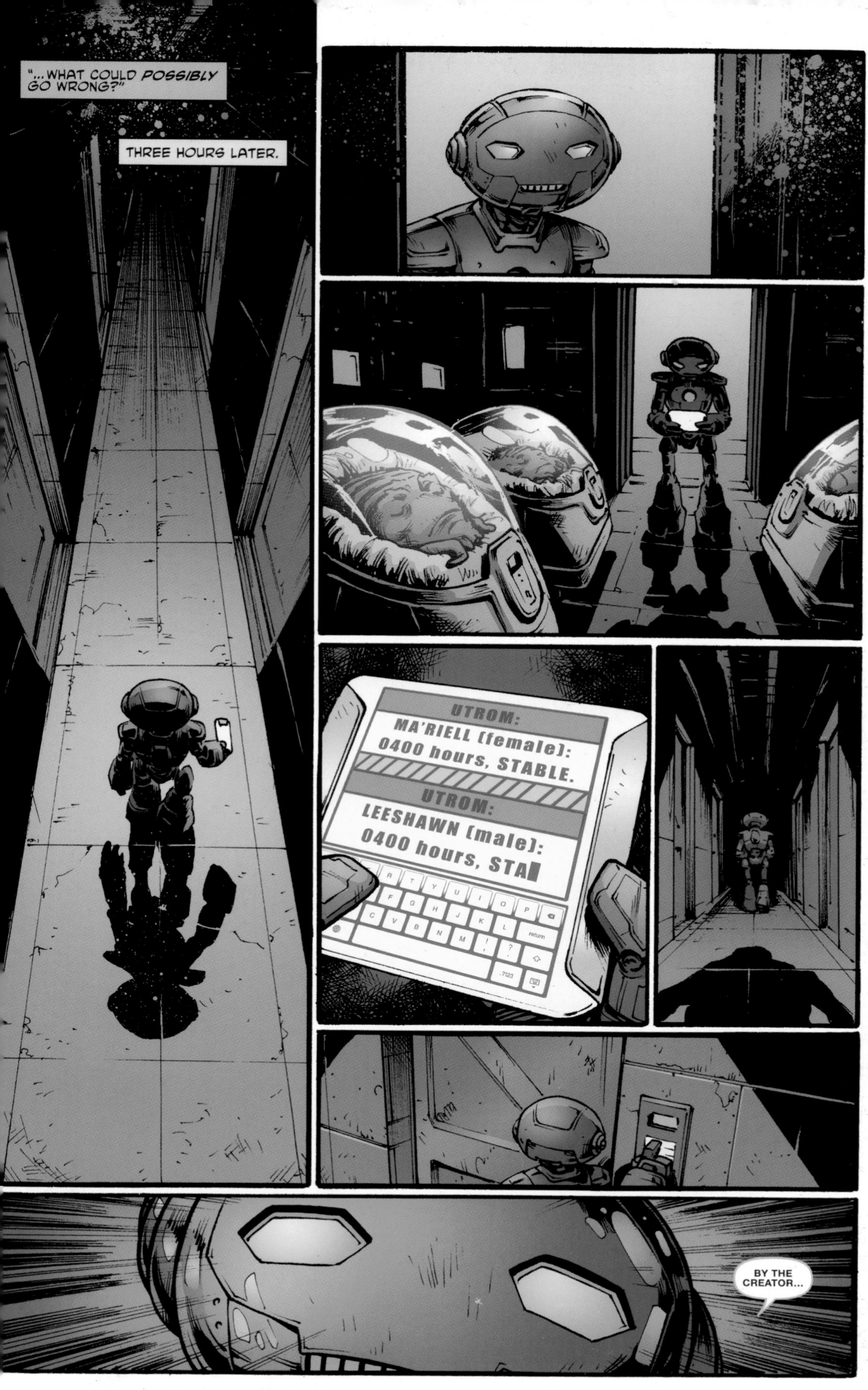
"...WHAT COULD POSSIBLY GO WRONG?"
THREE HOURS LATER.
UTROM:
MA'RIELL (female): 0400 hours, STABLE.
UTROM:
LEESHAWN (male): 0400 hours, STA
BY THE CREATOR...

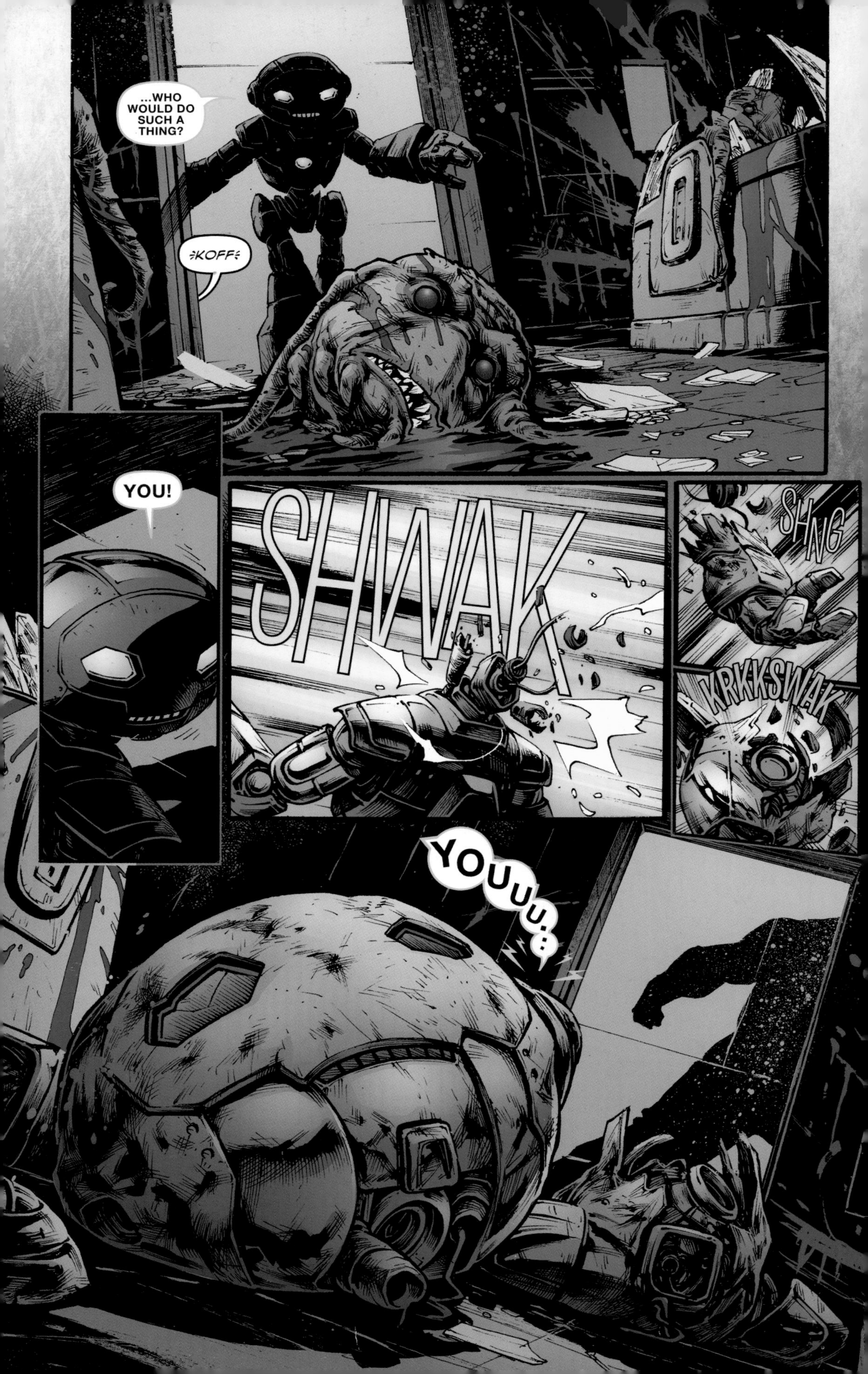
...WHO WOULD DO SUCH A THING?
KOFF
YOU!
SHWAK
SHNG
KRKKSWAK
YOUUU..

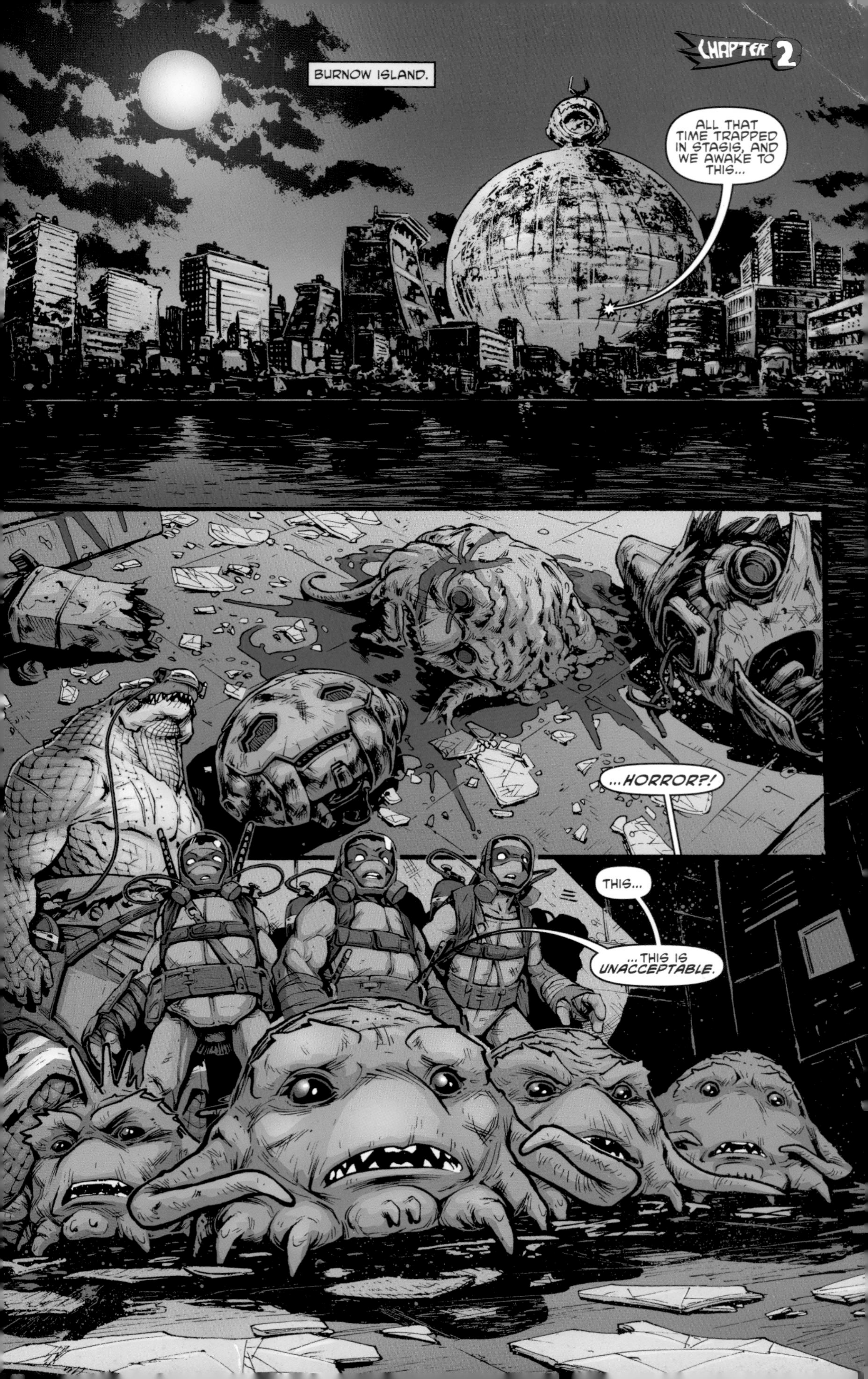
CHAPTER 2
BURNOW ISLAND.
ALL THAT TIME TRAPPED IN STASIS, AND WE AWAKE TO THIS...
...HORROR?!
THIS...
...THIS IS UNACCEPTABLE.

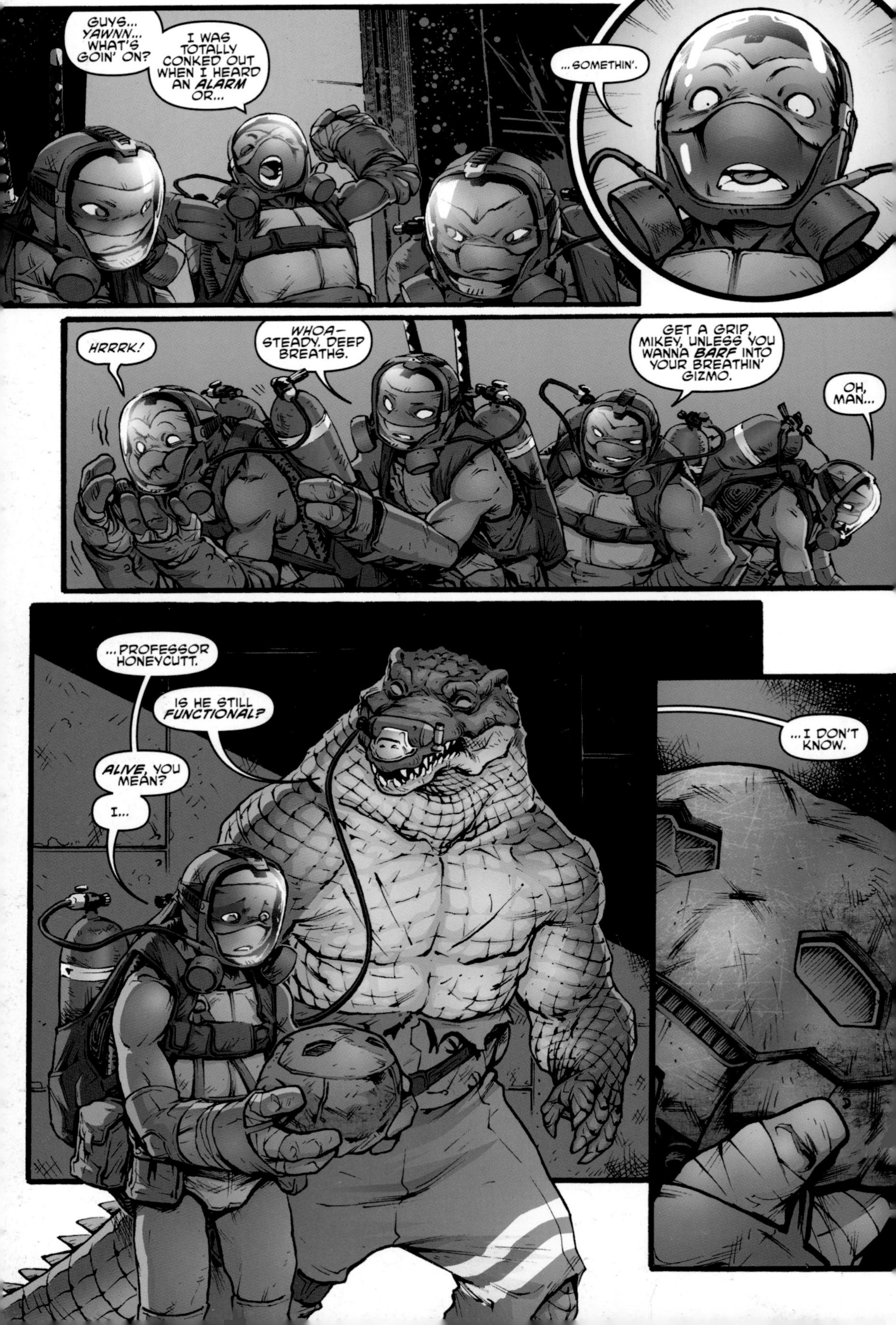
GUYS... YAWNN... WHAT'S GOIN' ON?
I WAS TOTALLY CONKED OUT WHEN I HEARD AN ALARM OR...
...SOMETHIN'.
HRRRK!
WHOA-- STEADY. DEEP BREATHS.
GET A GRIP, MIKEY, UNLESS YOU WANNA BARF INTO YOUR BREATHIN' GIZMO.
OH, MAN...
...PROFESSOR HONEYCUTT.
IS HE STILL FUNCTIONAL?
ALIVE, YOU MEAN?
I...
...I DON'T KNOW.

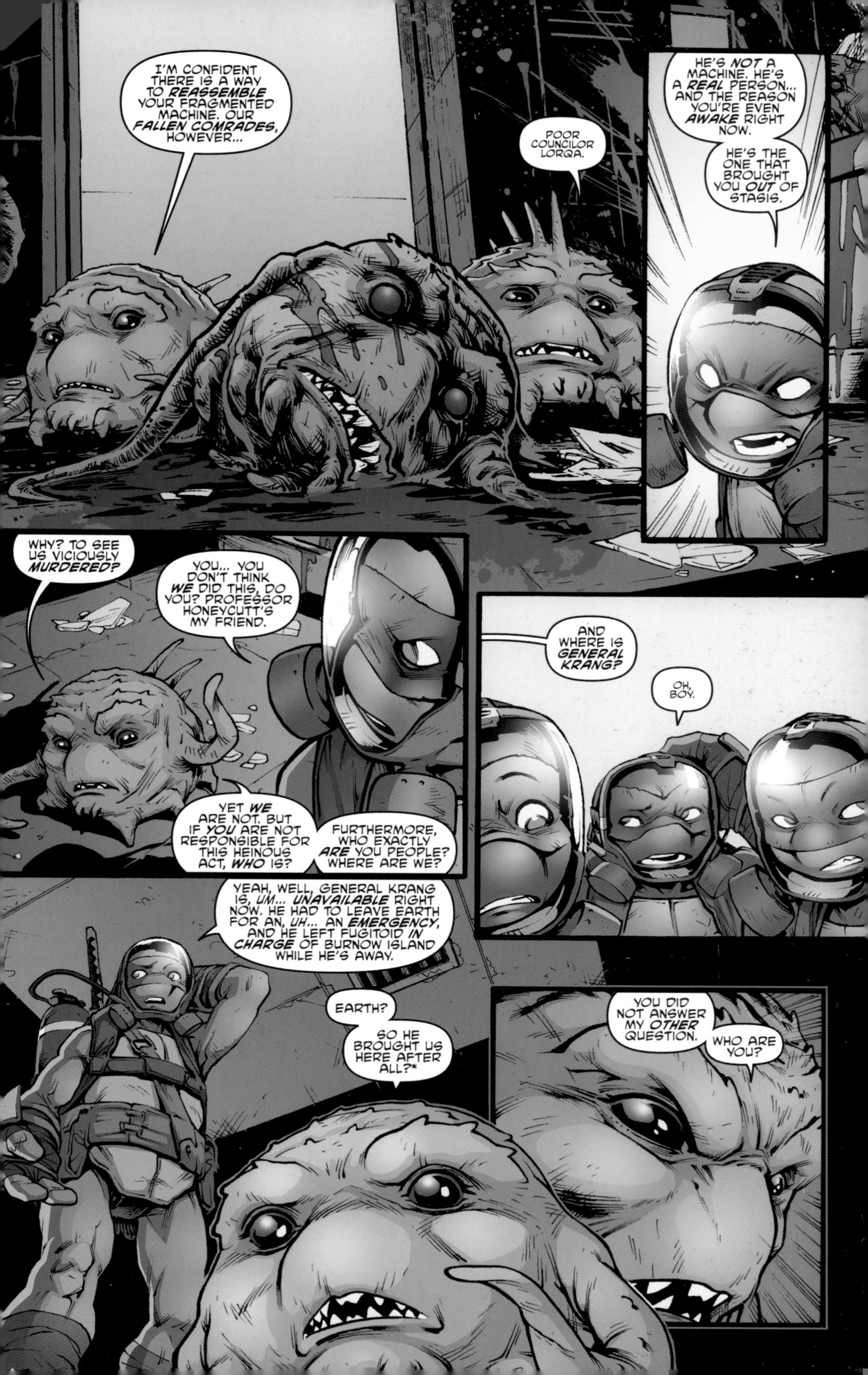
I'M CONFIDENT THERE IS A WAY TO REASSEMBLE YOUR FRAGMENTED MACHINE. OUR FALLEN COMRADES, HOWEVER...
POOR COUNCILOR LORQA.
HE'S NOT A MACHINE. HE'S A REAL PERSON... AND THE REASON YOU'RE EVEN AWAKE RIGHT NOW.
HE'S THE ONE THAT BROUGHT YOU OUT OF STASIS.
WHY? TO SEE US VICIOUSLY MURDERED?
YOU... YOU DON'T THINK WE DID THIS, DO YOU? PROFESSOR HONEYCUTT'S MY FRIEND.
YET WE ARE NOT. BUT IF YOU ARE NOT RESPONSIBLE FOR THIS HEINOUS ACT, WHO IS?
FURTHERMORE, WHO EXACTLY ARE YOU PEOPLE? WHERE ARE WE?
AND WHERE IS GENERAL KRANG?
OH, BOY.
YEAH, WELL, GENERAL KRANG IS, UM... UNAVAILABLE RIGHT NOW. HE HAD TO LEAVE EARTH FOR AN, UH... AN EMERGENCY, AND HE LEFT FUGITOID IN CHARGE OF BURNOW ISLAND WHILE HE'S AWAY.
EARTH?
SO HE BROUGHT US HERE AFTER ALL?*
YOU DID NOT ANSWER MY OTHER QUESTION.
WHO ARE YOU?

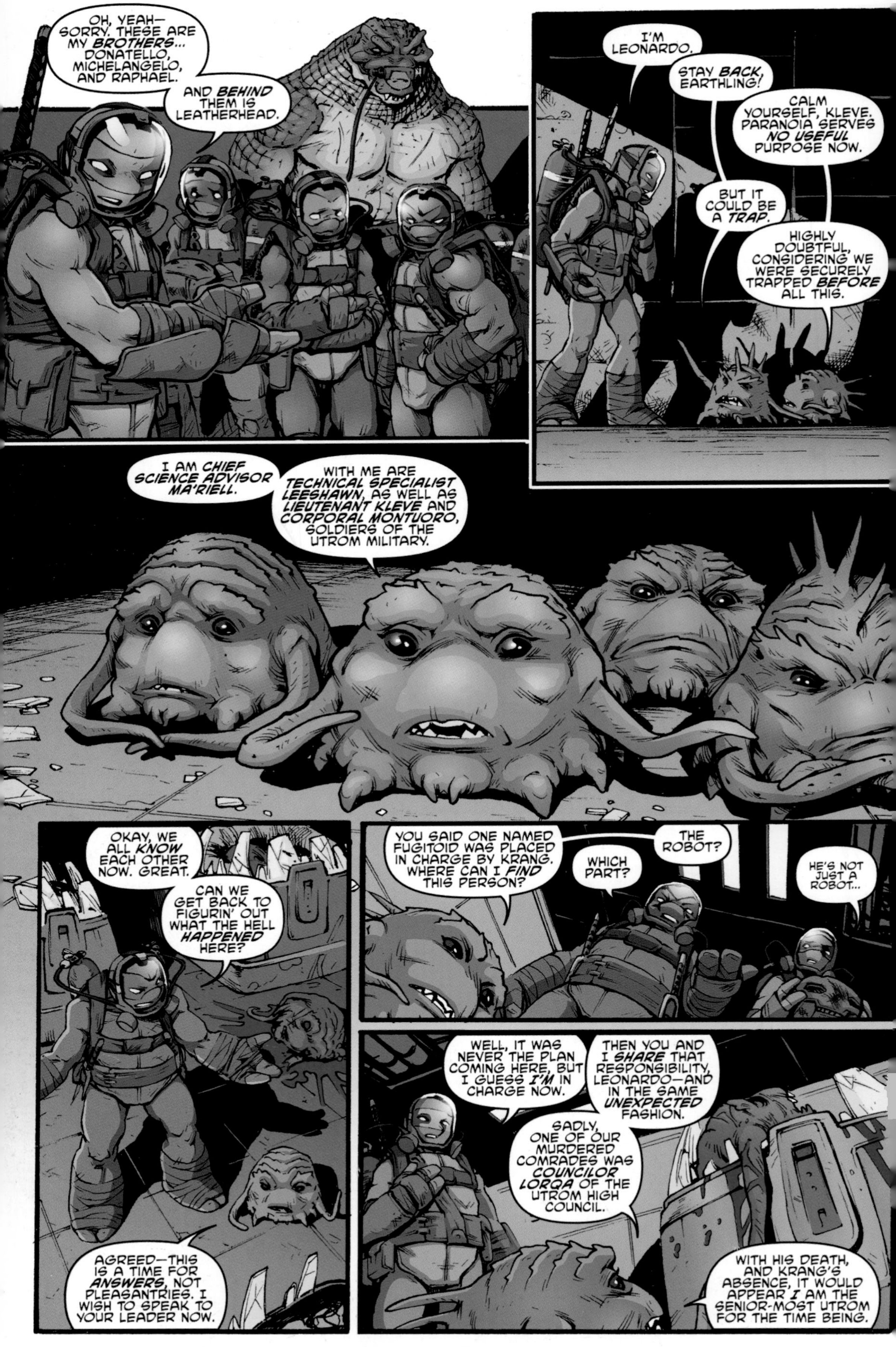
OH, YEAH— SORRY. THESE ARE MY BROTHERS... DONATELLO, MICHELANGELO, AND RAPHAEL.
AND BEHIND THEM IS LEATHERHEAD.
I'M LEONARDO.
STAY BACK, EARTHLING!
CALM YOURSELF, KLEVE. PARANOIA SERVES NO USEFUL PURPOSE NOW.
BUT IT COULD BE A TRAP.
HIGHLY DOUBTFUL, CONSIDERING WE WERE SECURELY TRAPPED BEFORE ALL THIS.
I AM CHIEF SCIENCE ADVISOR MA'RIELL.
WITH ME ARE TECHNICAL SPECIALIST LEESHAWN, AS WELL AS LIEUTENANT KLEVE AND CORPORAL MONTUORO, SOLDIERS OF THE UTROM MILITARY.
OKAY, WE ALL KNOW EACH OTHER NOW. GREAT.
CAN WE GET BACK TO FIGURIN' OUT WHAT THE HELL HAPPENED HERE?
AGREED—THIS IS A TIME FOR ANSWERS, NOT PLEASANTRIES. I WISH TO SPEAK TO YOUR LEADER NOW.
YOU SAID ONE NAMED FUGITOID WAS PLACED IN CHARGE BY KRANG. WHERE CAN I FIND THIS PERSON?
THE ROBOT?
WHICH PART?
HE'S NOT JUST A ROBOT...
WELL, IT WAS NEVER THE PLAN COMING HERE, BUT I GUESS I'M IN CHARGE NOW.
THEN YOU AND I SHARE THAT RESPONSIBILITY, LEONARDO—AND IN THE SAME UNEXPECTED FASHION.
SADLY, ONE OF OUR MURDERED COMRADES WAS COUNCILOR LORQA OF THE UTROM HIGH COUNCIL.
WITH HIS DEATH, AND KRANG'S ABSENCE, IT WOULD APPEAR I AM THE SENIOR-MOST UTROM FOR THE TIME BEING.

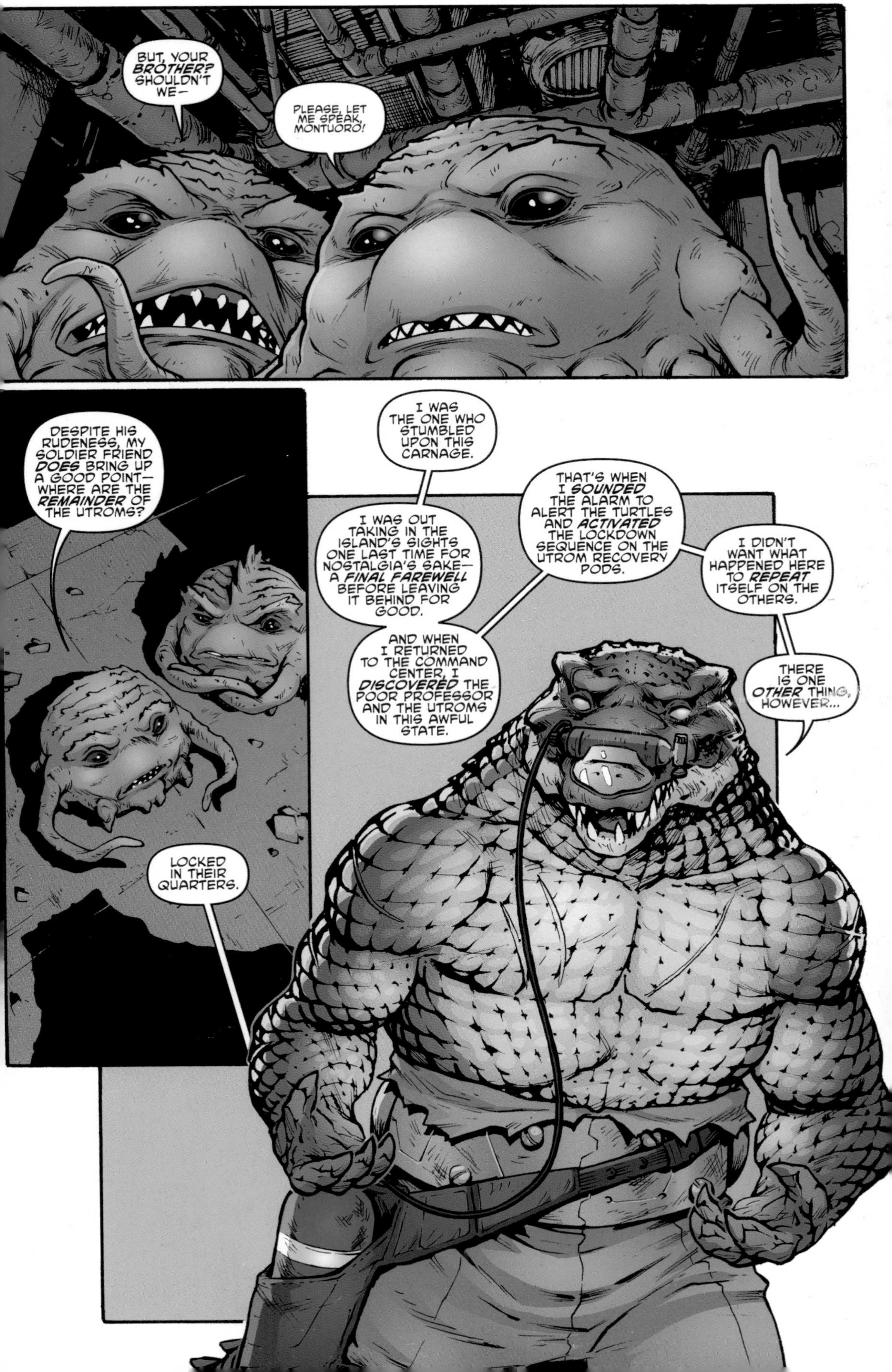
BUT, YOUR BROTHER? SHOULDN'T WE—
PLEASE, LET ME SPEAK, MONTUORO!
DESPITE HIS RUDENESS, MY SOLDIER FRIEND DOES BRING UP A GOOD POINT— WHERE ARE THE REMAINDER OF THE UTROMS?
LOCKED IN THEIR QUARTERS.
I WAS THE ONE WHO STUMBLED UPON THIS CARNAGE.
I WAS OUT TAKING IN THE ISLAND'S SIGHTS ONE LAST TIME FOR NOSTALGIA'S SAKE— A FINAL FAREWELL BEFORE LEAVING IT BEHIND FOR GOOD.
AND WHEN I RETURNED TO THE COMMAND CENTER, I DISCOVERED THE POOR PROFESSOR AND THE UTROMS IN THIS AWFUL STATE.
THAT'S WHEN I SOUNDED THE ALARM TO ALERT THE TURTLES AND ACTIVATED THE LOCKDOWN SEQUENCE ON THE UTROM RECOVERY PODS.
I DIDN'T WANT WHAT HAPPENED HERE TO REPEAT ITSELF ON THE OTHERS.
THERE IS ONE OTHER THING, HOWEVER...

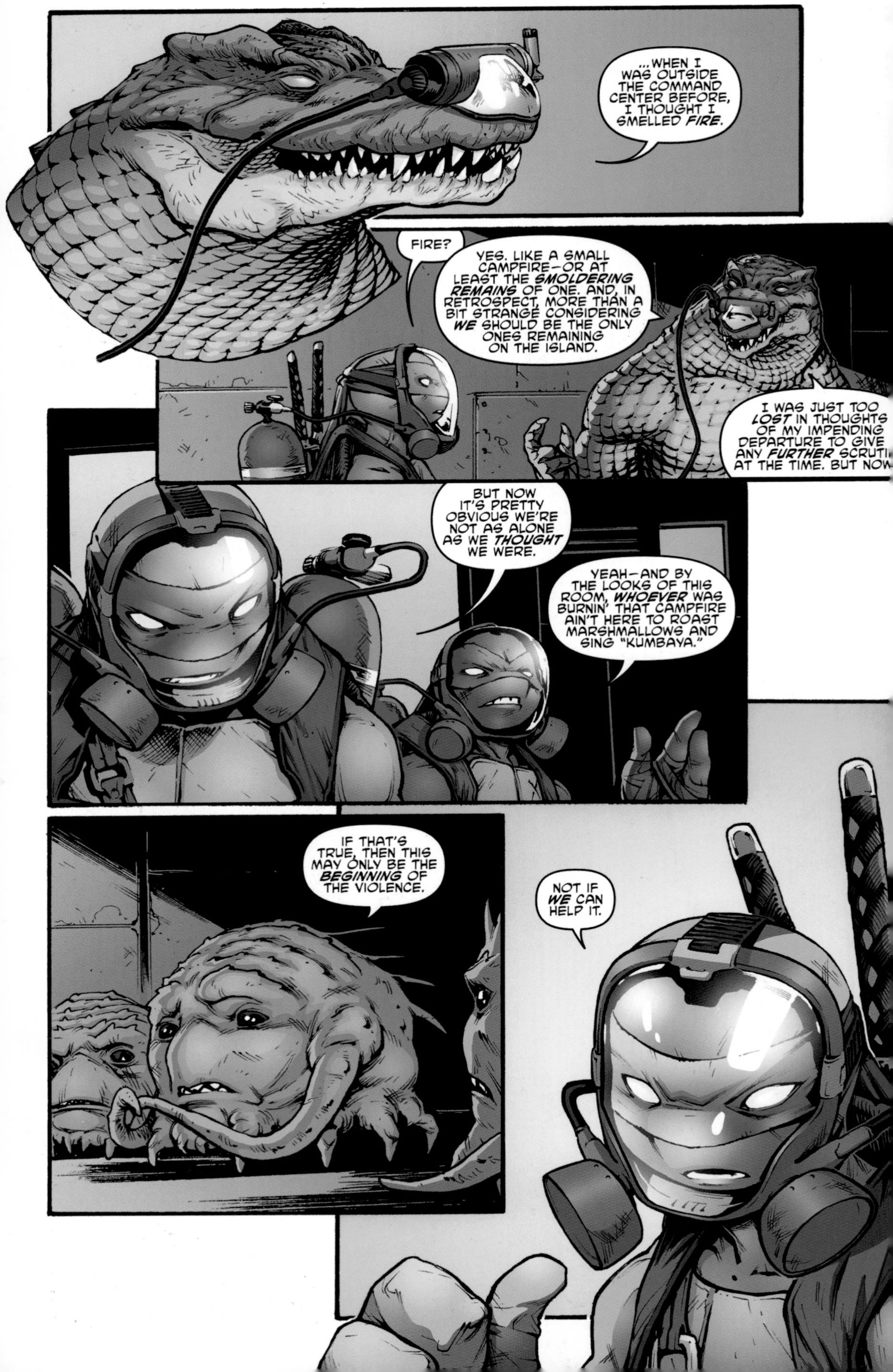
...WHEN I WAS OUTSIDE THE COMMAND CENTER BEFORE, I THOUGHT I SMELLED FIRE.
FIRE?
YES. LIKE A SMALL CAMPFIRE--OR AT LEAST THE SMOLDERING REMAINS OF ONE. AND, IN RETROSPECT, MORE THAN A BIT STRANGE CONSIDERING WE SHOULD BE THE ONLY ONES REMAINING ON THE ISLAND.
I WAS JUST TOO LOST IN THOUGHTS OF MY IMPENDING DEPARTURE TO GIVE ANY FURTHER SCRUTI AT THE TIME. BUT NOW
BUT NOW IT'S PRETTY OBVIOUS WE'RE NOT AS ALONE AS WE THOUGHT WE WERE.
YEAH--AND BY THE LOOKS OF THIS ROOM, WHOEVER WAS BURNIN' THAT CAMPFIRE AIN'T HERE TO ROAST MARSHMALLOWS AND SING "KUMBAYA."
IF THAT'S TRUE, THEN THIS MAY ONLY BE THE BEGINNING OF THE VIOLENCE.
NOT IF WE CAN HELP IT.

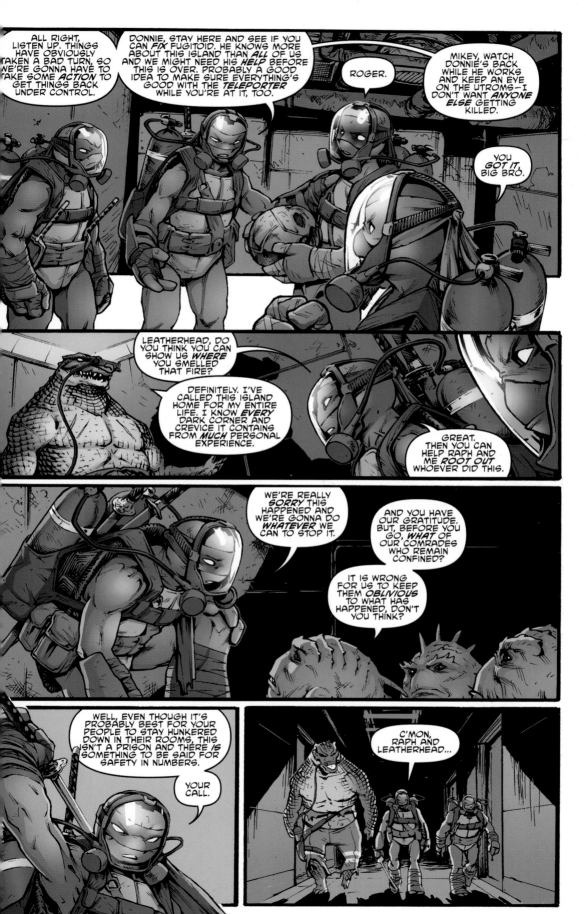

ALL RIGHT, LISTEN UP. THINGS HAVE OBVIOUSLY TAKEN A BAD TURN, SO WE'RE GONNA HAVE TO TAKE SOME *ACTION* TO GET THINGS BACK UNDER CONTROL.

DONNIE, STAY HERE AND SEE IF YOU CAN *FIX* FUGITOID. HE KNOWS MORE ABOUT THIS ISLAND THAN *ALL* OF US AND WE MIGHT NEED HIS *HELP* BEFORE THIS IS OVER. PROBABLY A GOOD IDEA TO MAKE SURE EVERYTHING'S GOOD WITH THE *TELEPORTER* WHILE YOU'RE AT IT, TOO.

ROGER.

MIKEY, WATCH DONNIE'S BACK WHILE HE WORKS AND KEEP AN EYE ON THE UTROMS—I DON'T WANT *ANYONE ELSE* GETTING KILLED.

YOU *GOT IT* BIG BRO.

LEATHERHEAD, DO YOU THINK YOU CAN SHOW US *WHERE* YOU SMELLED THAT FIRE?

DEFINITELY. I'VE CALLED THIS ISLAND HOME FOR MY ENTIRE LIFE. I KNOW *EVERY* DARK CORNER AND CREVICE IT CONTAINS FROM *MUCH* PERSONAL EXPERIENCE.

GREAT. THEN YOU CAN HELP RAPH AND ME *ROOT OUT* WHOEVER DID THIS.

WE'RE REALLY *SORRY* THIS HAPPENED AND WE'RE GONNA DO *WHATEVER* WE CAN TO STOP IT.

AND YOU HAVE OUR GRATITUDE. BUT, BEFORE YOU GO, *WHAT* OF OUR COMRADES WHO REMAIN CONFINED?

IT IS WRONG FOR US TO KEEP THEM *OBLIVIOUS* TO WHAT HAS HAPPENED, DON'T YOU THINK?

WELL, EVEN THOUGH IT'S PROBABLY BEST FOR YOUR PEOPLE TO STAY HUNKERED DOWN IN THEIR ROOMS, THIS ISN'T A PRISON AND THERE *IS* SOMETHING TO BE SAID FOR SAFETY IN NUMBERS.

YOUR CALL.

C'MON, RAPH AND LEATHERHEAD...

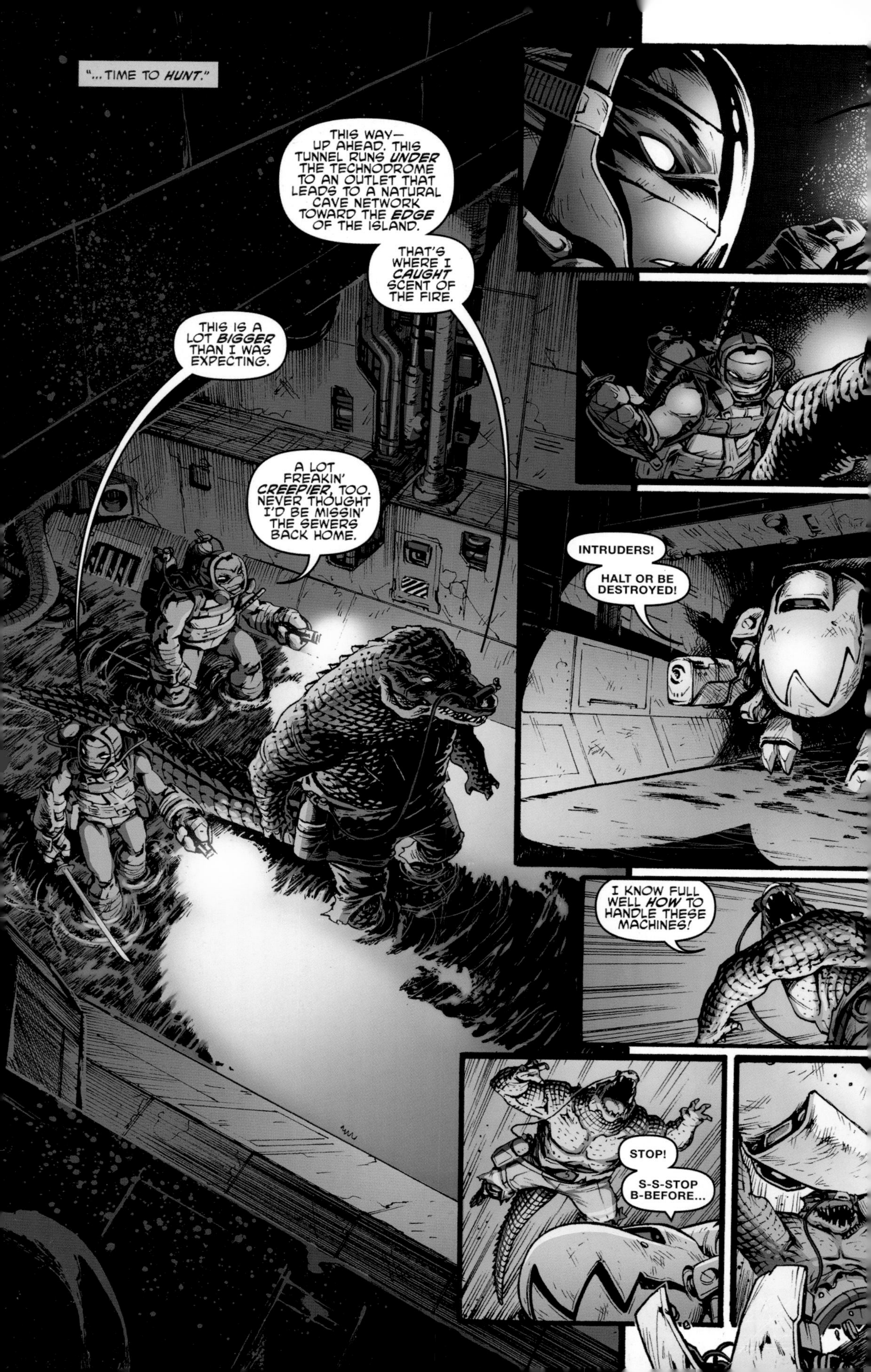
"...TIME TO HUNT."
THIS WAY— UP AHEAD. THIS TUNNEL RUNS UNDER THE TECHNODROME TO AN OUTLET THAT LEADS TO A NATURAL CAVE NETWORK TOWARD THE EDGE OF THE ISLAND.
THAT'S WHERE I CAUGHT SCENT OF THE FIRE.
THIS IS A LOT BIGGER THAN I WAS EXPECTING.
A LOT FREAKIN' CREEPIER, TOO. NEVER THOUGHT I'D BE MISSIN' THE SEWERS BACK HOME.
INTRUDERS!
HALT OR BE DESTROYED!
I KNOW FULL WELL HOW TO HANDLE THESE MACHINES!
STOP!
S-S-STOP B-BEFORE...

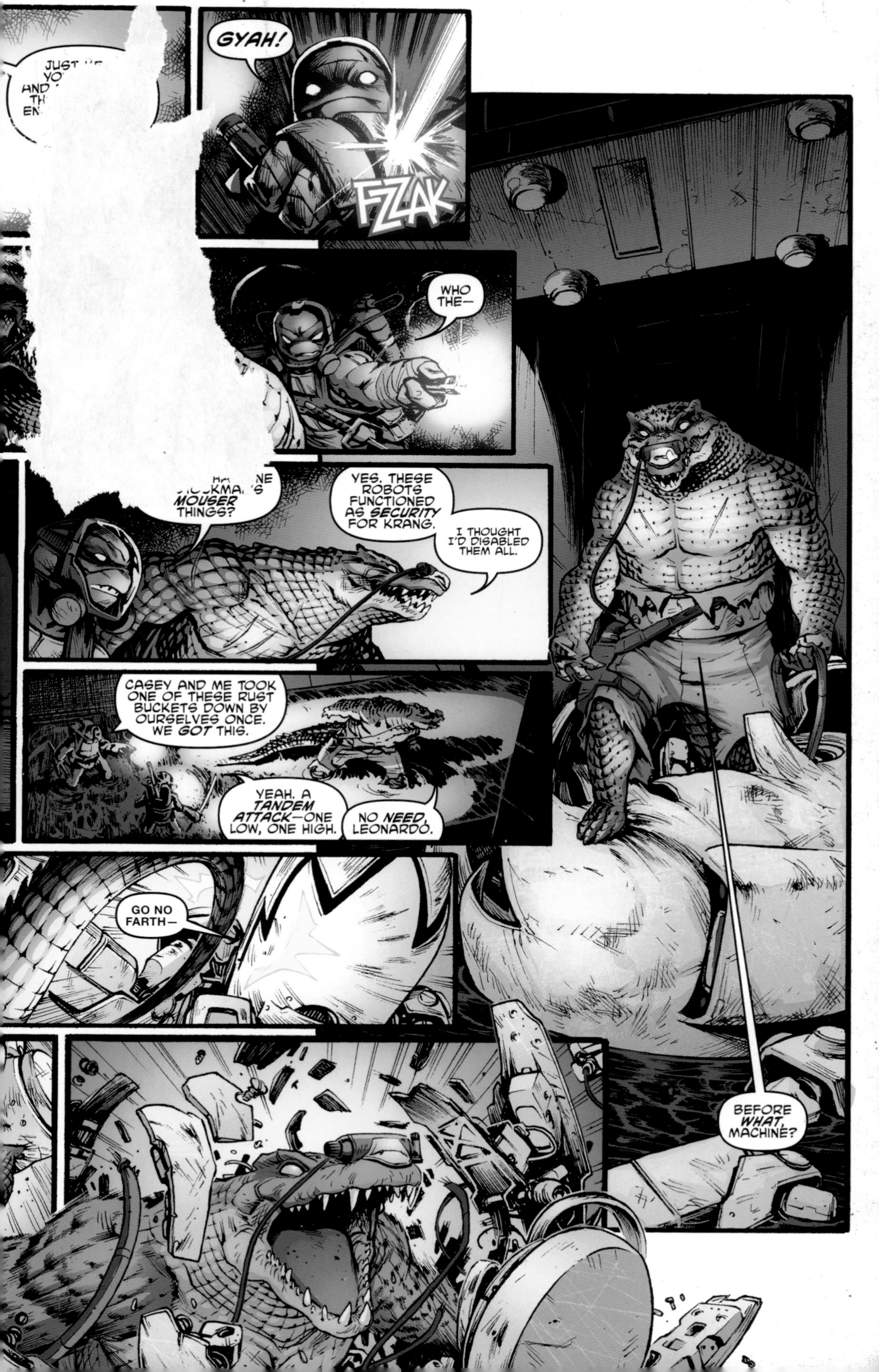
GYAH!
FZZAK
WHO THE—
MOUSER THINGS?
YES. THESE ROBOTS FUNCTIONED AS SECURITY FOR KRANG.
I THOUGHT I'D DISABLED THEM ALL.
CASEY AND ME TOOK ONE OF THESE RUST BUCKETS DOWN BY OURSELVES ONCE. WE GOT THIS.
YEAH. A TANDEM ATTACK—ONE LOW, ONE HIGH.
NO NEED, LEONARDO.
GO NO FARTH—
BEFORE WHAT, MACHINE?

YES, WELL...
SHALL WE
CONTINUE?

SKKZZXX

REMIND
ME TO NEVER
CHALLENGE
THAT GUY TO
A WRESTLIN'
MATCH.

YEAH.

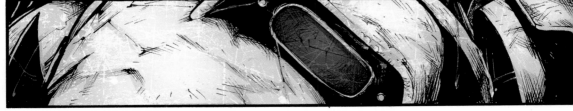

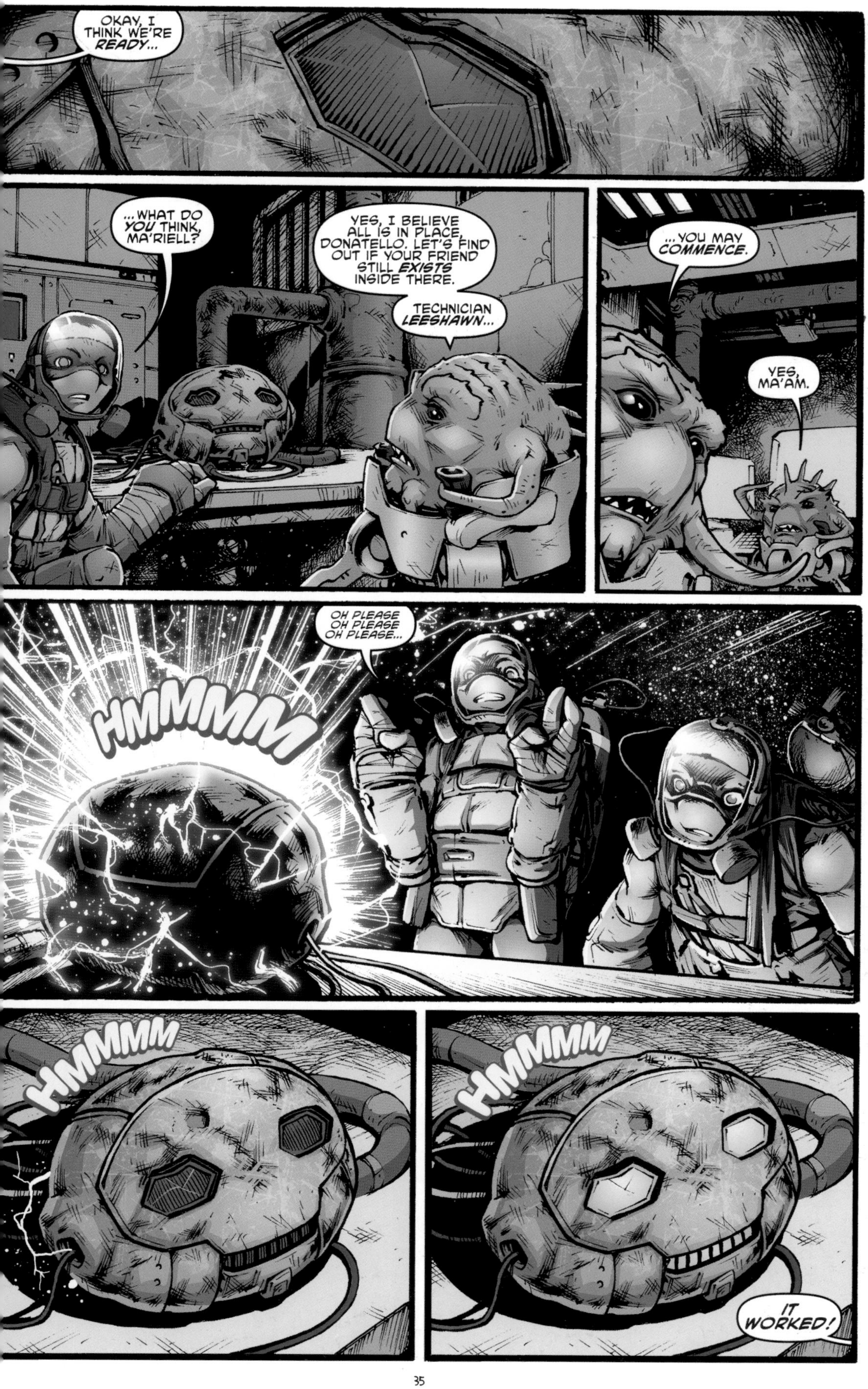
OKAY, I THINK WE'RE READY...
...WHAT DO YOU THINK, MA'RIELL?
YES, I BELIEVE ALL IS IN PLACE, DONATELLO. LET'S FIND OUT IF YOUR FRIEND STILL EXISTS INSIDE THERE.
TECHNICIAN LEESHAWN...
...YOU MAY COMMENCE.
YES, MA'AM.
HMMMM
OH PLEASE OH PLEASE OH PLEASE...
HMMMM
HMMMM
IT WORKED!

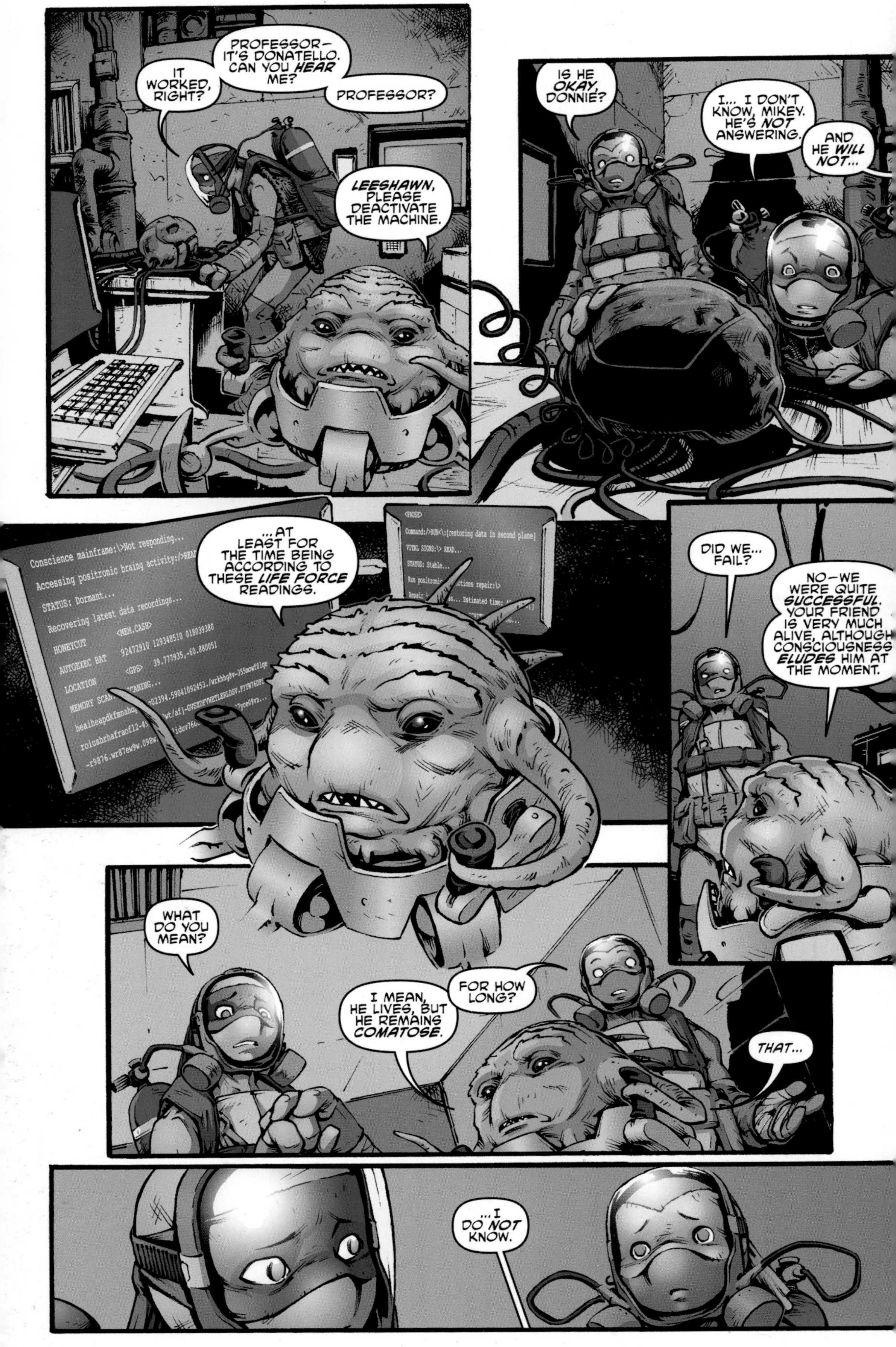

IT WORKED, RIGHT?
PROFESSOR– IT'S DONATELLO. CAN YOU *HEAR* ME?
PROFESSOR?
LEESHAWN, PLEASE DEACTIVATE THE MACHINE.
IS HE *OKAY,* DONNIE?
I... I DON'T KNOW, MIKEY. HE'S *NOT* ANSWERING.
AND HE *WILL NOT*...
Conscience mainframe:\>Not responding...
STATUS: Dormant...
Recovering latest data recordings...
...AT LEAST FOR THE TIME BEING ACCORDING TO THESE *LIFE FORCE* READINGS.
VITAL SIGNS:\> READ...
STATUS: Stable...
DID WE... FAIL?
NO–WE WERE QUITE *SUCCESSFUL.* YOUR FRIEND IS VERY MUCH ALIVE, ALTHOUGH CONSCIOUSNESS *ELUDES* HIM AT THE MOMENT.
WHAT DO YOU MEAN?
I MEAN, HE LIVES, BUT HE REMAINS *COMATOSE.*
FOR HOW LONG?
THAT...
...I DO *NOT* KNOW.

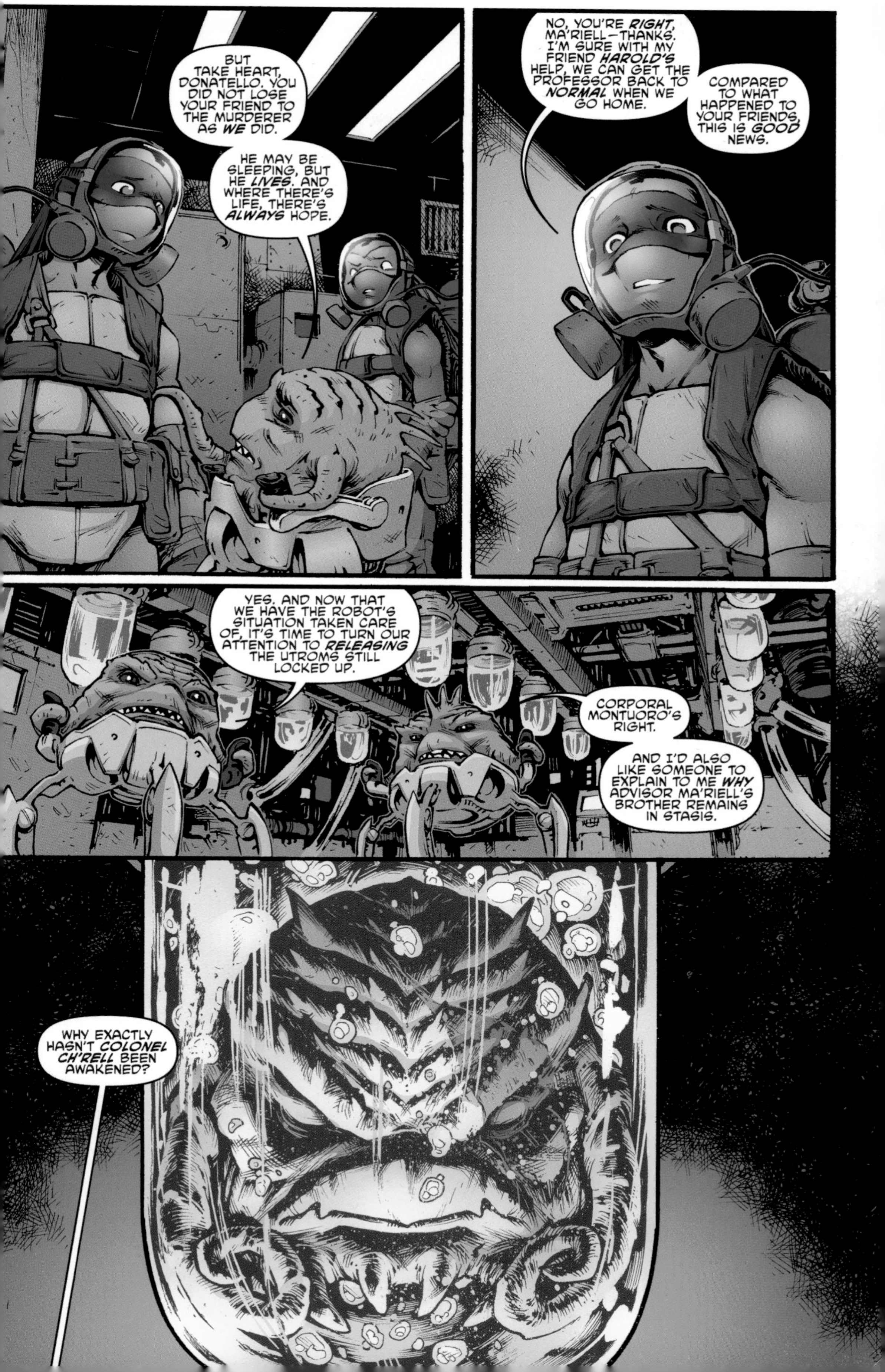

BUT TAKE HEART, DONATELLO. YOU DID NOT LOSE YOUR FRIEND TO THE MURDERER AS *WE* DID.
HE MAY BE SLEEPING, BUT HE *LIVES*. AND WHERE THERE'S LIFE, THERE'S *ALWAYS* HOPE.
NO, YOU'RE *RIGHT*, MA'RIELL—THANKS. I'M SURE WITH MY FRIEND *HAROLD'S* HELP, WE CAN GET THE PROFESSOR BACK TO *NORMAL* WHEN WE GO HOME.
COMPARED TO WHAT HAPPENED TO YOUR FRIENDS, THIS IS *GOOD* NEWS.
YES. AND NOW THAT WE HAVE THE ROBOT'S SITUATION TAKEN CARE OF, IT'S TIME TO TURN OUR ATTENTION TO *RELEASING* THE UTROMS STILL LOCKED UP.
CORPORAL MONTUORO'S RIGHT.
AND I'D ALSO LIKE SOMEONE TO EXPLAIN TO ME *WHY* ADVISOR MA'RIELL'S BROTHER REMAINS IN STASIS.
WHY EXACTLY HASN'T *COLONEL CH'RELL* BEEN AWAKENED?

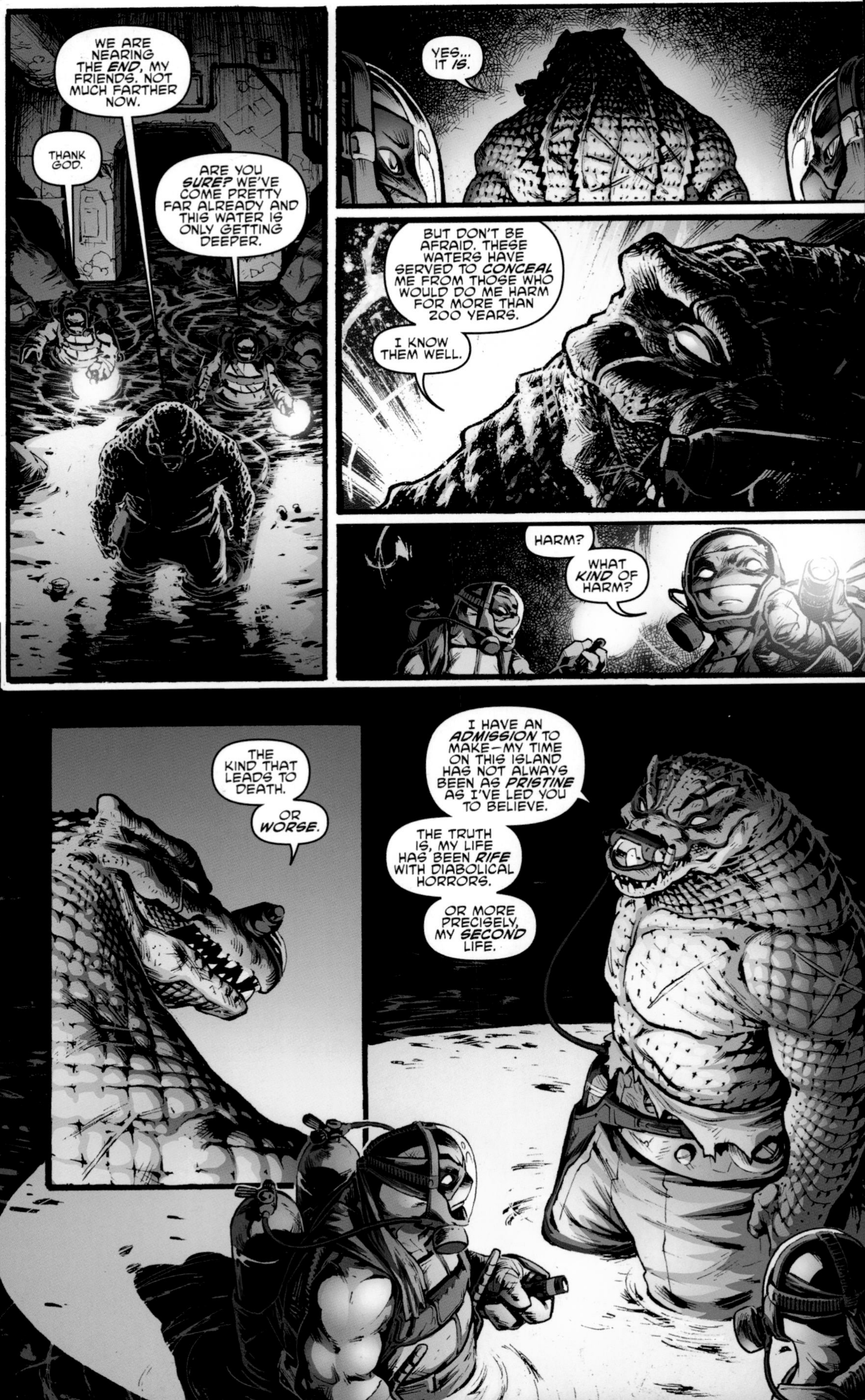
WE ARE NEARING THE END, MY FRIENDS. NOT MUCH FARTHER NOW.
THANK GOD.
ARE YOU SURE? WE'VE COME PRETTY FAR ALREADY AND THIS WATER IS ONLY GETTING DEEPER.
YES... IT IS.
BUT DON'T BE AFRAID. THESE WATERS HAVE SERVED TO CONCEAL ME FROM THOSE WHO WOULD DO ME HARM FOR MORE THAN 200 YEARS.
I KNOW THEM WELL.
HARM?
WHAT KIND OF HARM?
THE KIND THAT LEADS TO DEATH.
OR WORSE.
I HAVE AN ADMISSION TO MAKE—MY TIME ON THIS ISLAND HAS NOT ALWAYS BEEN AS PRISTINE AS I'VE LED YOU TO BELIEVE.
THE TRUTH IS, MY LIFE HAS BEEN RIFE WITH DIABOLICAL HORRORS.
OR MORE PRECISELY, MY SECOND LIFE.

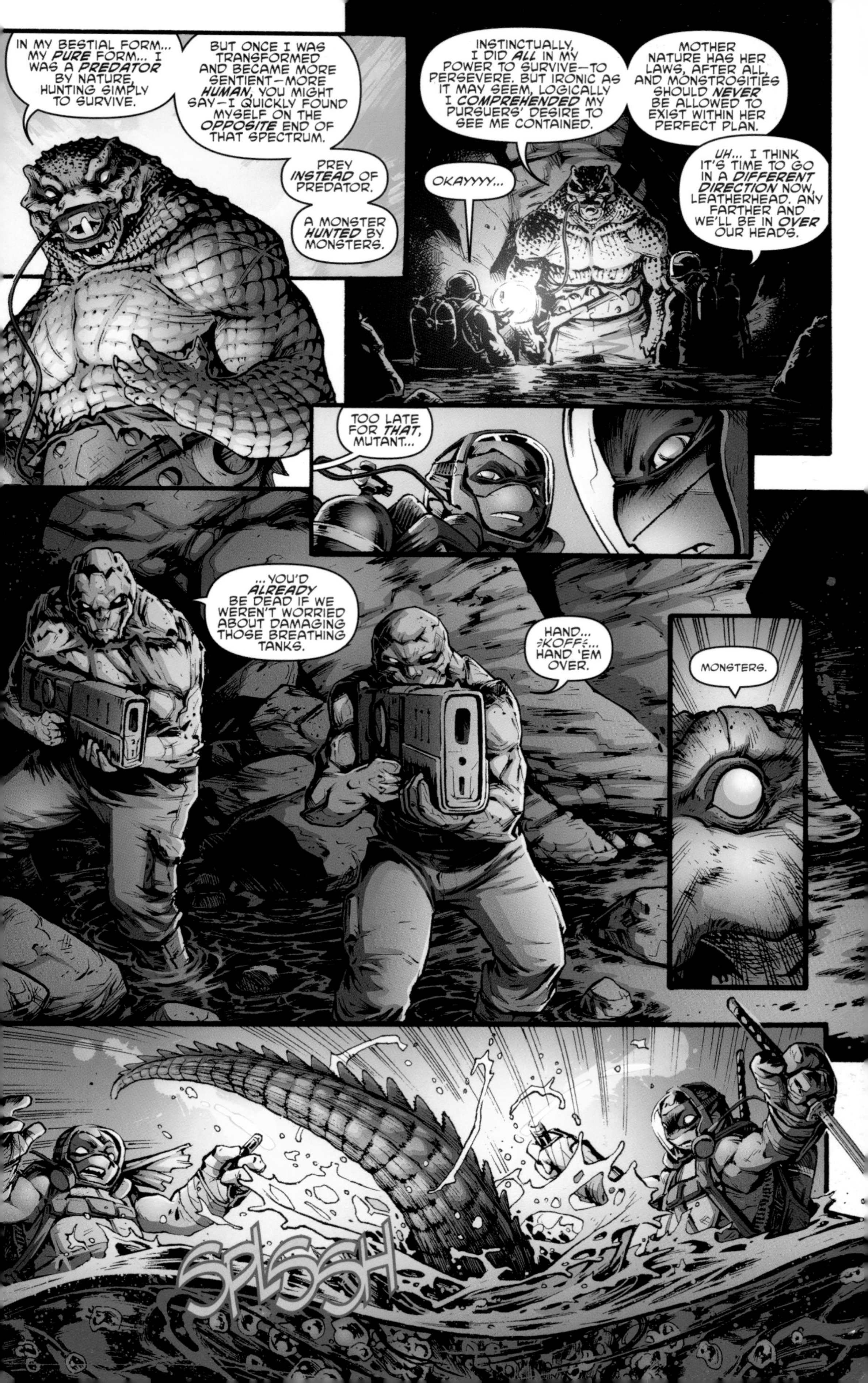
IN MY BESTIAL FORM... MY *PURE* FORM... I WAS A *PREDATOR* BY NATURE, HUNTING SIMPLY TO SURVIVE.
BUT ONCE I WAS TRANSFORMED AND BECAME MORE SENTIENT—MORE *HUMAN*, YOU MIGHT SAY—I QUICKLY FOUND MYSELF ON THE *OPPOSITE* END OF THAT SPECTRUM.
PREY *INSTEAD* OF PREDATOR.
A MONSTER *HUNTED* BY MONSTERS.
INSTINCTUALLY, I DID *ALL* IN MY POWER TO SURVIVE—TO PERSEVERE. BUT IRONIC AS IT MAY SEEM, LOGICALLY I *COMPREHENDED* MY PURSUERS' DESIRE TO SEE ME CONTAINED.
MOTHER NATURE HAS HER LAWS, AFTER ALL, AND MONSTROSITIES SHOULD *NEVER* BE ALLOWED TO EXIST WITHIN HER PERFECT PLAN.
OKAYYYY...
UH... I THINK IT'S TIME TO GO IN A *DIFFERENT DIRECTION* NOW, LEATHERHEAD. ANY FARTHER AND WE'LL BE IN *OVER* OUR HEADS.
TOO LATE FOR *THAT*, MUTANT...
...YOU'D *ALREADY* BE DEAD IF WE WEREN'T WORRIED ABOUT DAMAGING THOSE BREATHING TANKS.
HAND... *KOFF*... HAND 'EM OVER.
MONSTERS.
SPLSSH

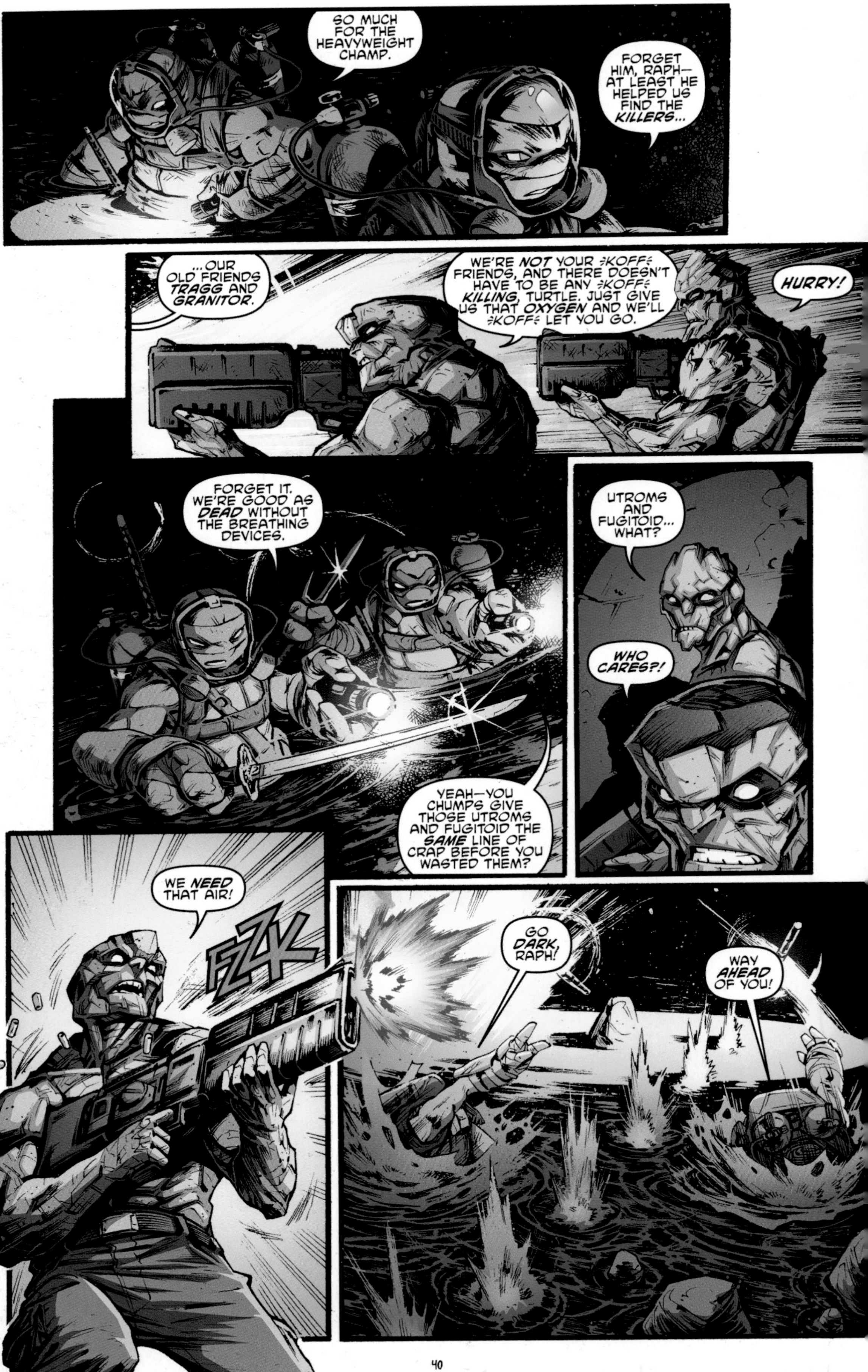
SO MUCH FOR THE HEAVYWEIGHT CHAMP.
FORGET HIM, RAPH— AT LEAST HE HELPED US FIND THE KILLERS...
...OUR OLD FRIENDS TRAGG AND GRANITOR.
WE'RE NOT YOUR ≠KOFF≠ FRIENDS, AND THERE DOESN'T HAVE TO BE ANY ≠KOFF≠ KILLING, TURTLE. JUST GIVE US THAT OXYGEN AND WE'LL ≠KOFF≠ LET YOU GO.
HURRY!
FORGET IT. WE'RE GOOD AS DEAD WITHOUT THE BREATHING DEVICES.
YEAH—YOU CHUMPS GIVE THOSE UTROMS AND FUGITOID THE SAME LINE OF CRAP BEFORE YOU WASTED THEM?
UTROMS AND FUGITOID... WHAT?
WHO CARES?!
WE NEED THAT AIR!
FZZK
GO DARK, RAPH!
WAY AHEAD OF YOU!

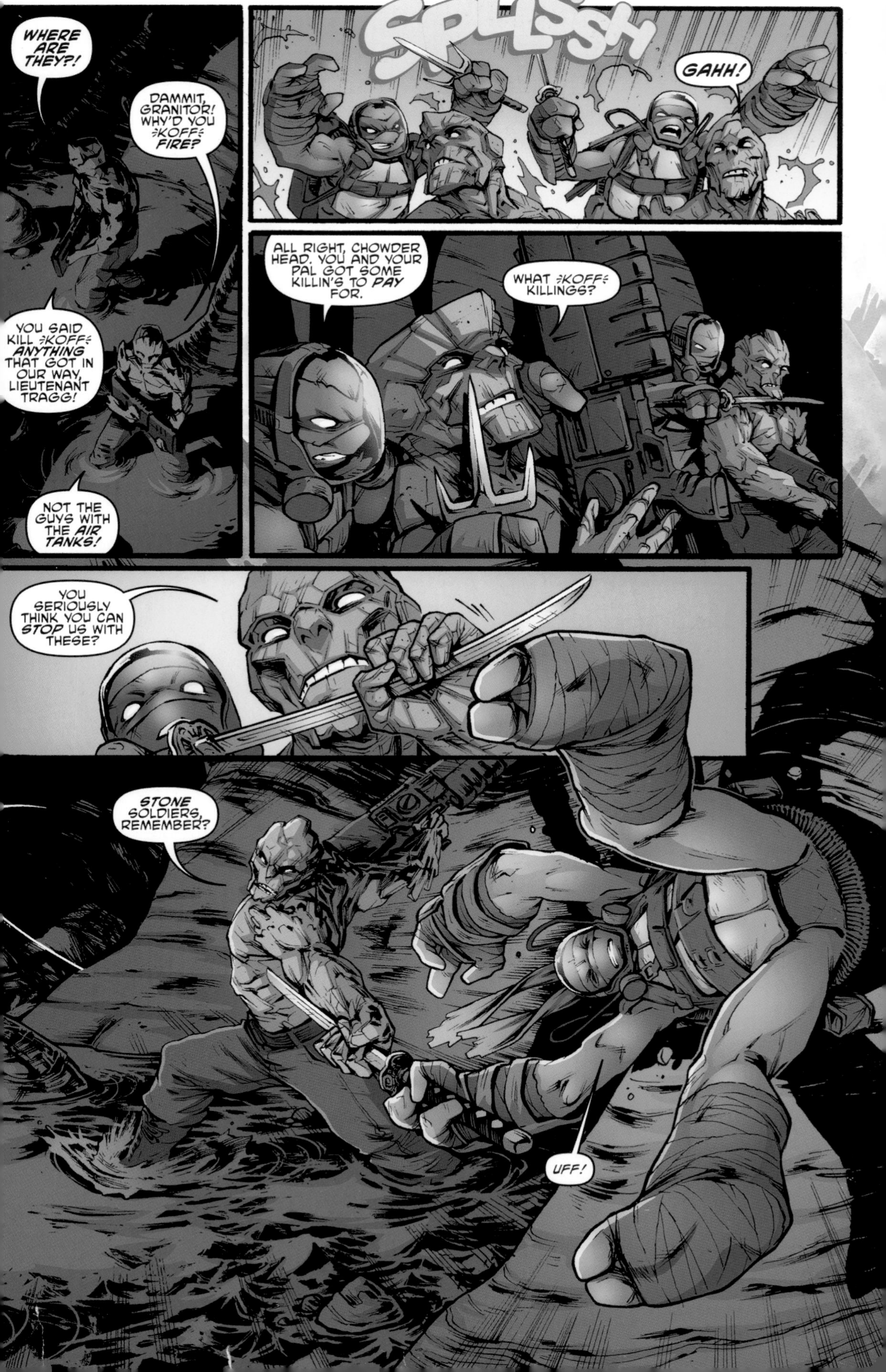
WHERE ARE THEY?!
DAMMIT, GRANITOR! WHY'D YOU *KOFF* FIRE?
YOU SAID KILL *KOFF* ANYTHING THAT GOT IN OUR WAY, LIEUTENANT TRAGG!
NOT THE GUYS WITH THE AIR TANKS!
SPLLSSH
GAHH!
ALL RIGHT, CHOWDER HEAD. YOU AND YOUR PAL GOT SOME KILLIN'S TO PAY FOR.
WHAT *KOFF* KILLINGS?
YOU SERIOUSLY THINK YOU CAN STOP US WITH THESE?
STONE SOLDIERS, REMEMBER?
UFF!

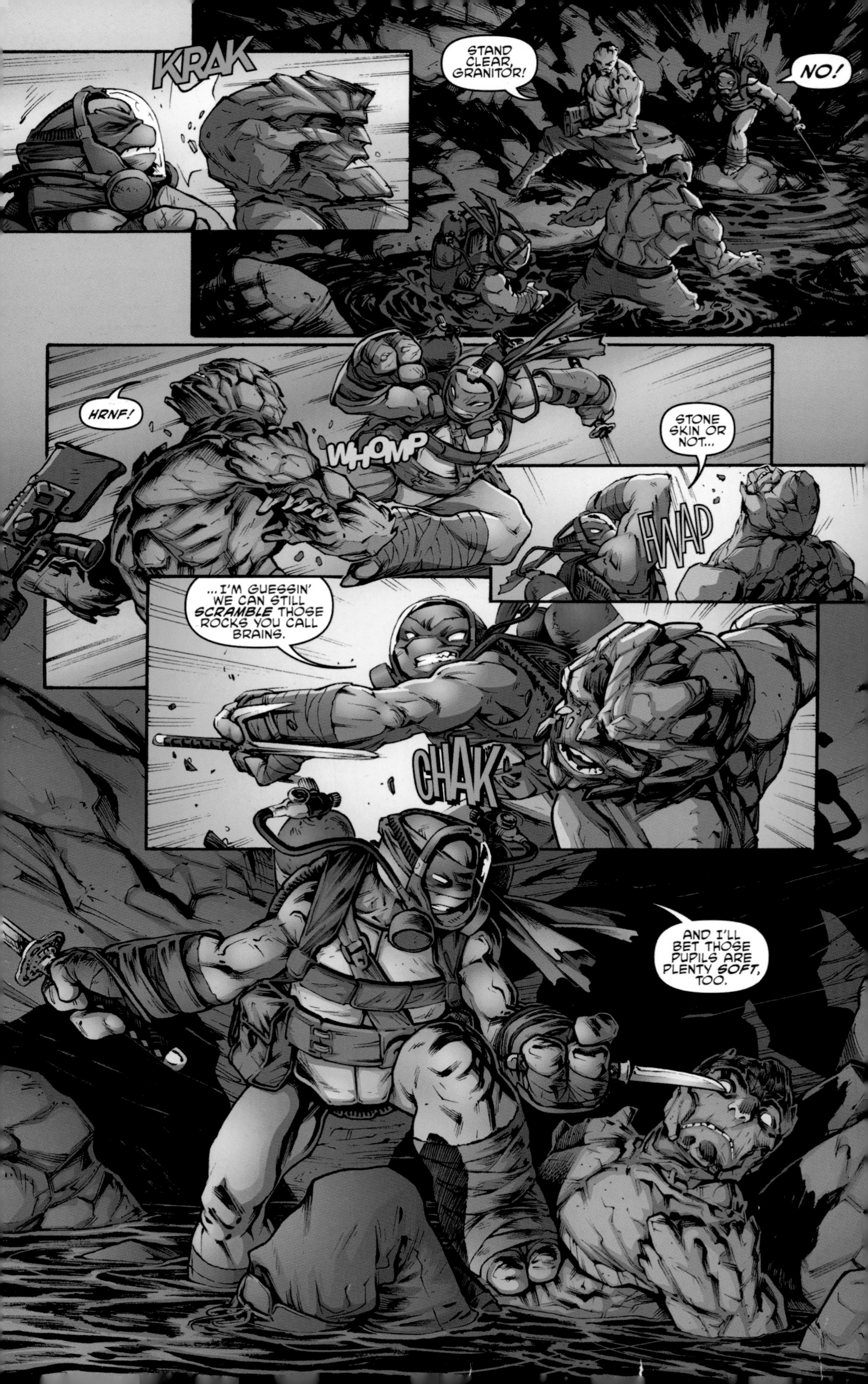
KRAK
STAND CLEAR, GRANITOR!
NO!
HRNF!
WHOMP
STONE SKIN OR NOT...
FWAP
...I'M GUESSIN' WE CAN STILL SCRAMBLE THOSE ROCKS YOU CALL BRAINS.
CHAK
AND I'LL BET THOSE PUPILS ARE PLENTY SOFT, TOO.

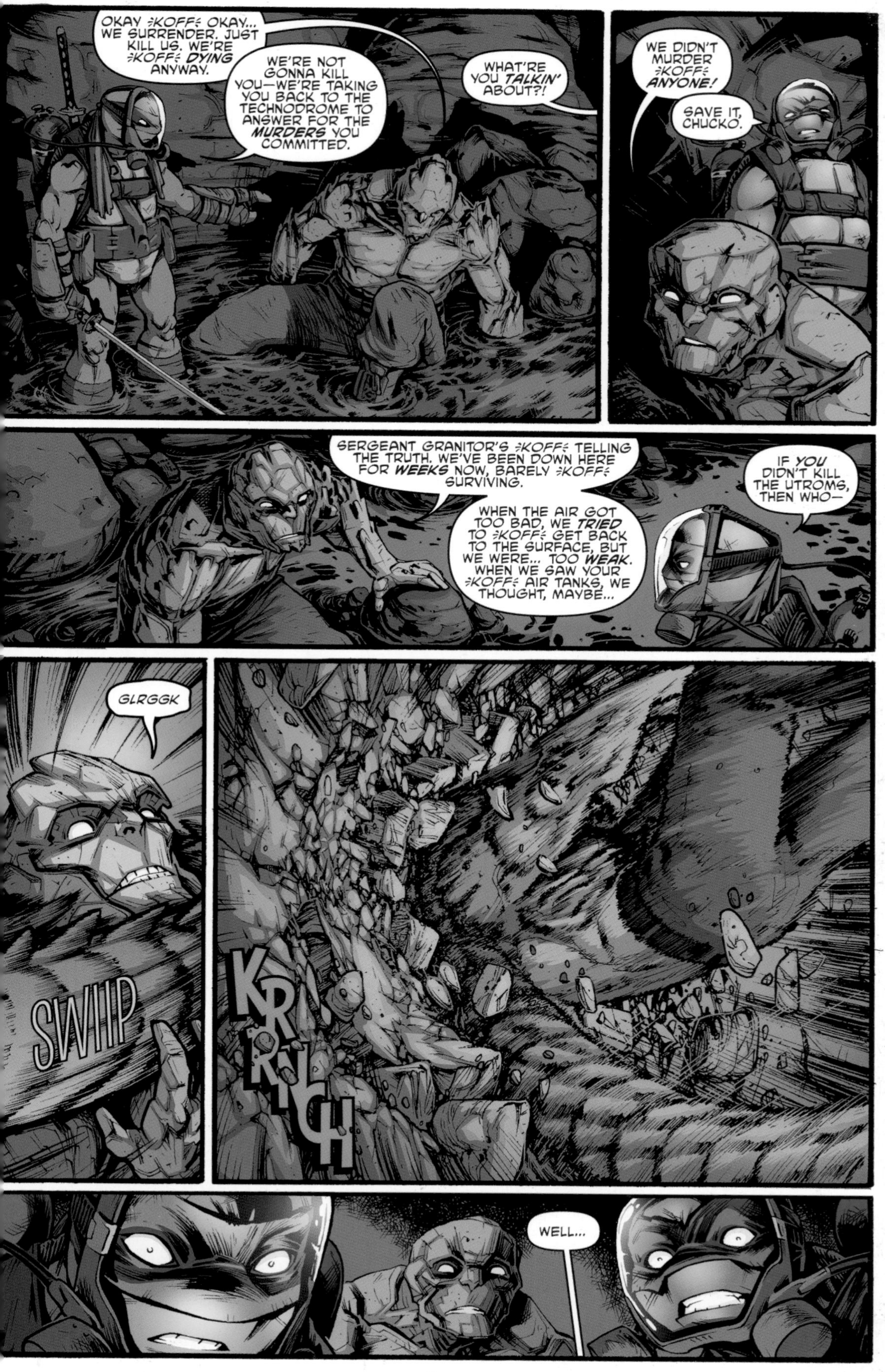
OKAY ≠KOFF≠ OKAY... WE SURRENDER. JUST KILL US. WE'RE ≠KOFF≠ DYING ANYWAY.
WE'RE NOT GONNA KILL YOU—WE'RE TAKING YOU BACK TO THE TECHNODROME TO ANSWER FOR THE MURDERS YOU COMMITTED.
WHAT'RE YOU TALKIN' ABOUT?!
WE DIDN'T MURDER ≠KOFF≠ ANYONE!
SAVE IT, CHUCKO.
SERGEANT GRANITOR'S ≠KOFF≠ TELLING THE TRUTH. WE'VE BEEN DOWN HERE FOR WEEKS NOW, BARELY ≠KOFF≠ SURVIVING.
WHEN THE AIR GOT TOO BAD, WE TRIED TO ≠KOFF≠ GET BACK TO THE SURFACE, BUT WE WERE... TOO WEAK. WHEN WE SAW YOUR ≠KOFF≠ AIR TANKS, WE THOUGHT, MAYBE...
IF YOU DIDN'T KILL THE UTROMS, THEN WHO—
GLRGGK
SWIIP
KRRNCH
WELL...

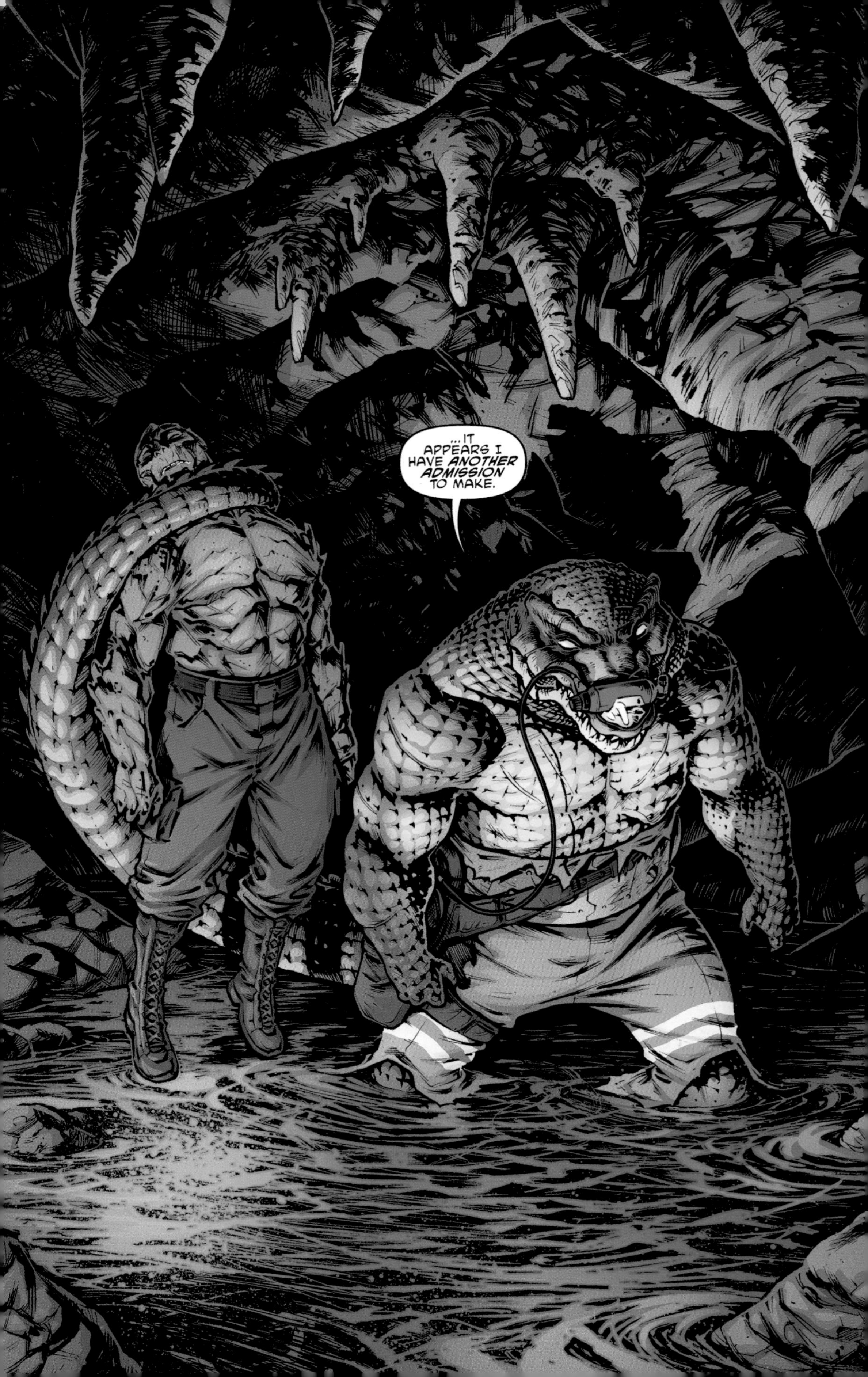
...IT APPEARS I HAVE ANOTHER ADMISSION TO MAKE.

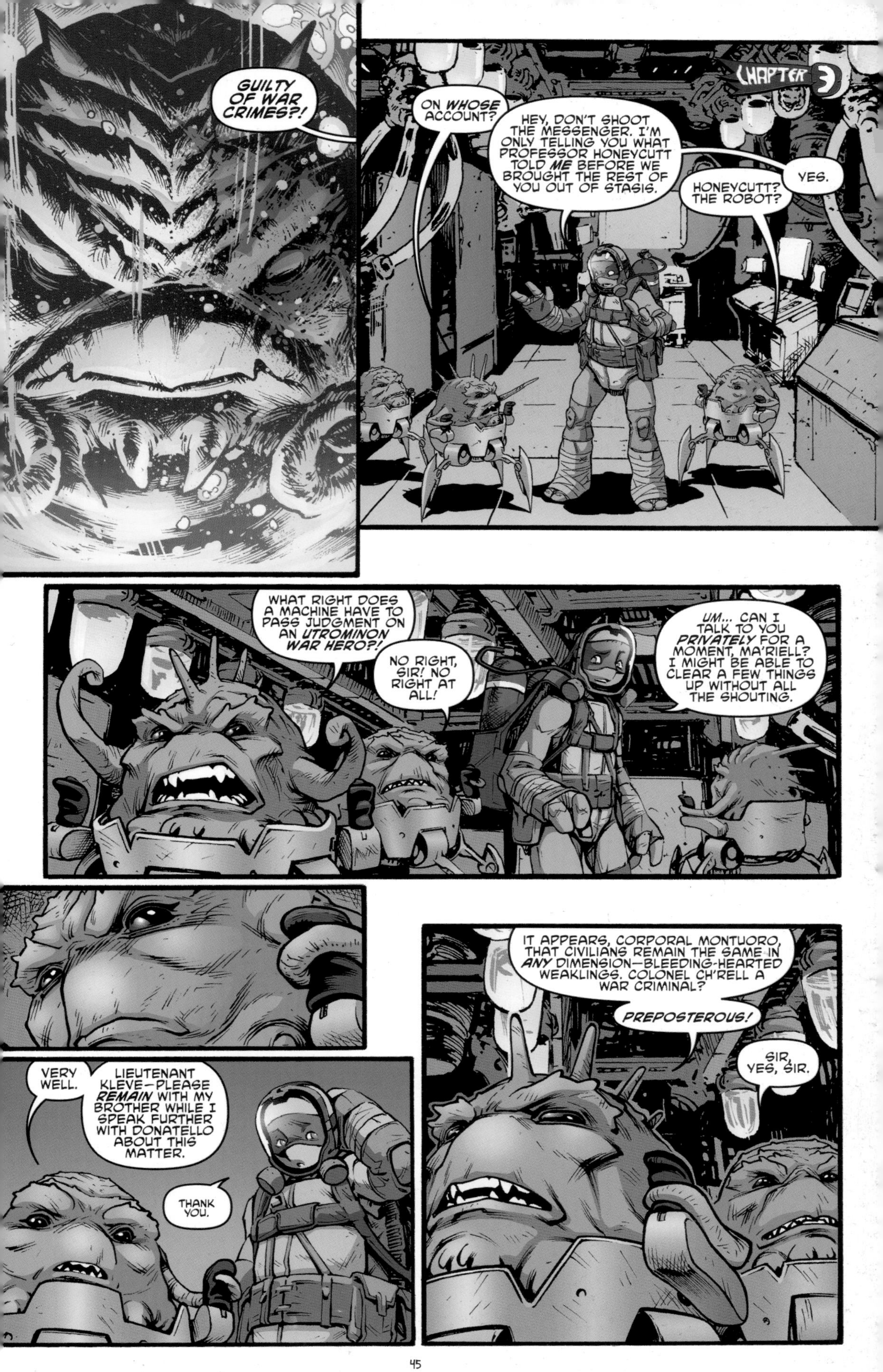

GUILTY OF WAR CRIMES?!
CHAPTER 3
ON WHOSE ACCOUNT?
HEY, DON'T SHOOT THE MESSENGER. I'M ONLY TELLING YOU WHAT PROFESSOR HONEYCUTT TOLD ME BEFORE WE BROUGHT THE REST OF YOU OUT OF STASIS.
HONEYCUTT? THE ROBOT?
YES.
WHAT RIGHT DOES A MACHINE HAVE TO PASS JUDGMENT ON AN UTROMINON WAR HERO?!
NO RIGHT, SIR! NO RIGHT AT ALL!
UM... CAN I TALK TO YOU PRIVATELY FOR A MOMENT, MA'RIELL? I MIGHT BE ABLE TO CLEAR A FEW THINGS UP WITHOUT ALL THE SHOUTING.
VERY WELL.
LIEUTENANT KLEVE—PLEASE REMAIN WITH MY BROTHER WHILE I SPEAK FURTHER WITH DONATELLO ABOUT THIS MATTER.
THANK YOU.
IT APPEARS, CORPORAL MONTUORO, THAT CIVILIANS REMAIN THE SAME IN ANY DIMENSION—BLEEDING-HEARTED WEAKLINGS. COLONEL CH'RELL A WAR CRIMINAL?
PREPOSTEROUS!
SIR, YES, SIR.

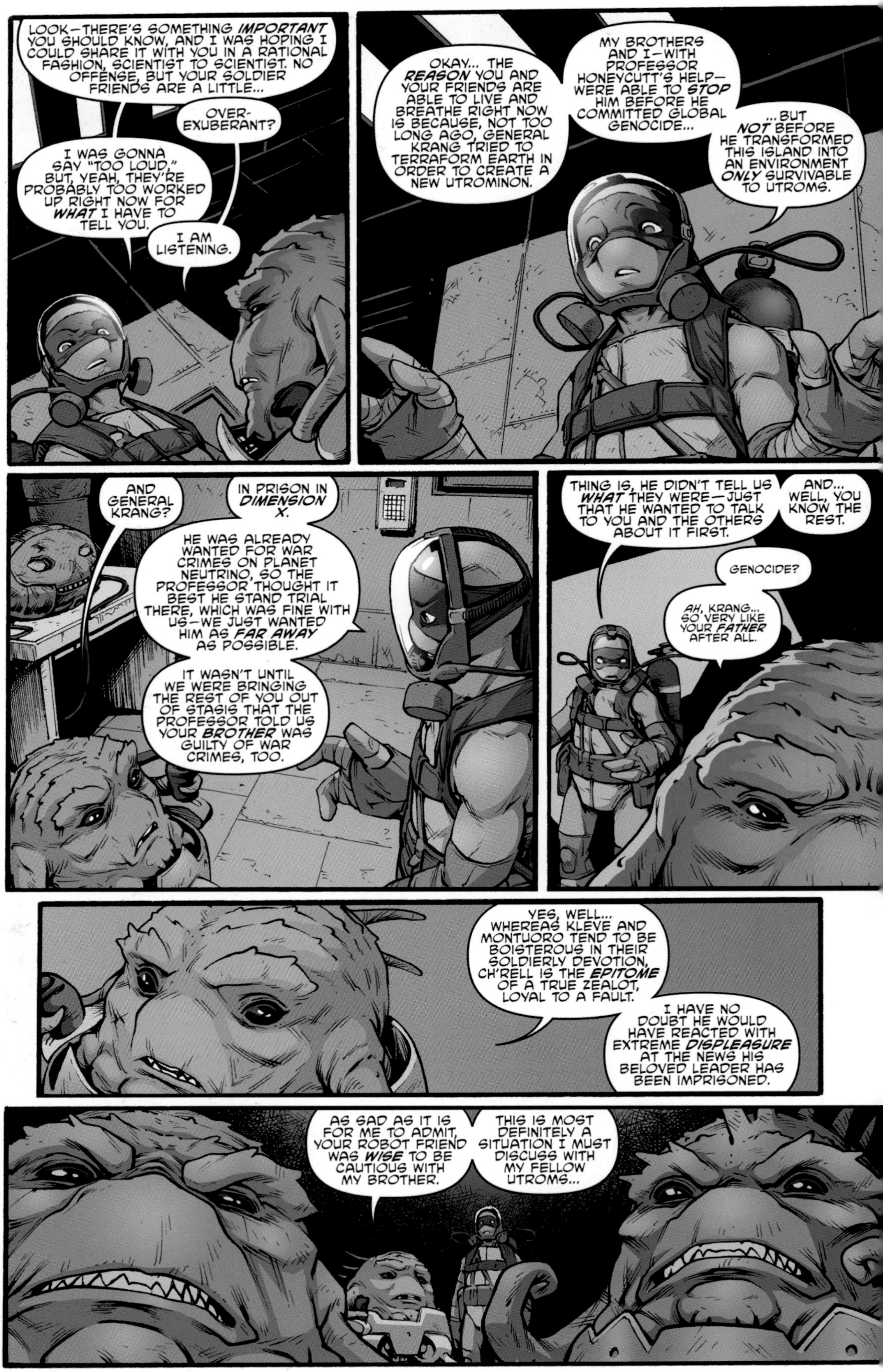
LOOK—THERE'S SOMETHING *IMPORTANT* YOU SHOULD KNOW, AND I WAS HOPING I COULD SHARE IT WITH YOU IN A RATIONAL FASHION, SCIENTIST TO SCIENTIST. NO OFFENSE, BUT YOUR SOLDIER FRIENDS ARE A LITTLE...
OVER-EXUBERANT?
I WAS GONNA SAY "TOO LOUD," BUT, YEAH, THEY'RE PROBABLY TOO WORKED UP RIGHT NOW FOR *WHAT* I HAVE TO TELL YOU.
I AM LISTENING.
OKAY... THE *REASON* YOU AND YOUR FRIENDS ARE ABLE TO LIVE AND BREATHE RIGHT NOW IS BECAUSE, NOT TOO LONG AGO, GENERAL KRANG TRIED TO TERRAFORM EARTH IN ORDER TO CREATE A NEW UTROMINON.
MY BROTHERS AND I—WITH PROFESSOR HONEYCUTT'S HELP—WERE ABLE TO *STOP* HIM BEFORE HE COMMITTED GLOBAL GENOCIDE...
...BUT *NOT* BEFORE HE TRANSFORMED THIS ISLAND INTO AN ENVIRONMENT *ONLY* SURVIVABLE TO UTROMS.
AND GENERAL KRANG?
IN PRISON IN *DIMENSION X.*
HE WAS ALREADY WANTED FOR WAR CRIMES ON PLANET NEUTRINO, SO THE PROFESSOR THOUGHT IT BEST HE STAND TRIAL THERE, WHICH WAS FINE WITH US—WE JUST WANTED HIM AS *FAR AWAY* AS POSSIBLE.
IT WASN'T UNTIL WE WERE BRINGING THE REST OF YOU OUT OF STASIS THAT THE PROFESSOR TOLD US YOUR *BROTHER* WAS GUILTY OF WAR CRIMES, TOO.
THING IS, HE DIDN'T TELL US *WHAT* THEY WERE—JUST THAT HE WANTED TO TALK TO YOU AND THE OTHERS ABOUT IT FIRST.
AND... WELL, YOU KNOW THE REST.
GENOCIDE?
AH, KRANG... SO VERY LIKE YOUR *FATHER* AFTER ALL.
YES, WELL... WHEREAS KLEVE AND MONTUORO TEND TO BE BOISTEROUS IN THEIR SOLDIERLY DEVOTION, CH'RELL IS THE *EPITOME* OF A TRUE ZEALOT, LOYAL TO A FAULT.
I HAVE NO DOUBT HE WOULD HAVE REACTED WITH EXTREME *DISPLEASURE* AT THE NEWS HIS BELOVED LEADER HAS BEEN IMPRISONED.
AS SAD AS IT IS FOR ME TO ADMIT, YOUR ROBOT FRIEND WAS *WISE* TO BE CAUTIOUS WITH MY BROTHER.
THIS IS MOST DEFINITELY A SITUATION I MUST DISCUSS WITH MY FELLOW UTROMS...

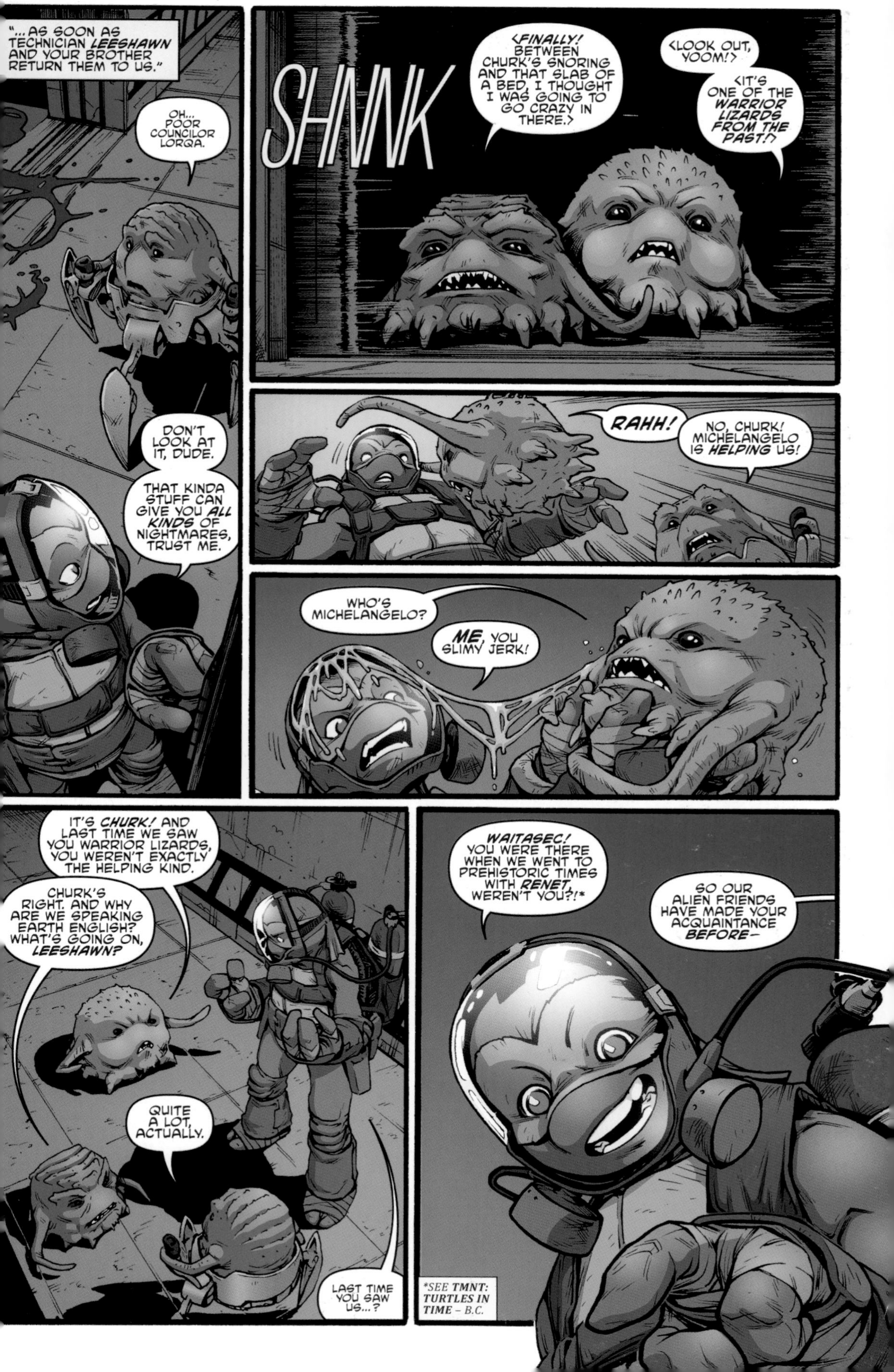
"...AS SOON AS TECHNICIAN LEESHAWN AND YOUR BROTHER RETURN THEM TO US."
OH... POOR COUNCILOR LORQA.
DON'T LOOK AT IT, DUDE.
THAT KINDA STUFF CAN GIVE YOU ALL KINDS OF NIGHTMARES, TRUST ME.
SHNNK
<FINALLY! BETWEEN CHURK'S SNORING AND THAT SLAB OF A BED, I THOUGHT I WAS GOING TO GO CRAZY IN THERE.>
<LOOK OUT, YOOM!>
<IT'S ONE OF THE WARRIOR LIZARDS FROM THE PAST!?>
RAHH!
NO, CHURK! MICHELANGELO IS HELPING US!
WHO'S MICHELANGELO?
ME, YOU SLIMY JERK!
IT'S CHURK! AND LAST TIME WE SAW YOU WARRIOR LIZARDS, YOU WEREN'T EXACTLY THE HELPING KIND.
CHURK'S RIGHT. AND WHY ARE WE SPEAKING EARTH ENGLISH? WHAT'S GOING ON, LEESHAWN?
QUITE A LOT, ACTUALLY.
LAST TIME YOU SAW US...?
WAITASEC! YOU WERE THERE WHEN WE WENT TO PREHISTORIC TIMES WITH RENET, WEREN'T YOU?!*
SO OUR ALIEN FRIENDS HAVE MADE YOUR ACQUAINTANCE BEFORE–
*SEE TMNT: TURTLES IN TIME – B.C.

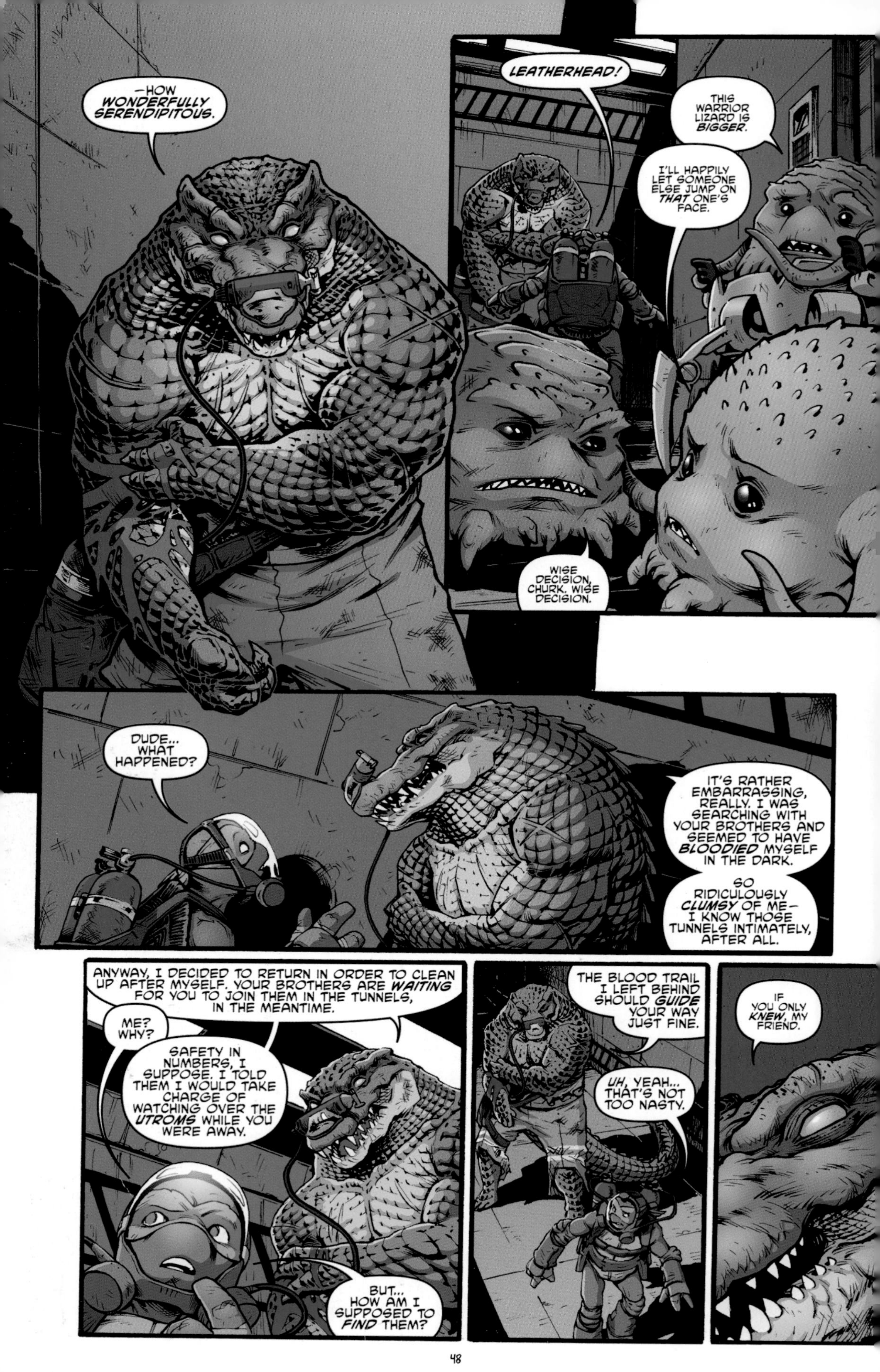

—HOW WONDERFULLY SERENDIPITOUS.
LEATHERHEAD!
THIS WARRIOR LIZARD IS BIGGER.
I'LL HAPPILY LET SOMEONE ELSE JUMP ON THAT ONE'S FACE.
WISE DECISION, CHURK. WISE DECISION.
DUDE... WHAT HAPPENED?
IT'S RATHER EMBARRASSING, REALLY. I WAS SEARCHING WITH YOUR BROTHERS AND SEEMED TO HAVE BLOODIED MYSELF IN THE DARK.
SO RIDICULOUSLY CLUMSY OF ME— I KNOW THOSE TUNNELS INTIMATELY, AFTER ALL.
ANYWAY, I DECIDED TO RETURN IN ORDER TO CLEAN UP AFTER MYSELF. YOUR BROTHERS ARE WAITING FOR YOU TO JOIN THEM IN THE TUNNELS, IN THE MEANTIME.
ME? WHY?
SAFETY IN NUMBERS, I SUPPOSE. I TOLD THEM I WOULD TAKE CHARGE OF WATCHING OVER THE UTROMS WHILE YOU WERE AWAY.
BUT... HOW AM I SUPPOSED TO FIND THEM?
THE BLOOD TRAIL I LEFT BEHIND SHOULD GUIDE YOUR WAY JUST FINE.
UH, YEAH... THAT'S NOT TOO NASTY.
IF YOU ONLY KNEW, MY FRIEND.

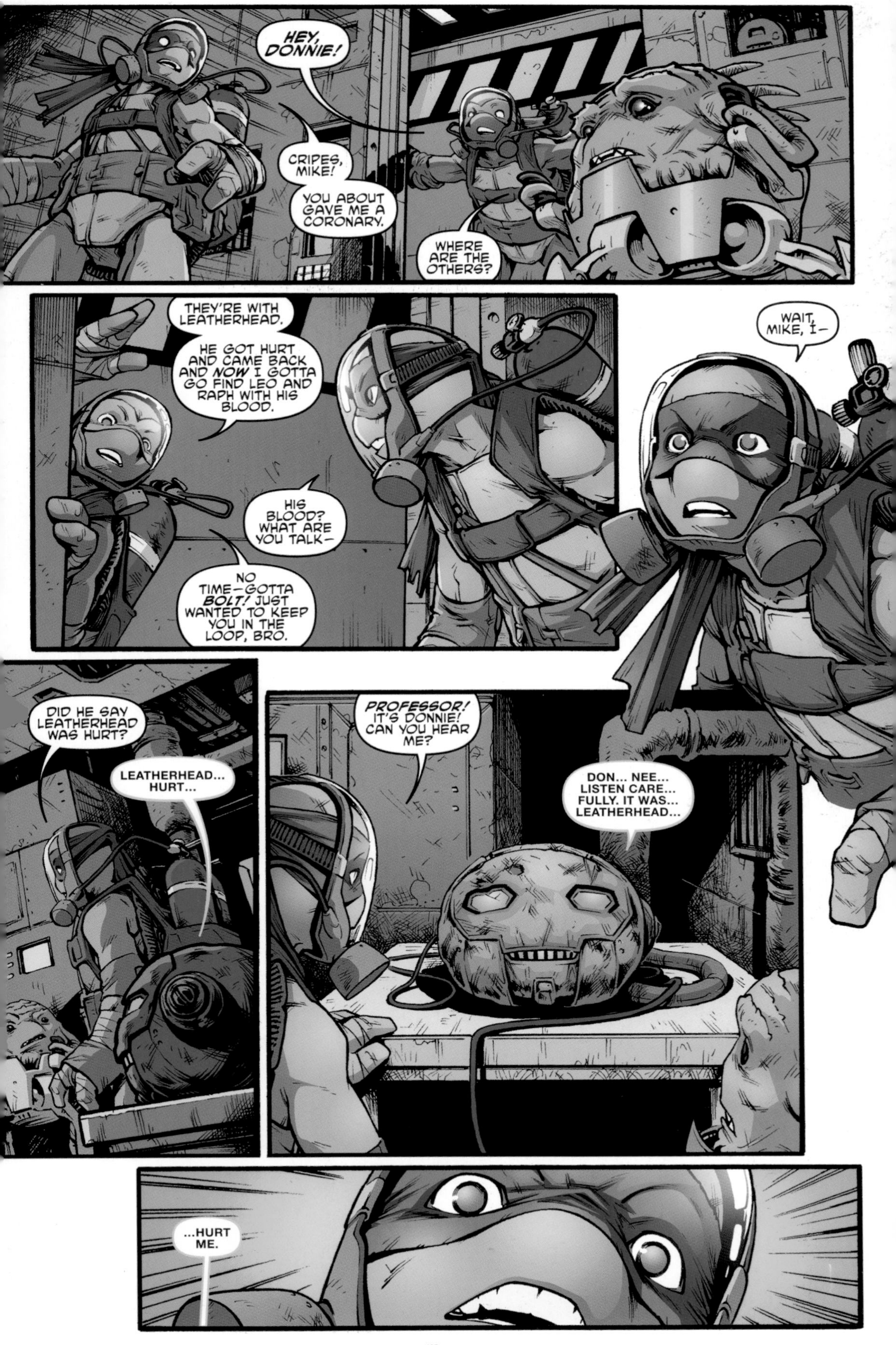
HEY, DONNIE!
CRIPES, MIKE!
YOU ABOUT GAVE ME A CORONARY.
WHERE ARE THE OTHERS?
THEY'RE WITH LEATHERHEAD.
HE GOT HURT AND CAME BACK AND NOW I GOTTA GO FIND LEO AND RAPH WITH HIS BLOOD.
HIS BLOOD? WHAT ARE YOU TALK—
NO TIME—GOTTA BOLT! JUST WANTED TO KEEP YOU IN THE LOOP, BRO.
WAIT, MIKE, I—
DID HE SAY LEATHERHEAD WAS HURT?
LEATHERHEAD... HURT...
PROFESSOR! IT'S DONNIE! CAN YOU HEAR ME?
DON... NEE... LISTEN CARE... FULLY. IT WAS... LEATHERHEAD...
...HURT ME.

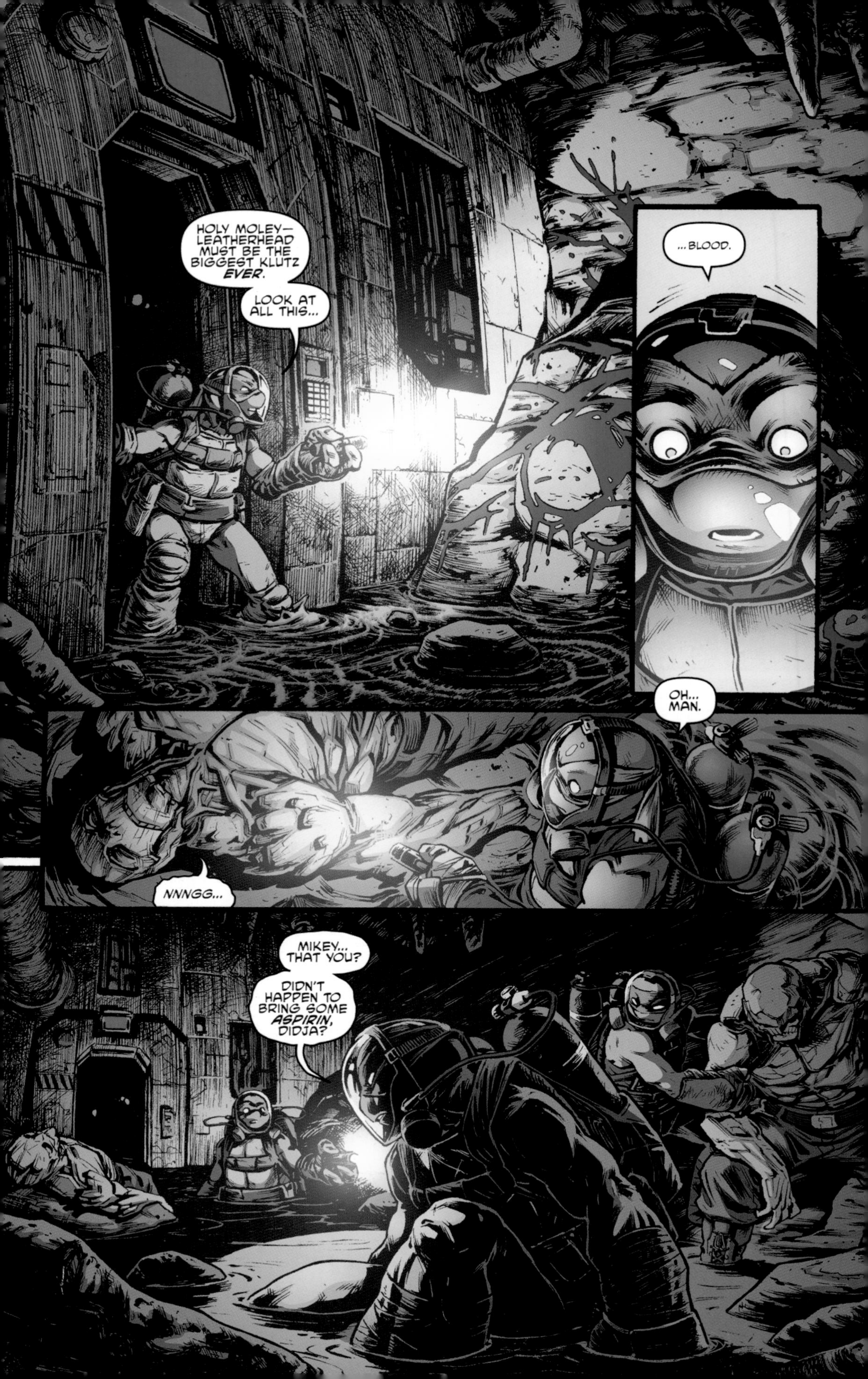
HOLY MOLEY— LEATHERHEAD MUST BE THE BIGGEST KLUTZ *EVER*.
LOOK AT ALL THIS...
...BLOOD.
OH... MAN.
NNNGG...
MIKEY... THAT YOU?
DIDN'T HAPPEN TO BRING SOME *ASPIRIN*, DIDJA?

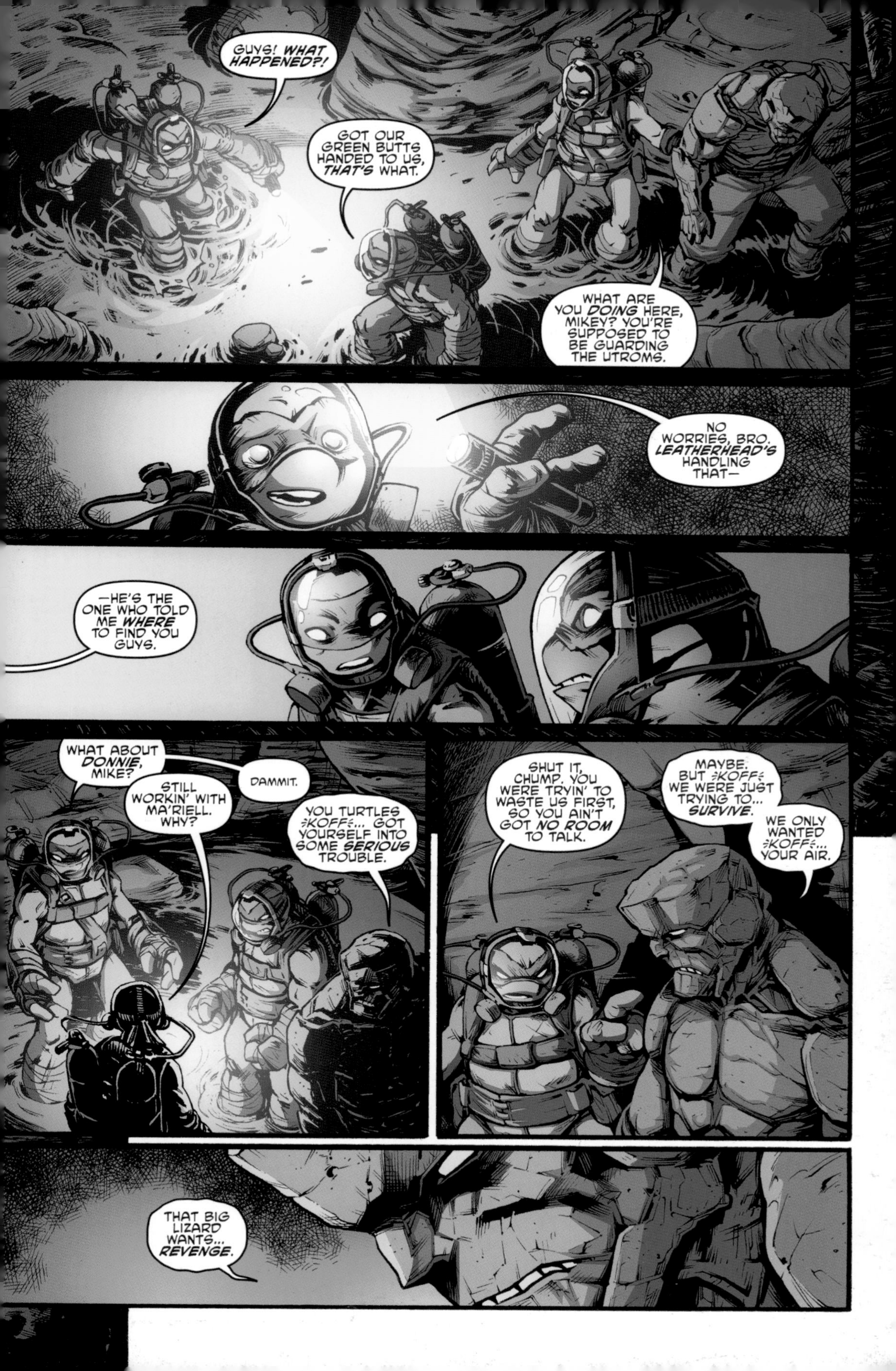
GUYS! WHAT HAPPENED?!
GOT OUR GREEN BUTTS HANDED TO US, THAT'S WHAT.
WHAT ARE YOU DOING HERE, MIKEY? YOU'RE SUPPOSED TO BE GUARDING THE UTROMS.
NO WORRIES, BRO. LEATHERHEAD'S HANDLING THAT—
—HE'S THE ONE WHO TOLD ME WHERE TO FIND YOU GUYS.
WHAT ABOUT DONNIE, MIKE?
DAMMIT.
STILL WORKIN' WITH MA'RIELL. WHY?
YOU TURTLES *KOFF*... GOT YOURSELF INTO SOME SERIOUS TROUBLE.
SHUT IT, CHUMP. YOU WERE TRYIN' TO WASTE US FIRST, SO YOU AIN'T GOT NO ROOM TO TALK.
MAYBE. BUT *KOFF* WE WERE JUST TRYING TO... SURVIVE.
WE ONLY WANTED *KOFF*... YOUR AIR.
THAT BIG LIZARD WANTS... REVENGE.

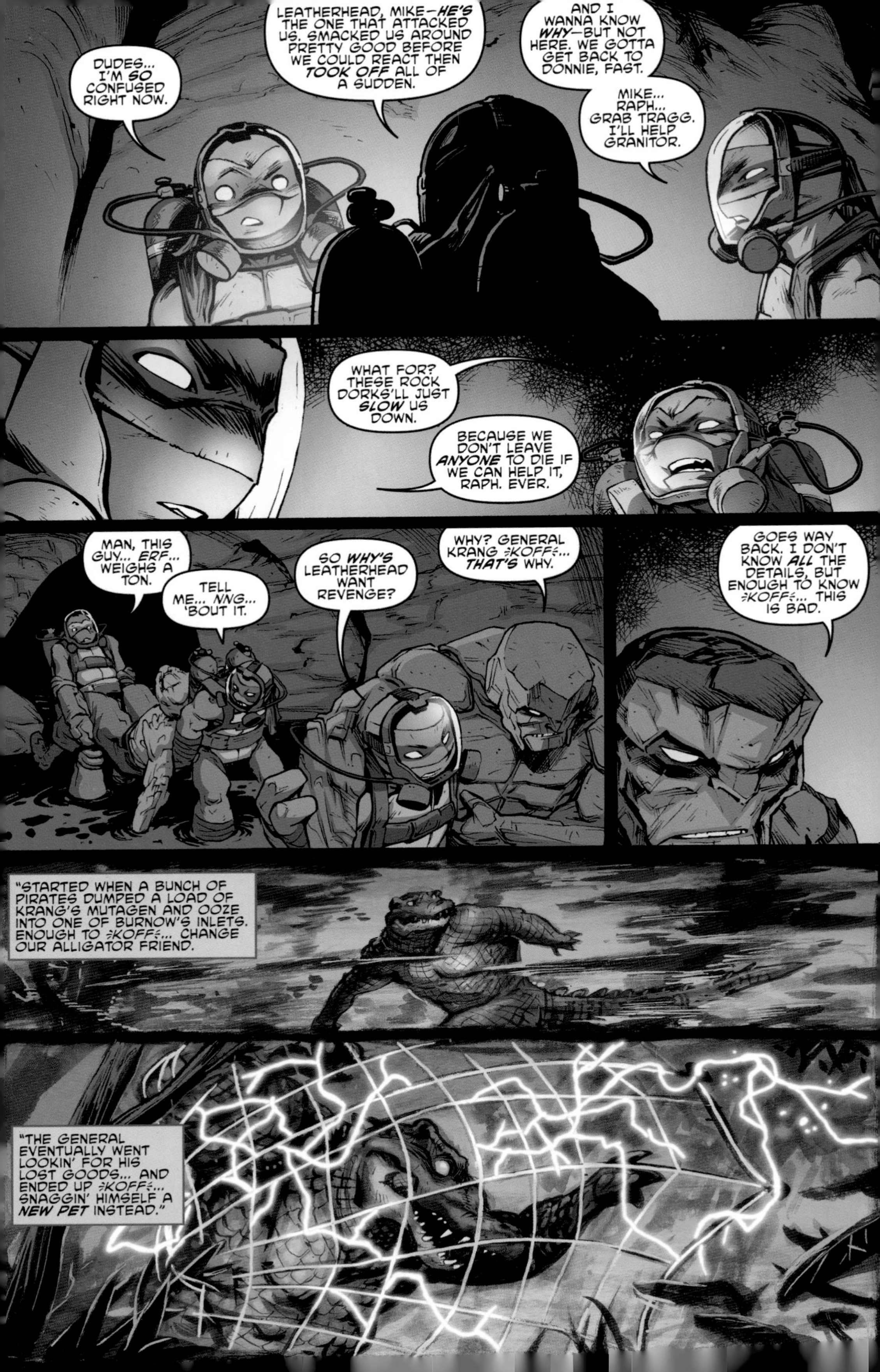
DUDES... I'M SO CONFUSED RIGHT NOW.
LEATHERHEAD, MIKE—HE'S THE ONE THAT ATTACKED US. SMACKED US AROUND PRETTY GOOD BEFORE WE COULD REACT THEN TOOK OFF ALL OF A SUDDEN.
AND I WANNA KNOW WHY—BUT NOT HERE. WE GOTTA GET BACK TO DONNIE, FAST.
MIKE... RAPH... GRAB TRAGG. I'LL HELP GRANITOR.
WHAT FOR? THESE ROCK DORKS'LL JUST SLOW US DOWN.
BECAUSE WE DON'T LEAVE ANYONE TO DIE IF WE CAN HELP IT, RAPH. EVER.
MAN, THIS GUY... ERF... WEIGHS A TON.
TELL ME... NNG... 'BOUT IT.
SO WHY'S LEATHERHEAD WANT REVENGE?
WHY? GENERAL KRANG ≠KOFF≠... THAT'S WHY.
GOES WAY BACK. I DON'T KNOW ALL THE DETAILS, BUT ENOUGH TO KNOW ≠KOFF≠... THIS IS BAD.
"STARTED WHEN A BUNCH OF PIRATES DUMPED A LOAD OF KRANG'S MUTAGEN AND OOZE INTO ONE OF BURNOW'S INLETS. ENOUGH TO ≠KOFF≠... CHANGE OUR ALLIGATOR FRIEND.
"THE GENERAL EVENTUALLY WENT LOOKIN' FOR HIS LOST GOODS... AND ENDED UP ≠KOFF≠... SNAGGIN' HIMSELF A NEW PET INSTEAD."

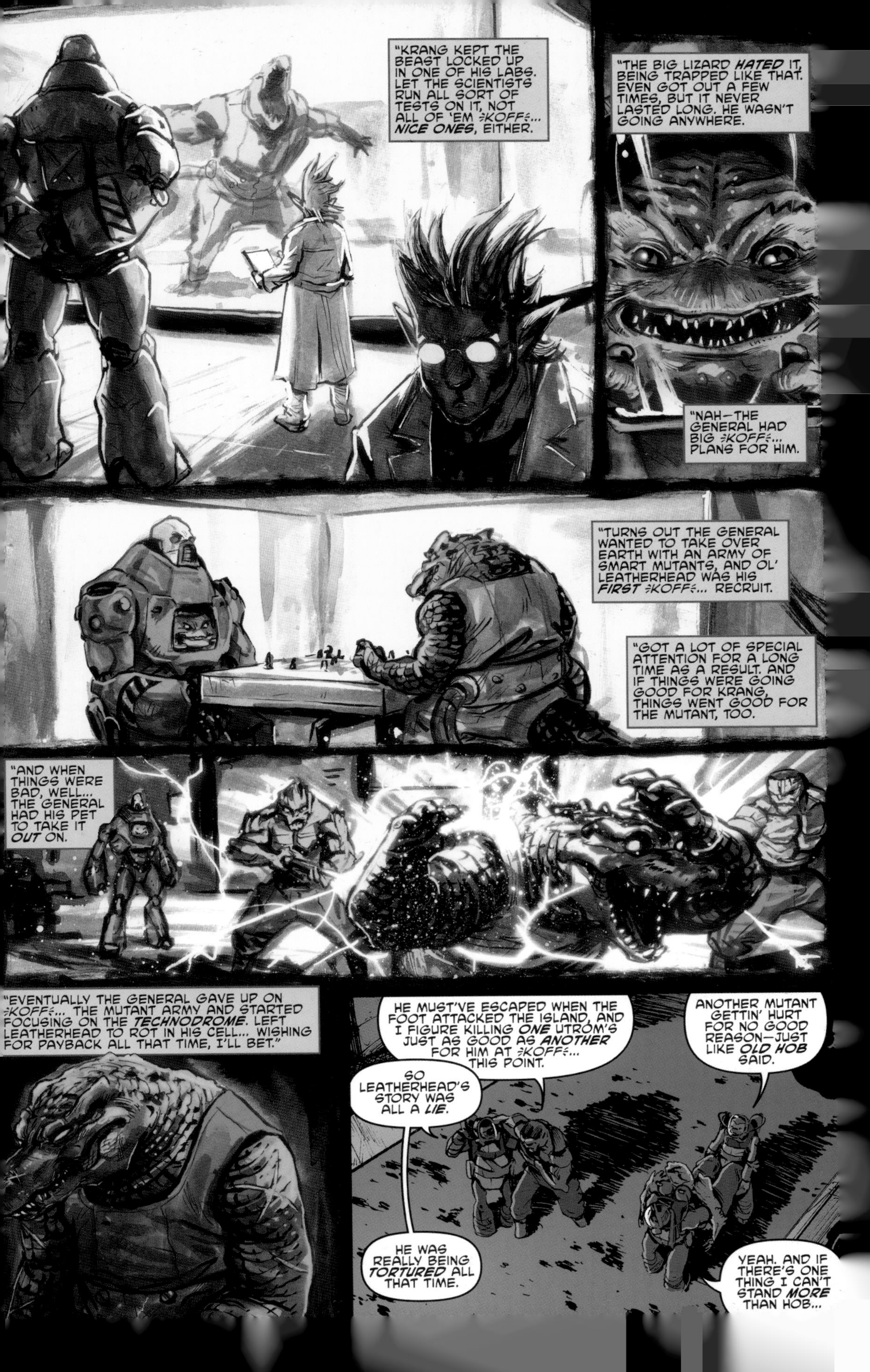
"KRANG KEPT THE BEAST LOCKED UP IN ONE OF HIS LABS. LET THE SCIENTISTS RUN ALL SORT OF TESTS ON IT, NOT ALL OF 'EM *KOFF*... *NICE ONES*, EITHER.
"THE BIG LIZARD *HATED* IT, BEING TRAPPED LIKE THAT. EVEN GOT OUT A FEW TIMES, BUT IT NEVER LASTED LONG. HE WASN'T GOING ANYWHERE.
"NAH—THE GENERAL HAD BIG *KOFF*... PLANS FOR HIM.
"TURNS OUT THE GENERAL WANTED TO TAKE OVER EARTH WITH AN ARMY OF SMART MUTANTS, AND OL' LEATHERHEAD WAS HIS *FIRST* *KOFF*... RECRUIT.
"GOT A LOT OF SPECIAL ATTENTION FOR A LONG TIME AS A RESULT. AND IF THINGS WERE GOING GOOD FOR KRANG, THINGS WENT GOOD FOR THE MUTANT, TOO.
"AND WHEN THINGS WERE BAD, WELL... THE GENERAL HAD HIS PET TO TAKE IT *OUT* ON.
"EVENTUALLY THE GENERAL GAVE UP ON *KOFF*... THE MUTANT ARMY AND STARTED FOCUSING ON THE *TECHNODROME*. LEFT LEATHERHEAD TO ROT IN HIS CELL... WISHING FOR PAYBACK ALL THAT TIME, I'LL BET."
HE MUST'VE ESCAPED WHEN THE FOOT ATTACKED THE ISLAND, AND I FIGURE KILLING *ONE* UTROM'S JUST AS GOOD AS *ANOTHER* FOR HIM AT *KOFF*... THIS POINT.
ANOTHER MUTANT GETTIN' HURT FOR NO GOOD REASON—JUST LIKE *OLD HOB* SAID.
SO LEATHERHEAD'S STORY WAS ALL A *LIE*.
HE WAS REALLY BEING *TORTURED* ALL THAT TIME.
YEAH. AND IF THERE'S ONE THING I CAN'T STAND *MORE* THAN HOB...

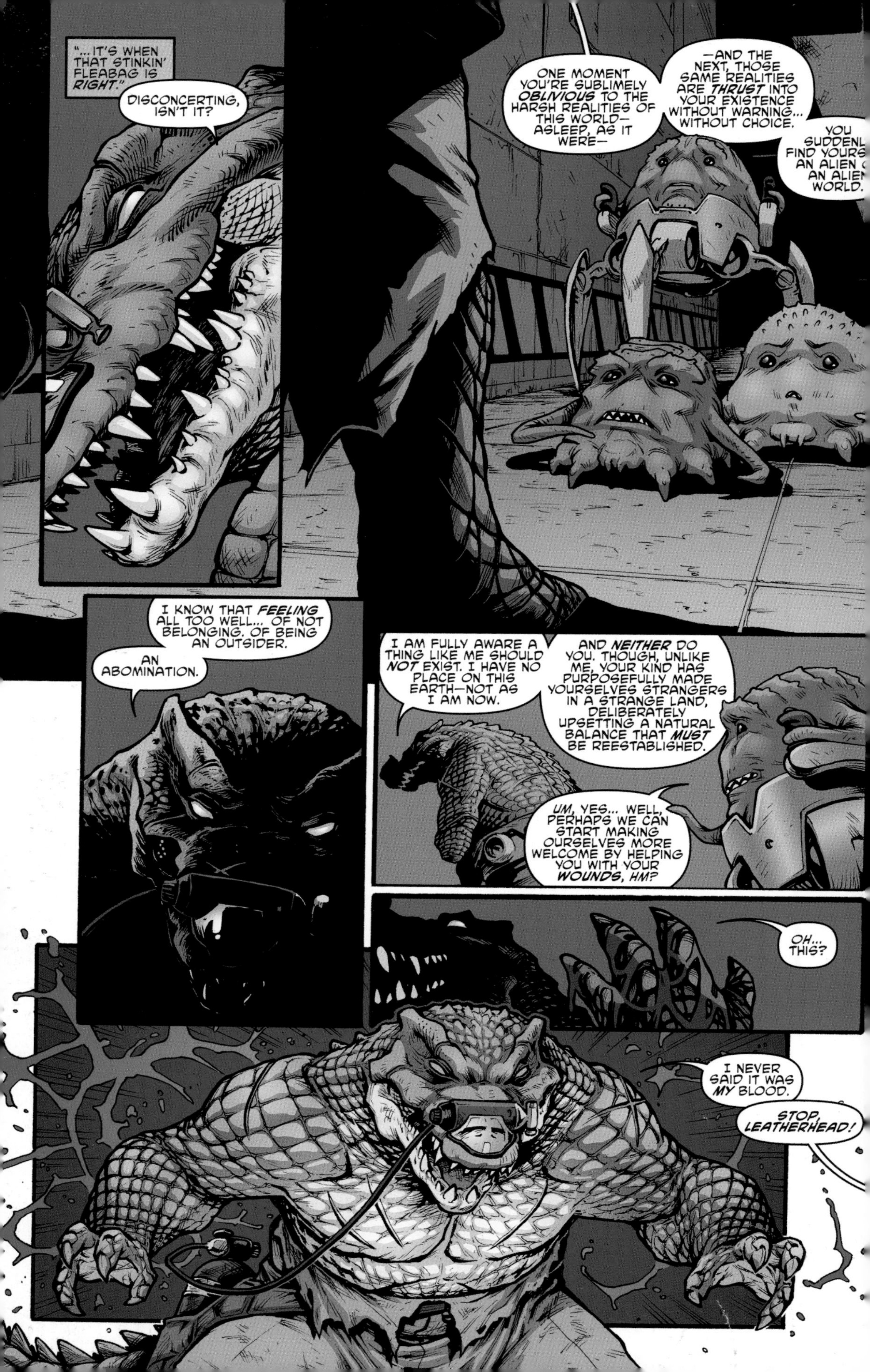
"...IT'S WHEN THAT STINKIN' FLEABAG IS *RIGHT*."
DISCONCERTING, ISN'T IT?
ONE MOMENT YOU'RE SUBLIMELY *OBLIVIOUS* TO THE HARSH REALITIES OF THIS WORLD— ASLEEP, AS IT WERE—
—AND THE NEXT, THOSE SAME REALITIES ARE *THRUST* INTO YOUR EXISTENCE WITHOUT WARNING... WITHOUT CHOICE.
I KNOW THAT *FEELING* ALL TOO WELL... OF NOT BELONGING. OF BEING AN OUTSIDER.
AN ABOMINATION.
I AM FULLY AWARE A THING LIKE ME SHOULD *NOT* EXIST. I HAVE NO PLACE ON THIS EARTH—NOT AS I AM NOW.
AND *NEITHER* DO YOU. THOUGH, UNLIKE ME, YOUR KIND HAS PURPOSEFULLY MADE YOURSELVES STRANGERS IN A STRANGE LAND, DELIBERATELY UPSETTING A NATURAL BALANCE THAT *MUST* BE REESTABLISHED.
UM, YES... WELL, PERHAPS WE CAN START MAKING OURSELVES MORE WELCOME BY HELPING YOU WITH YOUR *WOUNDS*, HM?
OH... THIS?
I NEVER SAID IT WAS *MY* BLOOD.
STOP, LEATHERHEAD!

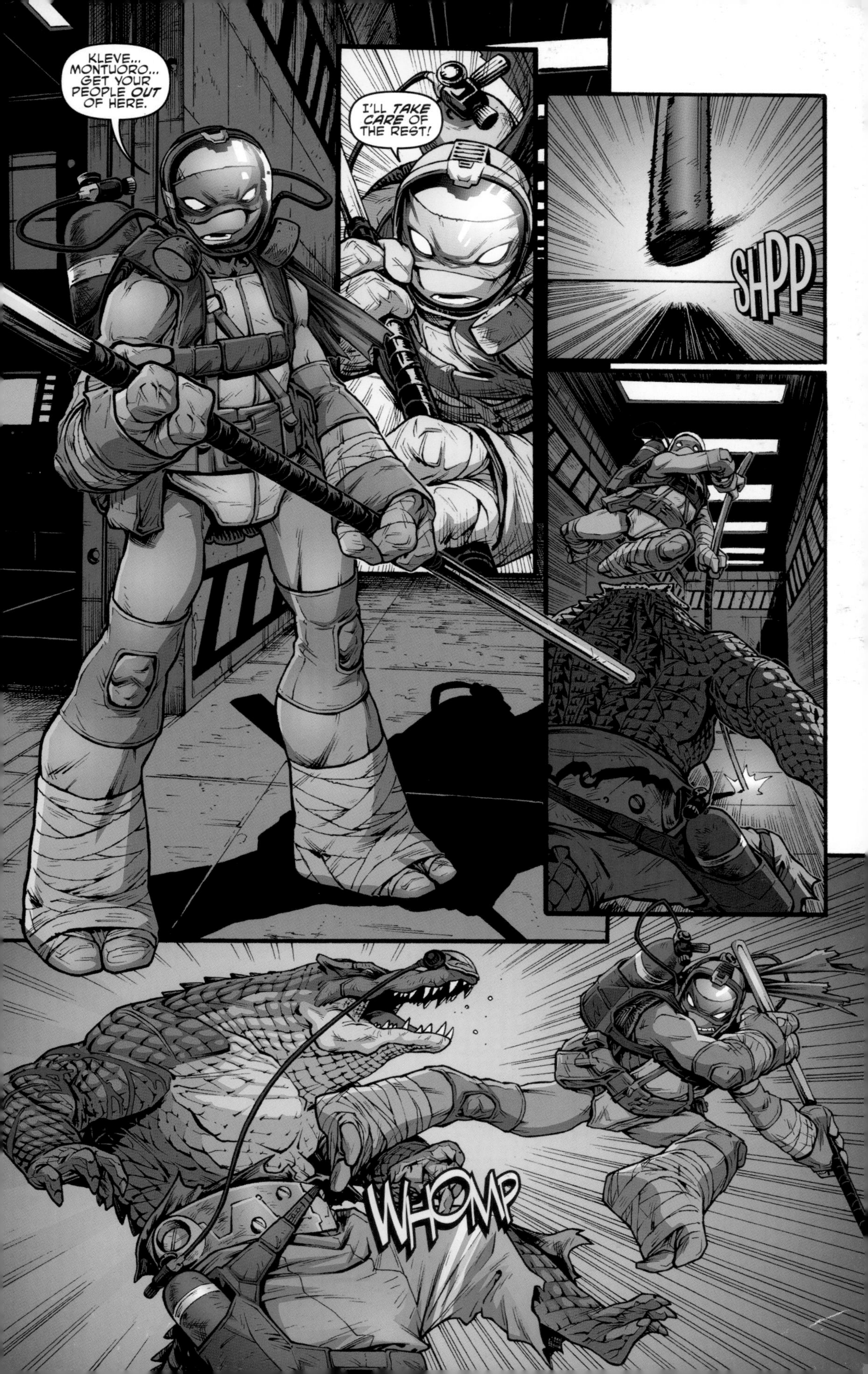
KLEVE... MONTUORO... GET YOUR PEOPLE *OUT* OF HERE.
I'LL *TAKE CARE* OF THE REST!
SHPP
WHOMP

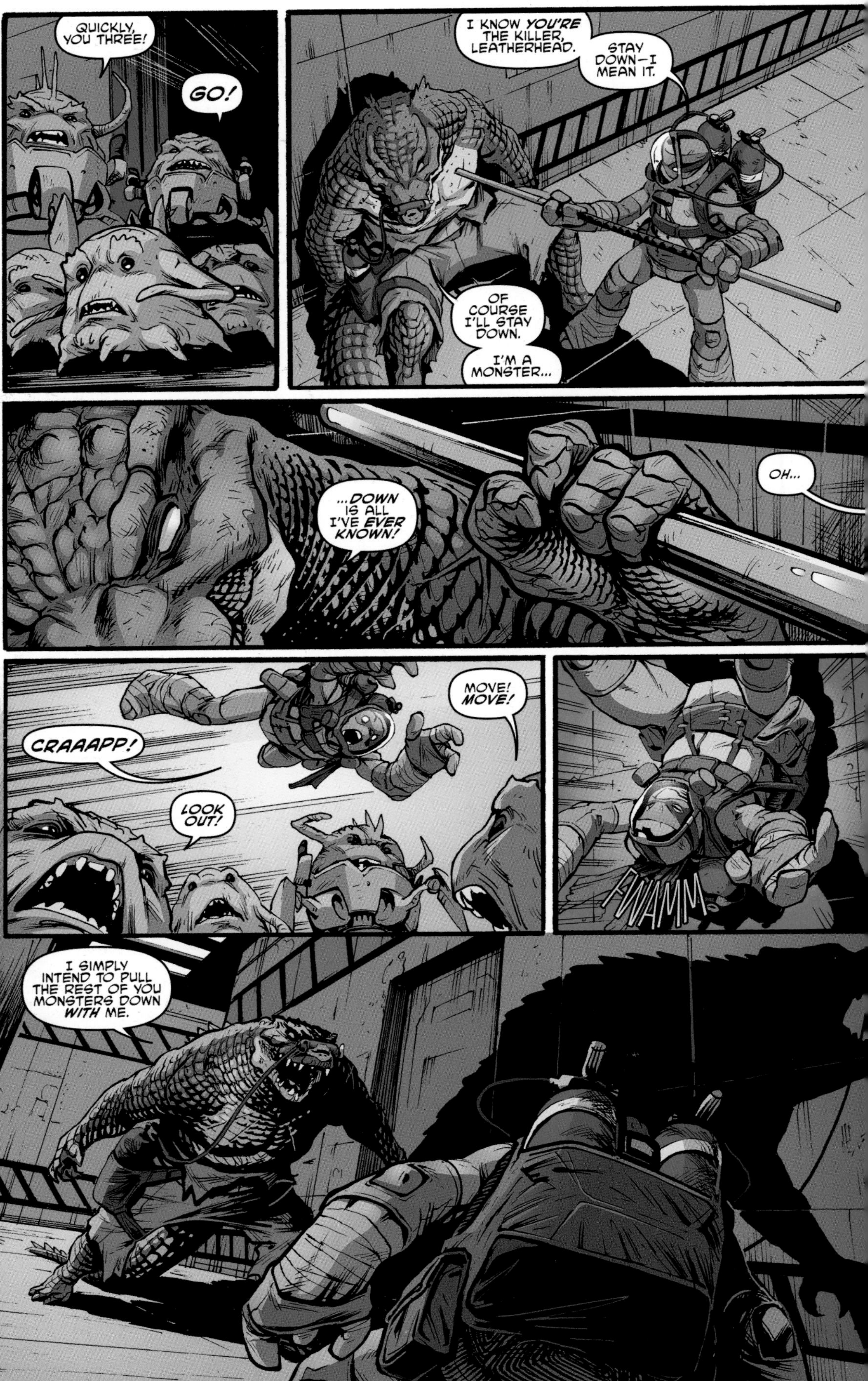
QUICKLY, YOU THREE!
GO!
I KNOW YOU'RE THE KILLER, LEATHERHEAD.
STAY DOWN—I MEAN IT.
OF COURSE I'LL STAY DOWN.
I'M A MONSTER...
...DOWN IS ALL I'VE EVER KNOWN!
OH...
MOVE! MOVE!
CRAAAPP!
LOOK OUT!
FWAMM
I SIMPLY INTEND TO PULL THE REST OF YOU MONSTERS DOWN WITH ME.

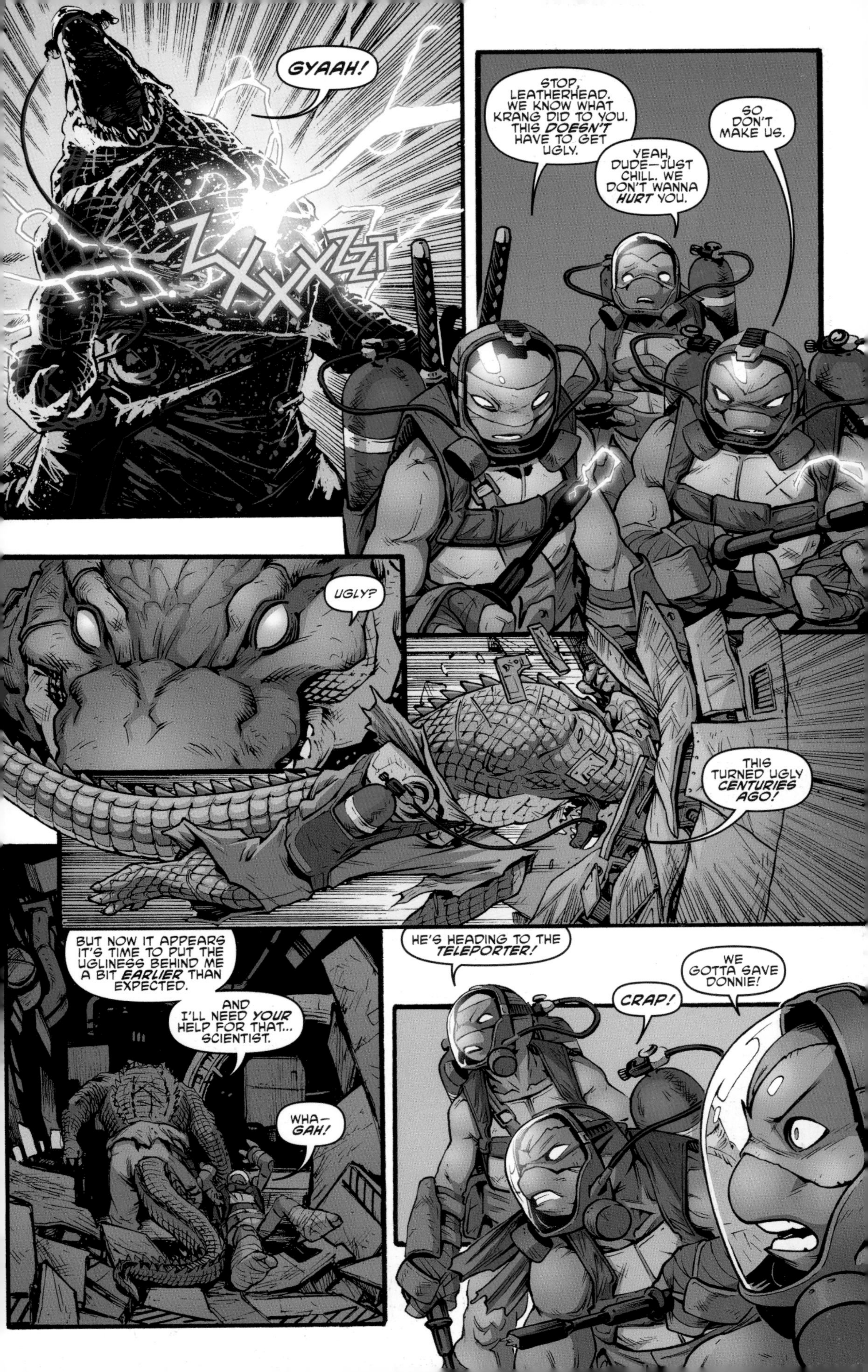
GYAAH!
ZZXXXZZT
STOP, LEATHERHEAD. WE KNOW WHAT KRANG DID TO YOU. THIS DOESN'T HAVE TO GET UGLY.
YEAH, DUDE—JUST CHILL. WE DON'T WANNA HURT YOU.
SO DON'T MAKE US.
UGLY?
THIS TURNED UGLY CENTURIES AGO!
BUT NOW IT APPEARS IT'S TIME TO PUT THE UGLINESS BEHIND ME A BIT EARLIER THAN EXPECTED.
AND I'LL NEED YOUR HELP FOR THAT... SCIENTIST.
WHA—GAH!
HE'S HEADING TO THE TELEPORTER!
CRAP!
WE GOTTA SAVE DONNIE!

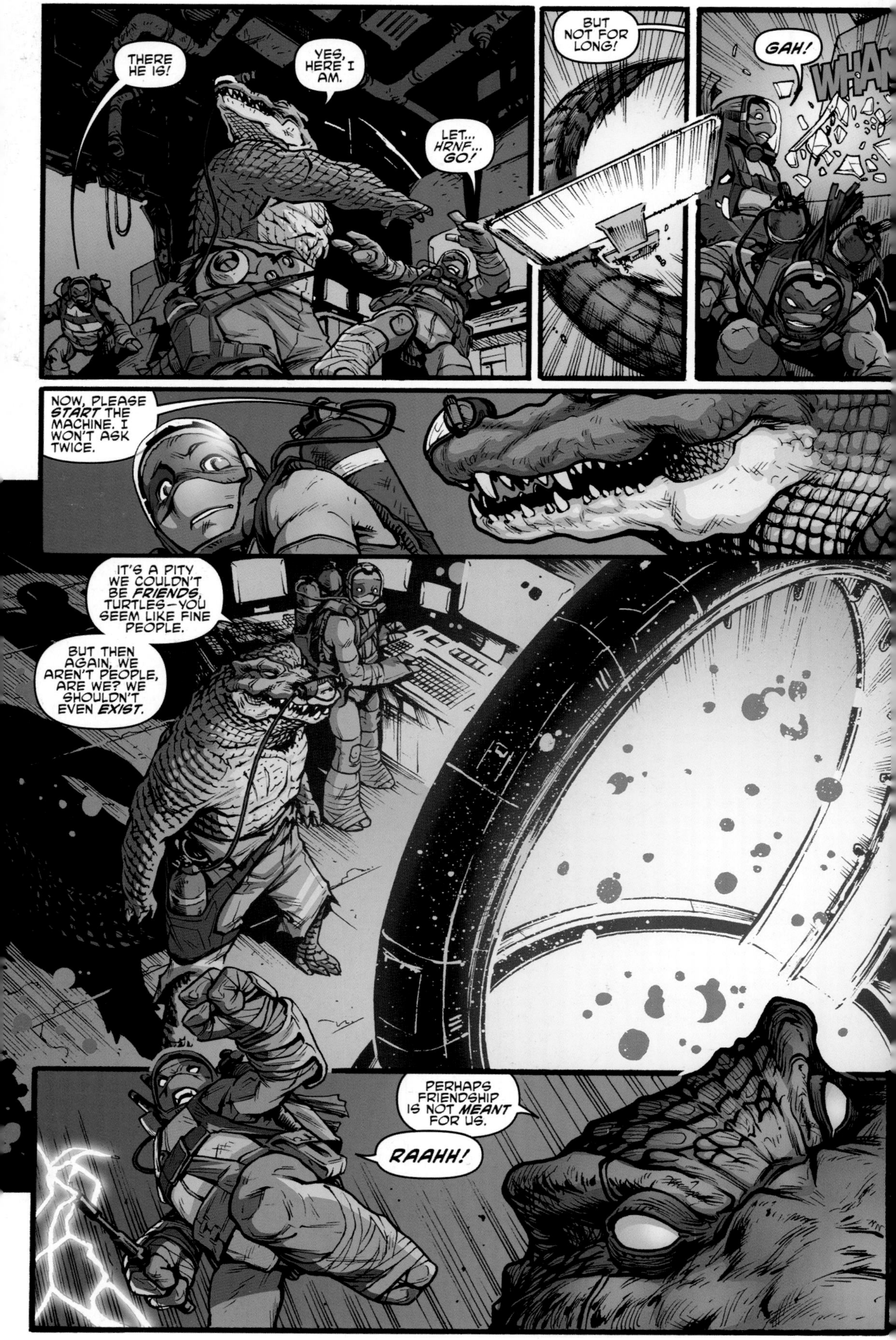
THERE HE IS!
YES, HERE I AM.
LET... HRNF... GO!
BUT NOT FOR LONG!
GAH!
WHAM
NOW, PLEASE START THE MACHINE. I WON'T ASK TWICE.
IT'S A PITY WE COULDN'T BE FRIENDS, TURTLES—YOU SEEM LIKE FINE PEOPLE.
BUT THEN AGAIN, WE AREN'T PEOPLE, ARE WE? WE SHOULDN'T EVEN EXIST.
PERHAPS FRIENDSHIP IS NOT MEANT FOR US.
RAAHH!

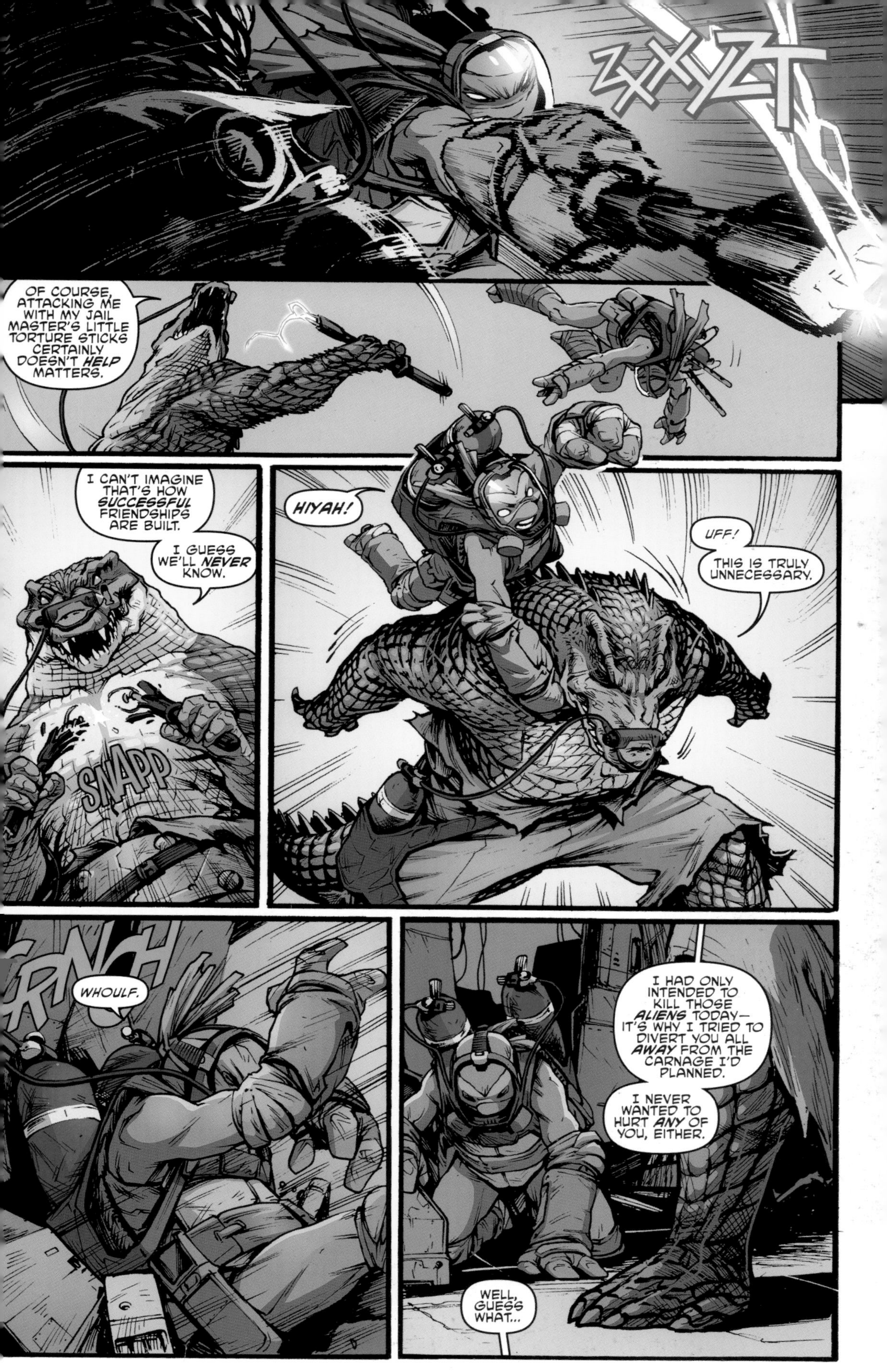
ZXXZT
OF COURSE, ATTACKING ME WITH MY JAIL MASTER'S LITTLE TORTURE STICKS CERTAINLY DOESN'T HELP MATTERS.
I CAN'T IMAGINE THAT'S HOW SUCCESSFUL FRIENDSHIPS ARE BUILT.
I GUESS WE'LL NEVER KNOW.
SNAPP
HIYAH!
UFF!
THIS IS TRULY UNNECESSARY.
WHOULF.
I HAD ONLY INTENDED TO KILL THOSE ALIENS TODAY— IT'S WHY I TRIED TO DIVERT YOU ALL AWAY FROM THE CARNAGE I'D PLANNED.
I NEVER WANTED TO HURT ANY OF YOU, EITHER.
WELL, GUESS WHAT...

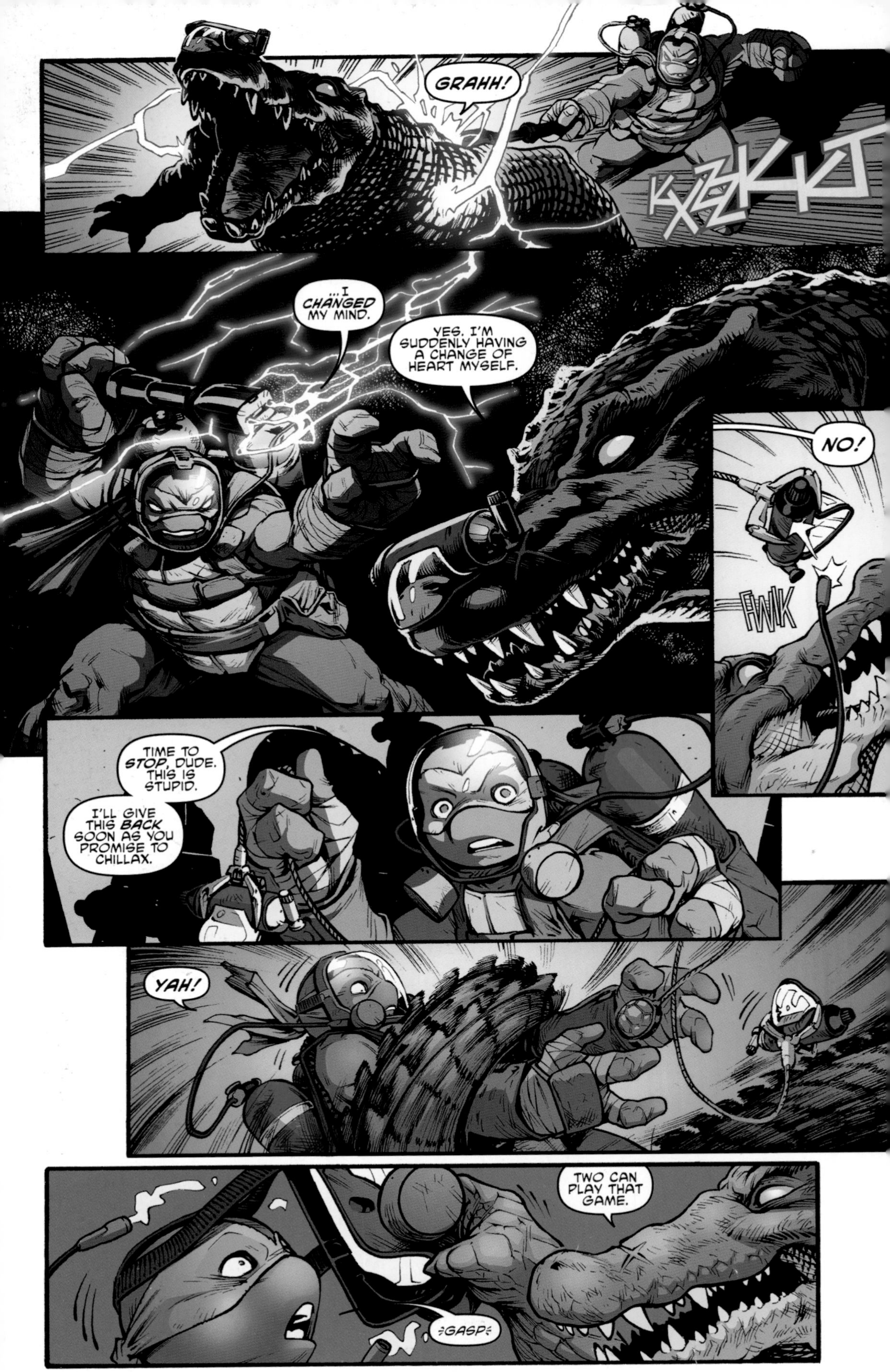
GRAHH!
KZZKKT
...I CHANGED MY MIND.
YES. I'M SUDDENLY HAVING A CHANGE OF HEART MYSELF.
NO!
FWIK
TIME TO STOP, DUDE. THIS IS STUPID.
I'LL GIVE THIS BACK SOON AS YOU PROMISE TO CHILLAX.
YAH!
TWO CAN PLAY THAT GAME.
GASP

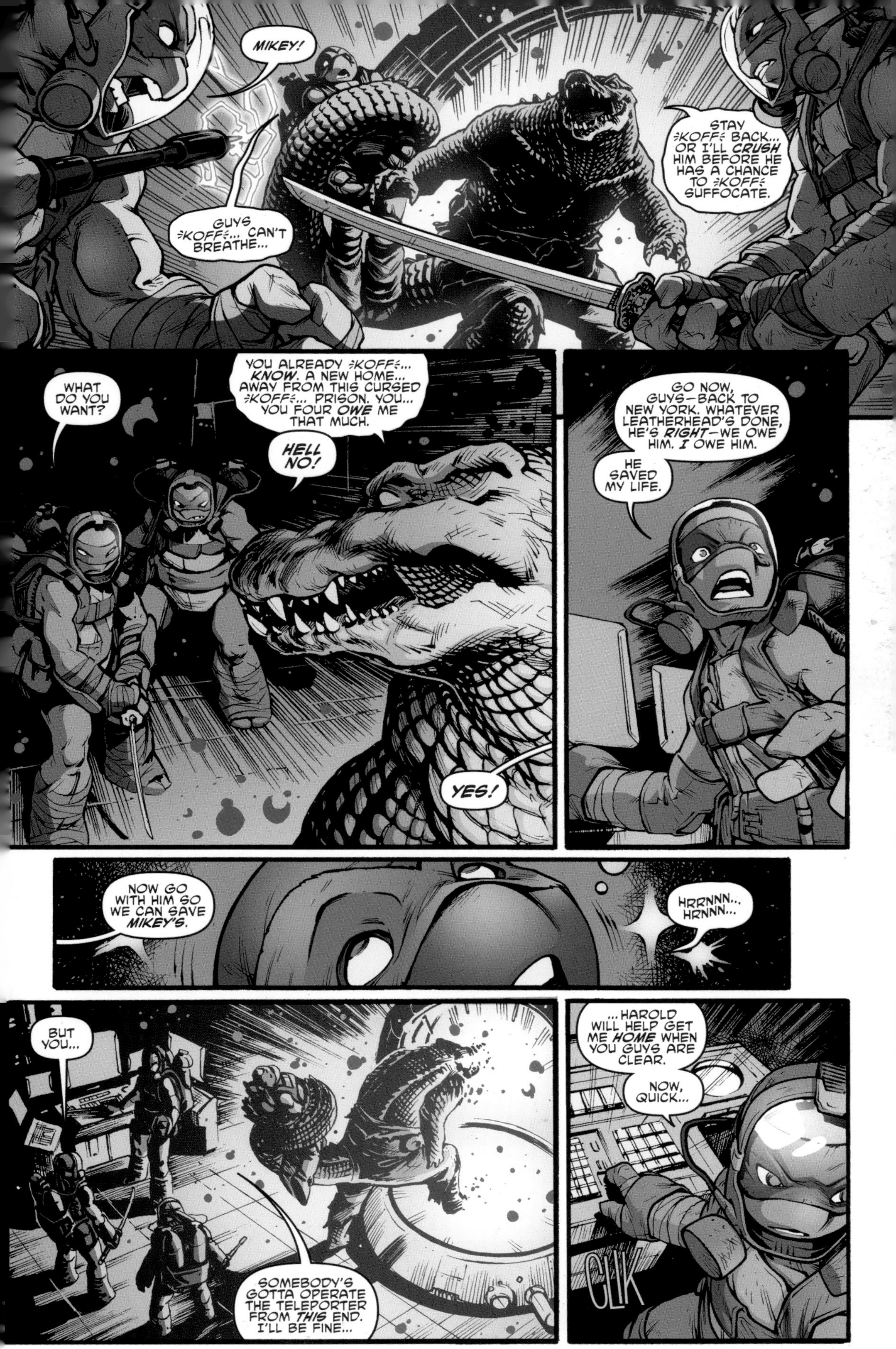
MIKEY!
GUYS ≶KOFF≶... CAN'T BREATHE...
STAY ≶KOFF≶ BACK... OR I'LL *CRUSH* HIM BEFORE HE HAS A CHANCE TO ≶KOFF≶ SUFFOCATE.
WHAT DO YOU WANT?
YOU ALREADY ≶KOFF≶... *KNOW*. A NEW HOME... AWAY FROM THIS CURSED ≶KOFF≶... PRISON. YOU... YOU FOUR *OWE* ME THAT MUCH.
HELL NO!
YES!
GO NOW, GUYS—BACK TO NEW YORK. WHATEVER LEATHERHEAD'S DONE, HE'S *RIGHT*—WE OWE HIM. *I* OWE HIM.
HE SAVED MY LIFE.
NOW GO WITH HIM SO WE CAN SAVE *MIKEY'S*.
HRNNN... HRNNN...
BUT YOU...
SOMEBODY'S GOTTA OPERATE THE TELEPORTER FROM *THIS* END. I'LL BE FINE...
...HAROLD WILL HELP GET ME *HOME* WHEN YOU GUYS ARE CLEAR.
NOW, QUICK...
CLIK

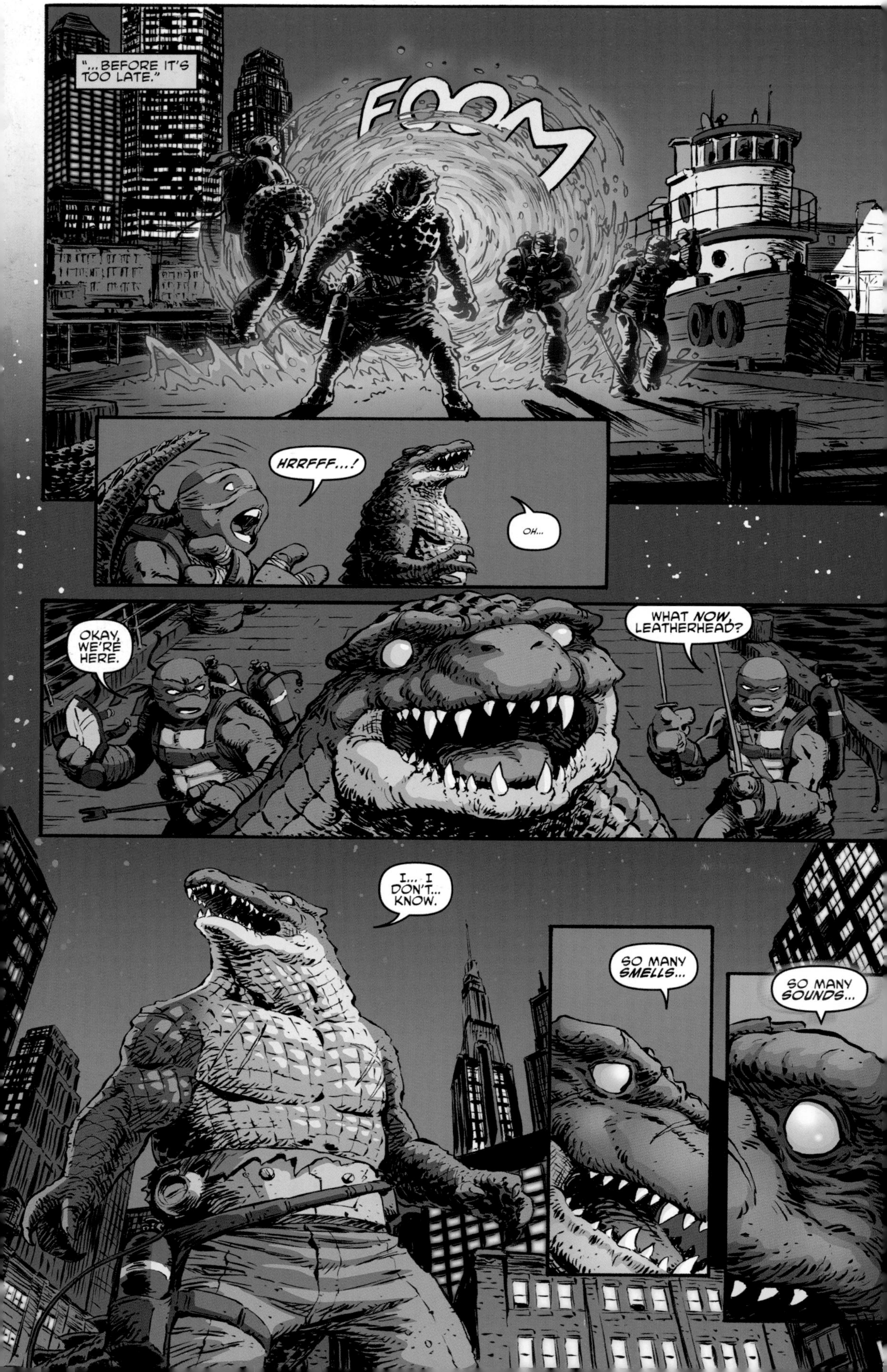
"...BEFORE IT'S TOO LATE."
FOOM
HRRFFF...!
OH...
OKAY, WE'RE HERE.
WHAT NOW, LEATHERHEAD?
I... I DON'T... KNOW.
SO MANY SMELLS...
SO MANY SOUNDS...

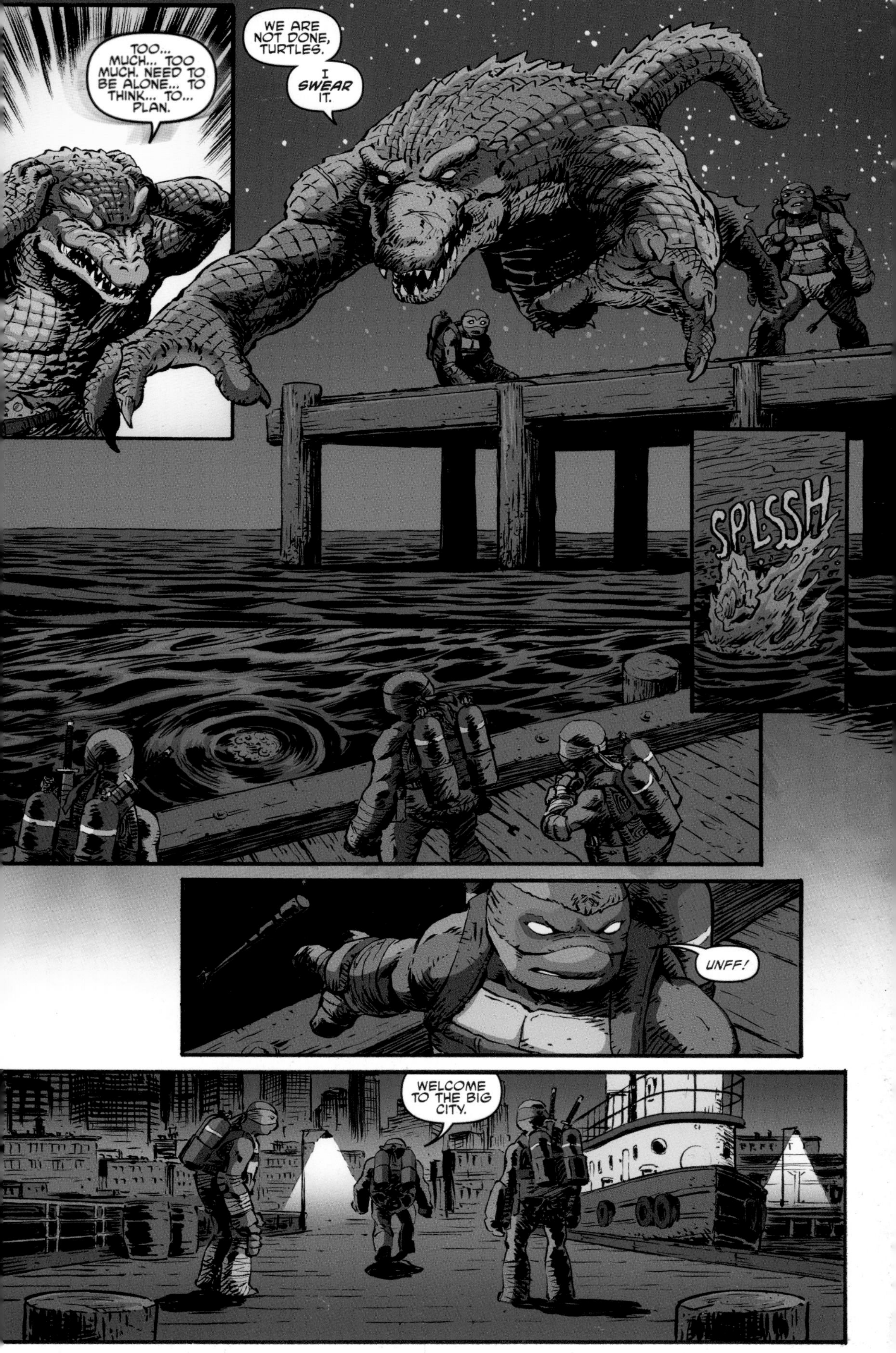
TOO... MUCH... TOO MUCH. NEED TO BE ALONE... TO THINK... TO... PLAN.
WE ARE NOT DONE, TURTLES.
I SWEAR IT.
SPLSSH
UNFF!
WELCOME TO THE BIG CITY.

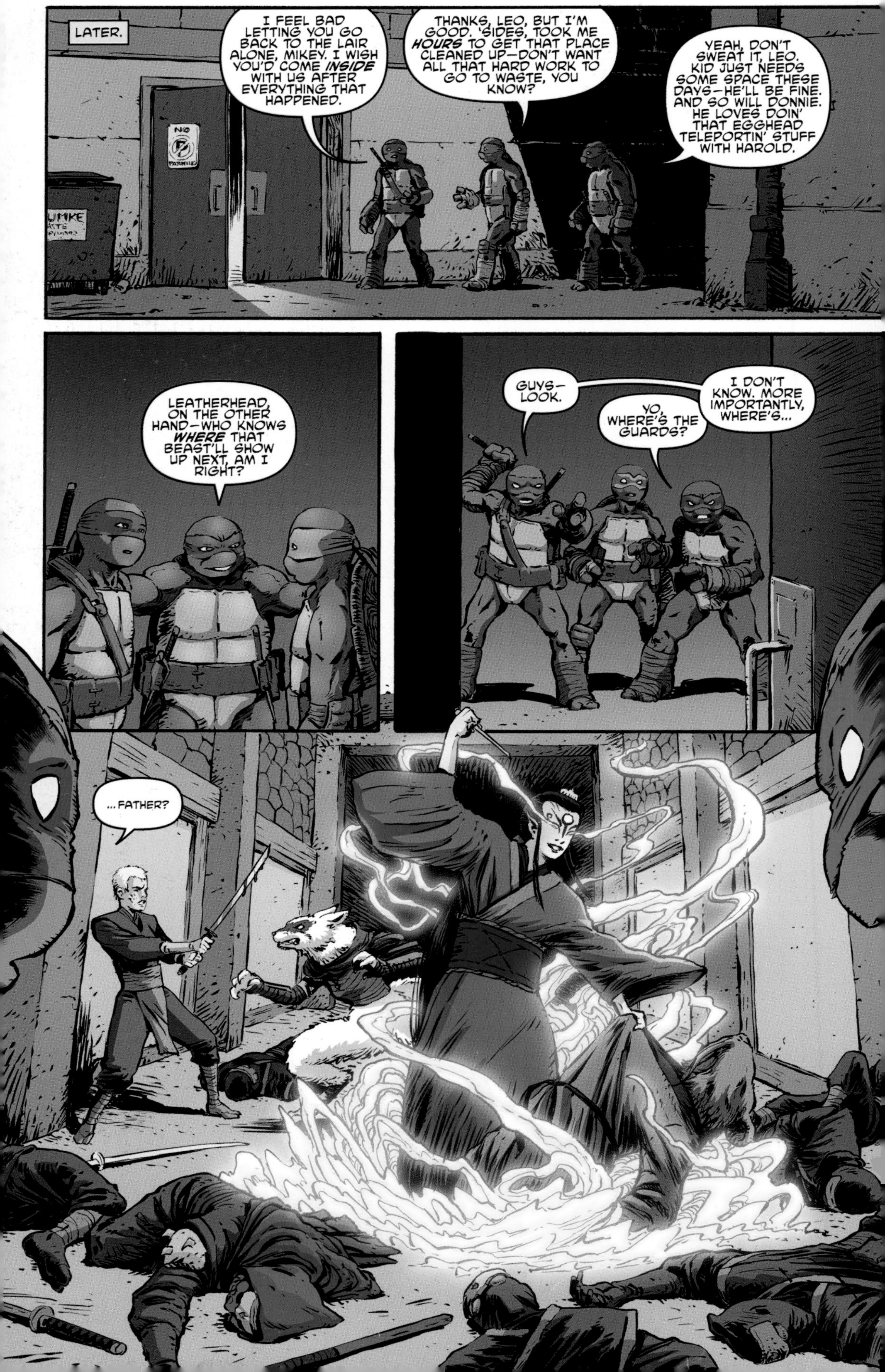
LATER.
I FEEL BAD LETTING YOU GO BACK TO THE LAIR ALONE, MIKEY. I WISH YOU'D COME INSIDE WITH US AFTER EVERYTHING THAT HAPPENED.
THANKS, LEO, BUT I'M GOOD. 'SIDES, TOOK ME HOURS TO GET THAT PLACE CLEANED UP—DON'T WANT ALL THAT HARD WORK TO GO TO WASTE, YOU KNOW?
YEAH, DON'T SWEAT IT, LEO. KID JUST NEEDS SOME SPACE THESE DAYS—HE'LL BE FINE. AND SO WILL DONNIE. HE LOVES DOIN' THAT EGGHEAD TELEPORTIN' STUFF WITH HAROLD.
NO PARKING
LEATHERHEAD, ON THE OTHER HAND—WHO KNOWS WHERE THAT BEAST'LL SHOW UP NEXT, AM I RIGHT?
GUYS—LOOK.
YO, WHERE'S THE GUARDS?
I DON'T KNOW. MORE IMPORTANTLY, WHERE'S...
...FATHER?

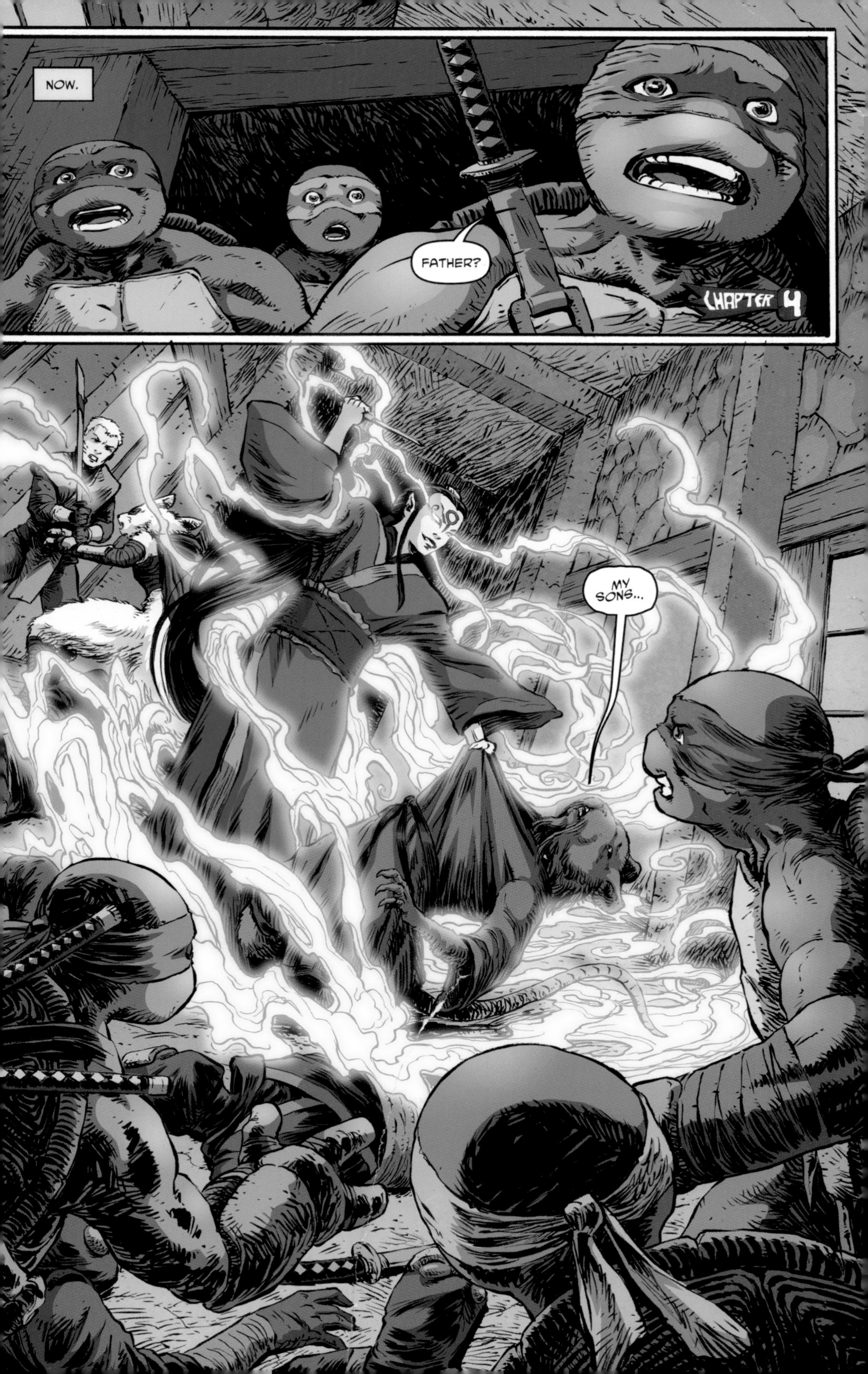
NOW.
FATHER?
CHAPTER 4
MY SONS...

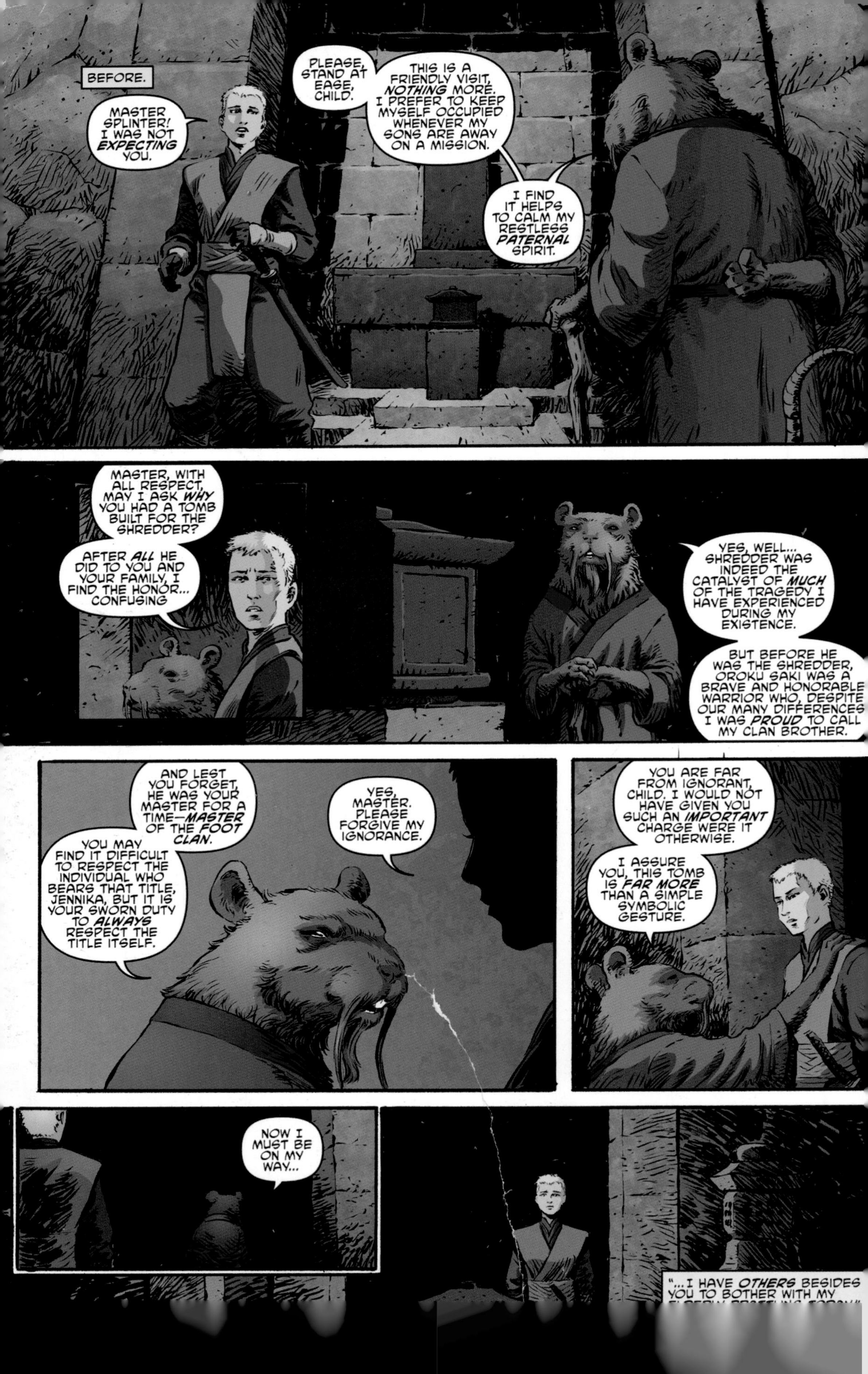
BEFORE.
MASTER SPLINTER! I WAS NOT EXPECTING YOU.
PLEASE, STAND AT EASE, CHILD.
THIS IS A FRIENDLY VISIT, NOTHING MORE. I PREFER TO KEEP MYSELF OCCUPIED WHENEVER MY SONS ARE AWAY ON A MISSION.
I FIND IT HELPS TO CALM MY RESTLESS PATERNAL SPIRIT.
MASTER, WITH ALL RESPECT, MAY I ASK WHY YOU HAD A TOMB BUILT FOR THE SHREDDER?
AFTER ALL HE DID TO YOU AND YOUR FAMILY, I FIND THE HONOR... CONFUSING
YES, WELL... SHREDDER WAS INDEED THE CATALYST OF MUCH OF THE TRAGEDY I HAVE EXPERIENCED DURING MY EXISTENCE.
BUT BEFORE HE WAS THE SHREDDER, OROKU SAKI WAS A BRAVE AND HONORABLE WARRIOR WHO, DESPITE OUR MANY DIFFERENCES I WAS PROUD TO CALL MY CLAN BROTHER.
AND LEST YOU FORGET, HE WAS YOUR MASTER FOR A TIME—MASTER OF THE FOOT CLAN.
YOU MAY FIND IT DIFFICULT TO RESPECT THE INDIVIDUAL WHO BEARS THAT TITLE, JENNIKA, BUT IT IS YOUR SWORN DUTY TO ALWAYS RESPECT THE TITLE ITSELF.
YES, MASTER. PLEASE FORGIVE MY IGNORANCE.
YOU ARE FAR FROM IGNORANT, CHILD. I WOULD NOT HAVE GIVEN YOU SUCH AN IMPORTANT CHARGE WERE IT OTHERWISE.
I ASSURE YOU, THIS TOMB IS FAR MORE THAN A SIMPLE SYMBOLIC GESTURE.
NOW I MUST BE ON MY WAY...
"...I HAVE OTHERS BESIDES YOU TO BOTHER WITH MY

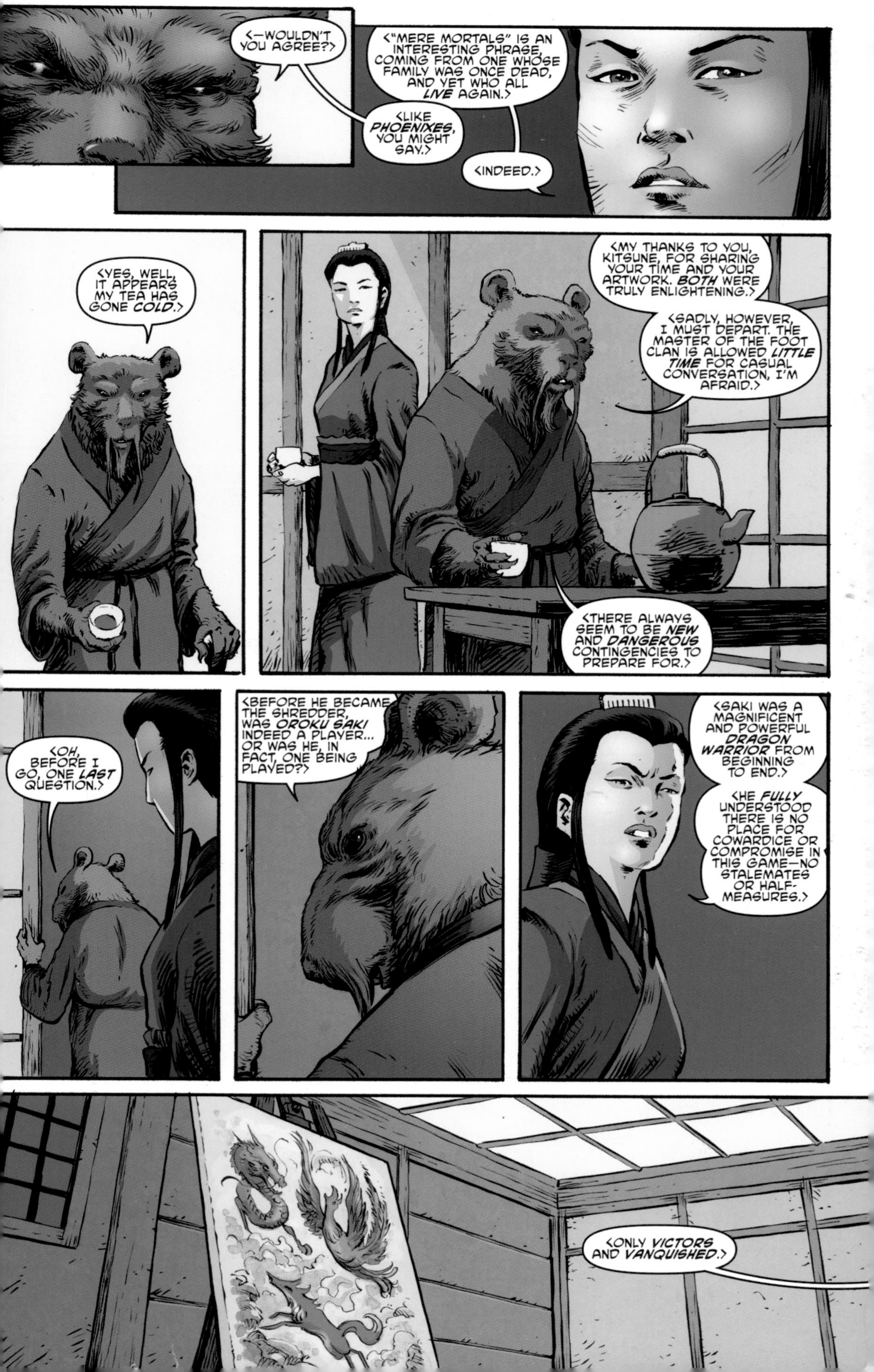
<—WOULDN'T YOU AGREE?>
<"MERE MORTALS" IS AN INTERESTING PHRASE, COMING FROM ONE WHOSE FAMILY WAS ONCE DEAD, AND YET WHO ALL LIVE AGAIN.>
<LIKE PHOENIXES, YOU MIGHT SAY.>
<INDEED.>
<YES, WELL, IT APPEARS MY TEA HAS GONE COLD.>
<MY THANKS TO YOU, KITSUNE, FOR SHARING YOUR TIME AND YOUR ARTWORK. BOTH WERE TRULY ENLIGHTENING.>
<SADLY, HOWEVER, I MUST DEPART. THE MASTER OF THE FOOT CLAN IS ALLOWED LITTLE TIME FOR CASUAL CONVERSATION, I'M AFRAID.>
<THERE ALWAYS SEEM TO BE NEW AND DANGEROUS CONTINGENCIES TO PREPARE FOR.>
<OH, BEFORE I GO, ONE LAST QUESTION.>
<BEFORE HE BECAME THE SHREDDER, WAS OROKU SAKI INDEED A PLAYER... OR WAS HE, IN FACT, ONE BEING PLAYED?>
<SAKI WAS A MAGNIFICENT AND POWERFUL DRAGON WARRIOR FROM BEGINNING TO END.>
<HE FULLY UNDERSTOOD THERE IS NO PLACE FOR COWARDICE OR COMPROMISE IN THIS GAME—NO STALEMATES OR HALF-MEASURES.>
<ONLY VICTORS AND VANQUISHED.>

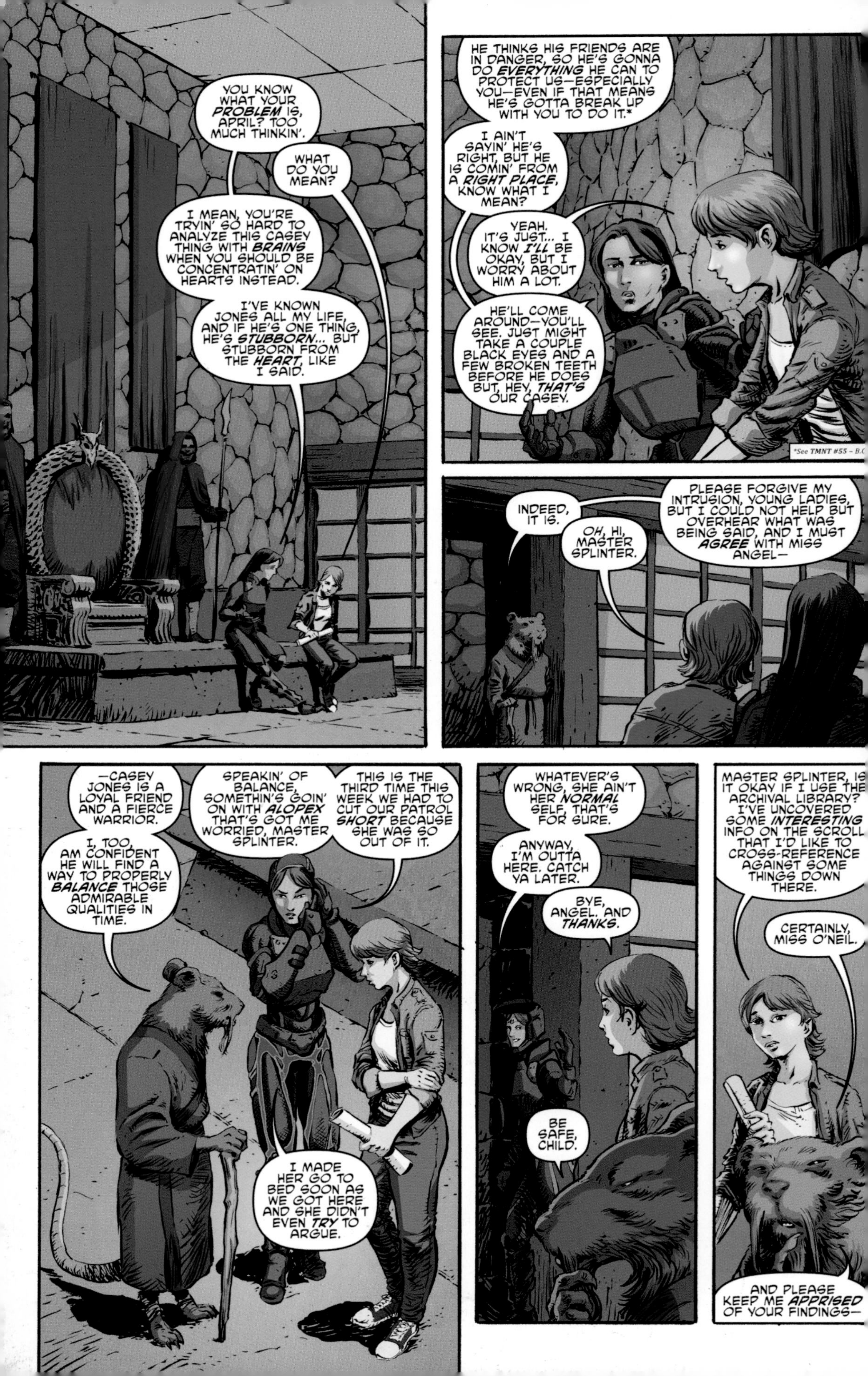
YOU KNOW WHAT YOUR PROBLEM IS, APRIL? TOO MUCH THINKIN'.
WHAT DO YOU MEAN?
I MEAN, YOU'RE TRYIN' SO HARD TO ANALYZE THIS CASEY THING WITH BRAINS WHEN YOU SHOULD BE CONCENTRATIN' ON HEARTS INSTEAD.
I'VE KNOWN JONES ALL MY LIFE, AND IF HE'S ONE THING, HE'S STUBBORN... BUT STUBBORN FROM THE HEART, LIKE I SAID.
HE THINKS HIS FRIENDS ARE IN DANGER, SO HE'S GONNA DO EVERYTHING HE CAN TO PROTECT US—ESPECIALLY YOU—EVEN IF THAT MEANS HE'S GOTTA BREAK UP WITH YOU TO DO IT.*
I AIN'T SAYIN' HE'S RIGHT, BUT HE IS COMIN' FROM A RIGHT PLACE, KNOW WHAT I MEAN?
YEAH. IT'S JUST... I KNOW I'LL BE OKAY, BUT I WORRY ABOUT HIM A LOT.
HE'LL COME AROUND—YOU'LL SEE. JUST MIGHT TAKE A COUPLE BLACK EYES AND A FEW BROKEN TEETH BEFORE HE DOES BUT, HEY, THAT'S OUR CASEY.
*See TMNT #55 – B.C
PLEASE FORGIVE MY INTRUSION, YOUNG LADIES, BUT I COULD NOT HELP BUT OVERHEAR WHAT WAS BEING SAID, AND I MUST AGREE WITH MISS ANGEL—
OH, HI, MASTER SPLINTER.
INDEED, IT IS.
—CASEY JONES IS A LOYAL FRIEND AND A FIERCE WARRIOR.
I, TOO, AM CONFIDENT HE WILL FIND A WAY TO PROPERLY BALANCE THOSE ADMIRABLE QUALITIES IN TIME.
SPEAKIN' OF BALANCE, SOMETHIN'S GOIN' ON WITH ALOPEX THAT'S GOT ME WORRIED, MASTER SPLINTER.
THIS IS THE THIRD TIME THIS WEEK WE HAD TO CUT OUR PATROL SHORT BECAUSE SHE WAS SO OUT OF IT.
I MADE HER GO TO BED SOON AS WE GOT HERE AND SHE DIDN'T EVEN TRY TO ARGUE.
WHATEVER'S WRONG, SHE AIN'T HER NORMAL SELF, THAT'S FOR SURE.
ANYWAY, I'M OUTTA HERE. CATCH YA LATER.
BYE, ANGEL. AND THANKS.
BE SAFE, CHILD.
MASTER SPLINTER, IS IT OKAY IF I USE THE ARCHIVAL LIBRARY? I'VE UNCOVERED SOME INTERESTING INFO ON THE SCROLL THAT I'D LIKE TO CROSS-REFERENCE AGAINST SOME THINGS DOWN THERE.
CERTAINLY, MISS O'NEIL.
AND PLEASE KEEP ME APPRISED OF YOUR FINDINGS—

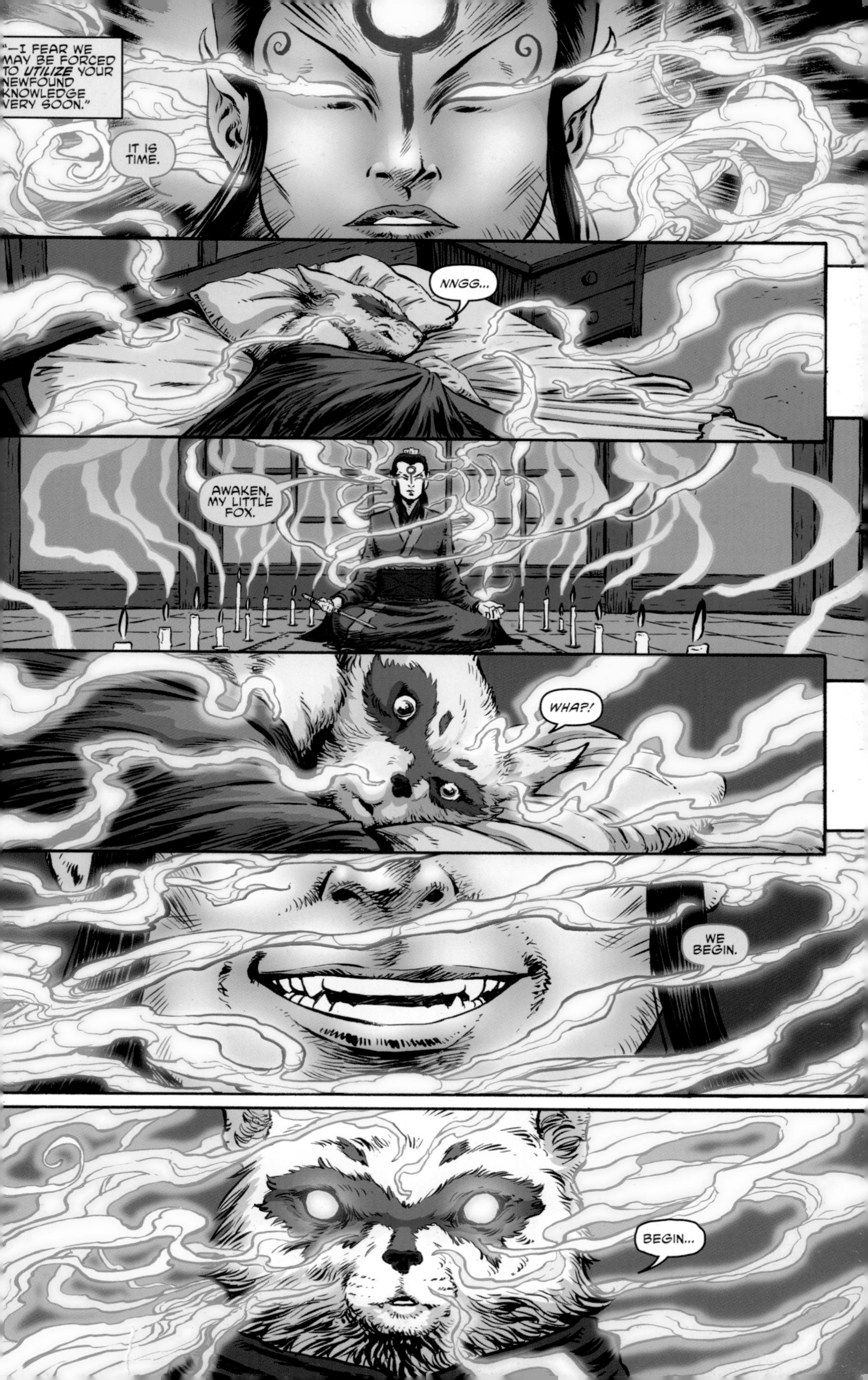
"—I FEAR WE MAY BE FORCED TO *UTILIZE* YOUR NEWFOUND KNOWLEDGE VERY SOON."
IT IS TIME.
NNGG...
AWAKEN, MY LITTLE FOX.
WHA?!
WE BEGIN.
BEGIN...

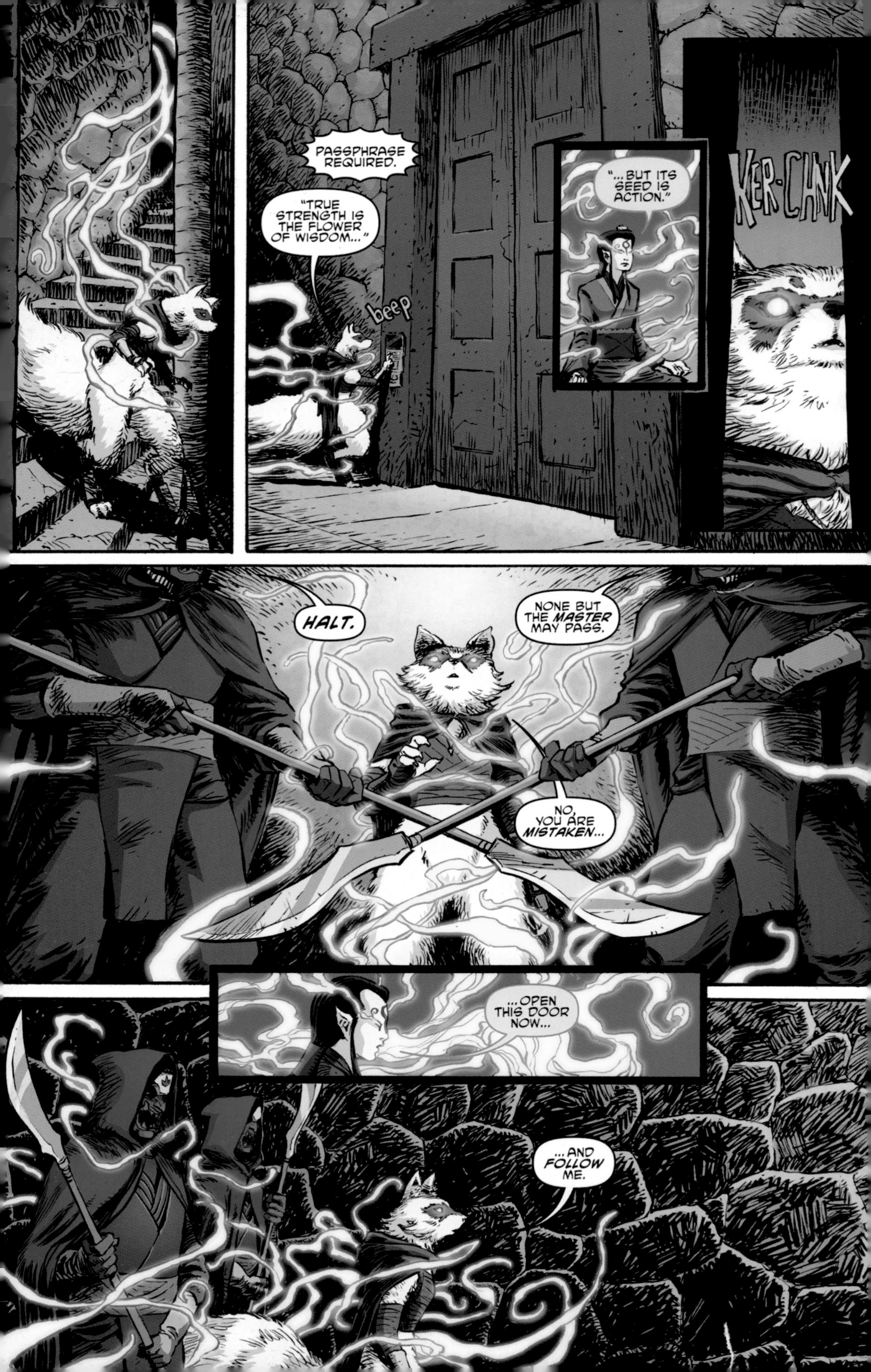

PASSPHRASE REQUIRED.
"TRUE STRENGTH IS THE FLOWER OF WISDOM..."
beep
"...BUT ITS SEED IS ACTION."
KER-CHNK
HALT.
NONE BUT THE MASTER MAY PASS.
NO, YOU ARE MISTAKEN...
...OPEN THIS DOOR NOW...
...AND FOLLOW ME.

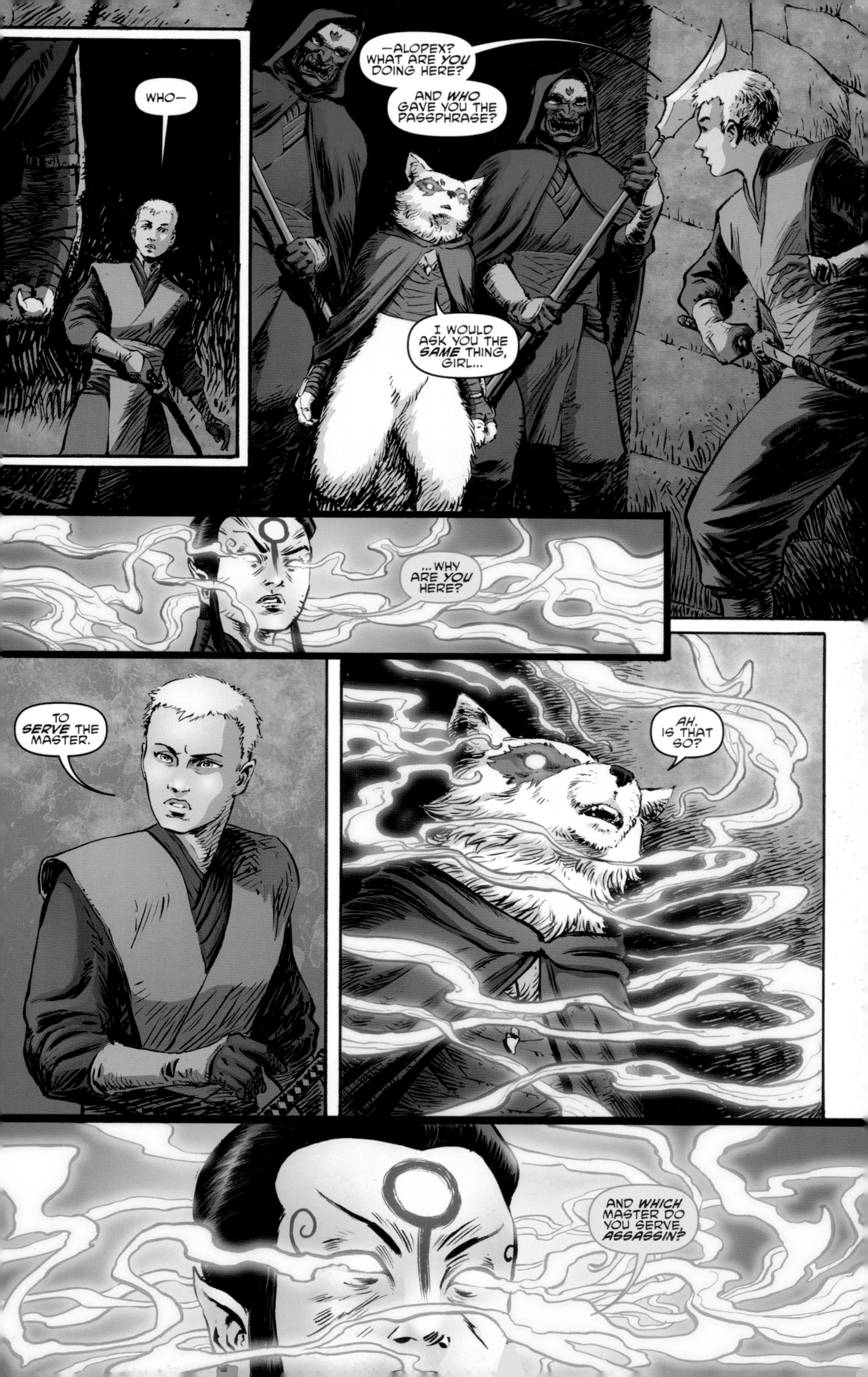
WHO—
—ALOPEX? WHAT ARE YOU DOING HERE?
AND WHO GAVE YOU THE PASSPHRASE?
I WOULD ASK YOU THE SAME THING, GIRL...
...WHY ARE YOU HERE?
TO SERVE THE MASTER.
AH. IS THAT SO?
AND WHICH MASTER DO YOU SERVE, ASSASSIN?

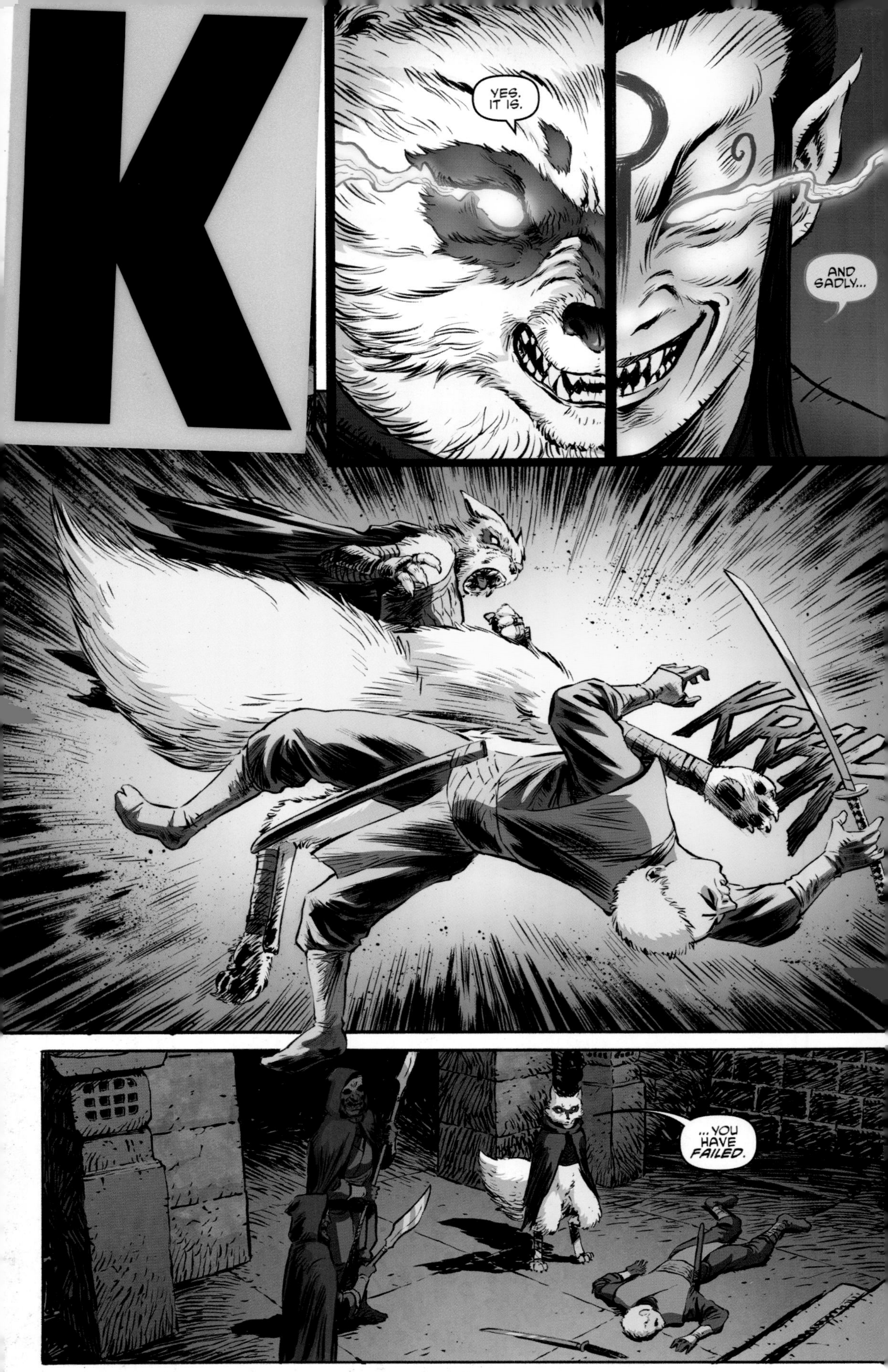
K
YES. IT IS.
AND SADLY...
...YOU HAVE FAILED.

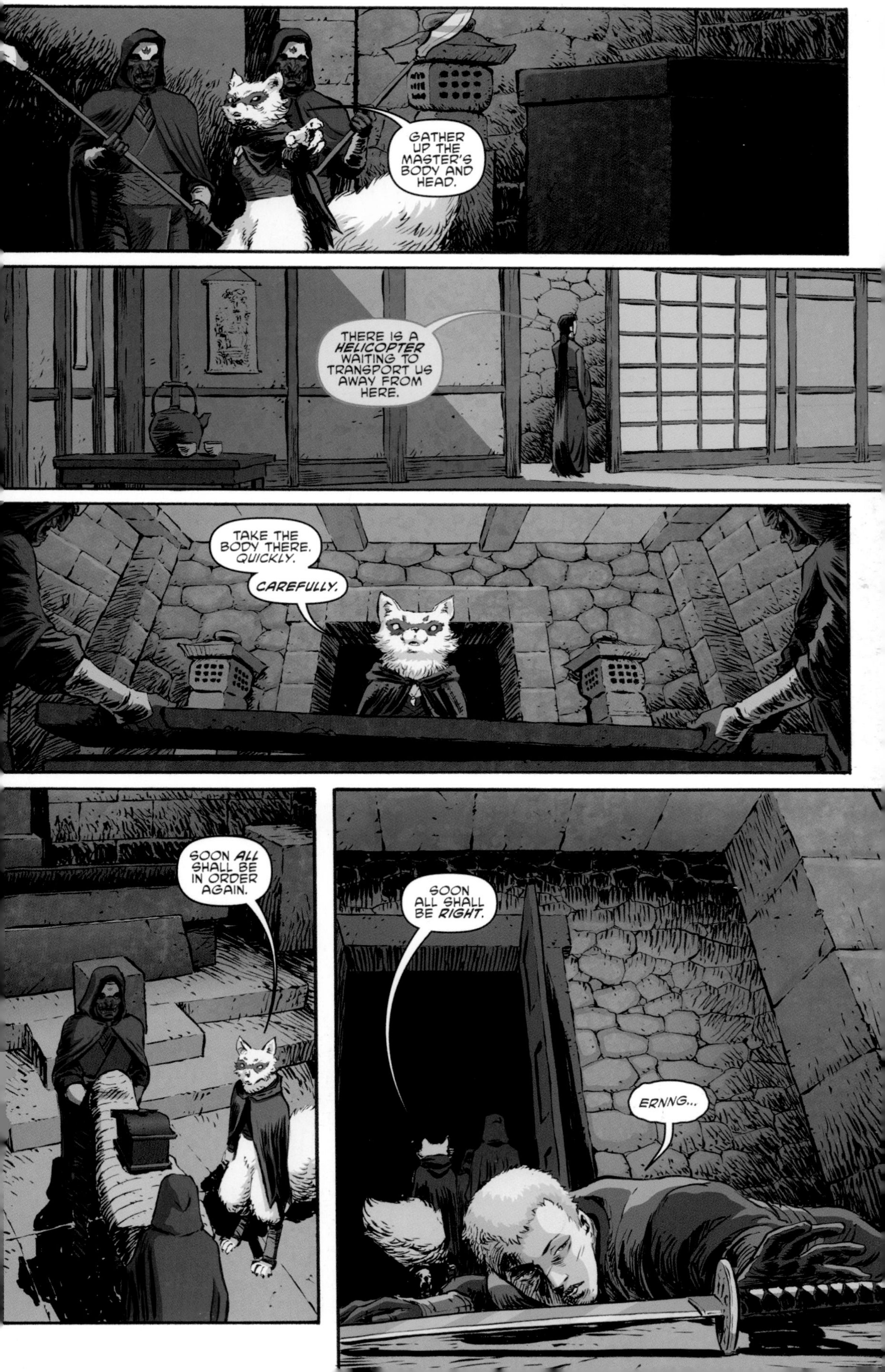
GATHER UP THE MASTER'S BODY AND HEAD.
THERE IS A *HELICOPTER* WAITING TO TRANSPORT US AWAY FROM HERE.
TAKE THE BODY THERE. *QUICKLY.*
CAREFULLY.
SOON *ALL* SHALL BE IN ORDER AGAIN.
SOON ALL SHALL BE *RIGHT*.
ERNNG...

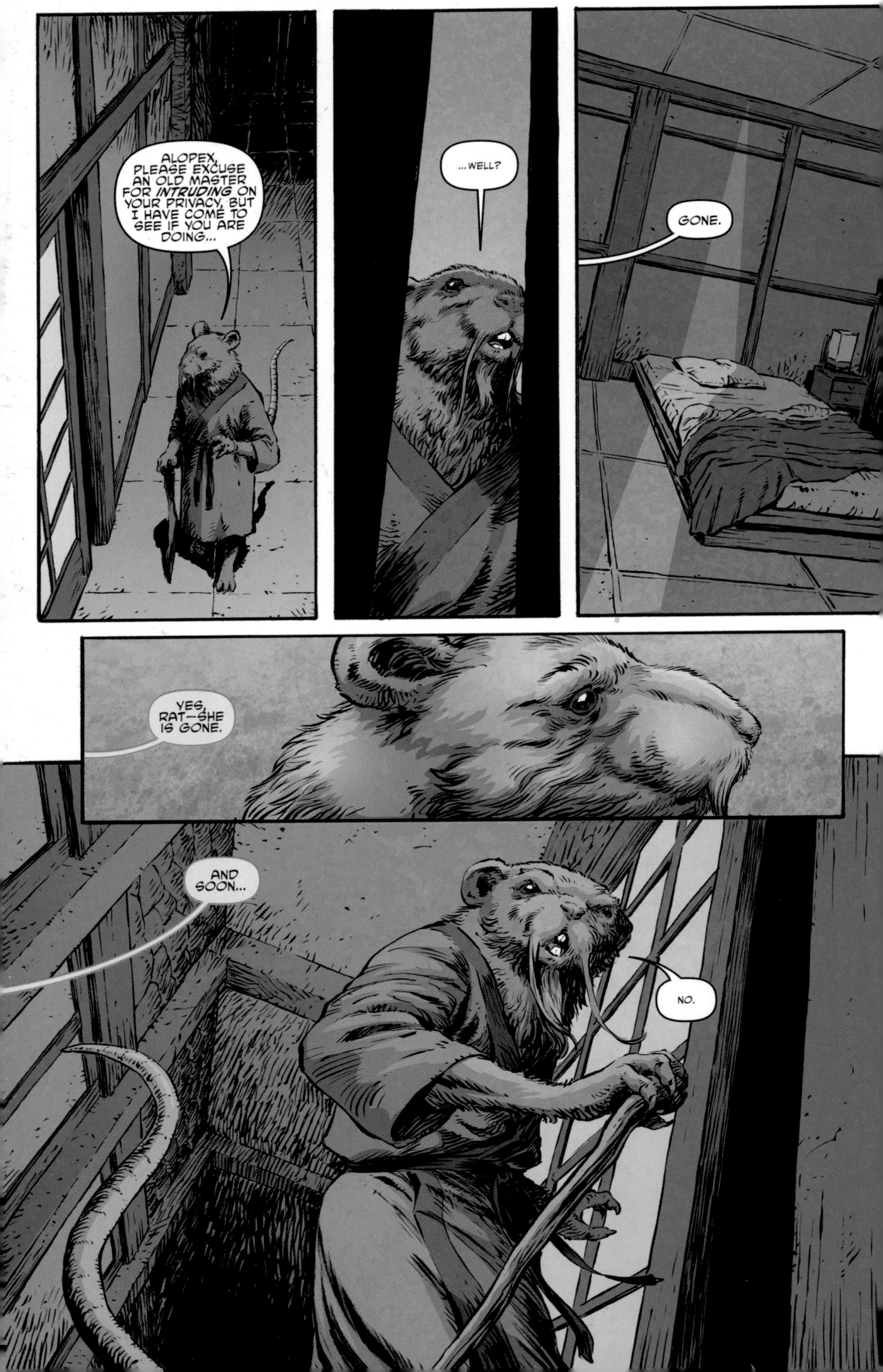
ALOPEX, PLEASE EXCUSE AN OLD MASTER FOR *INTRUDING* ON YOUR PRIVACY, BUT I HAVE COME TO SEE IF YOU ARE DOING...
...WELL?
GONE.
YES, RAT—SHE IS GONE.
AND SOON...
NO.

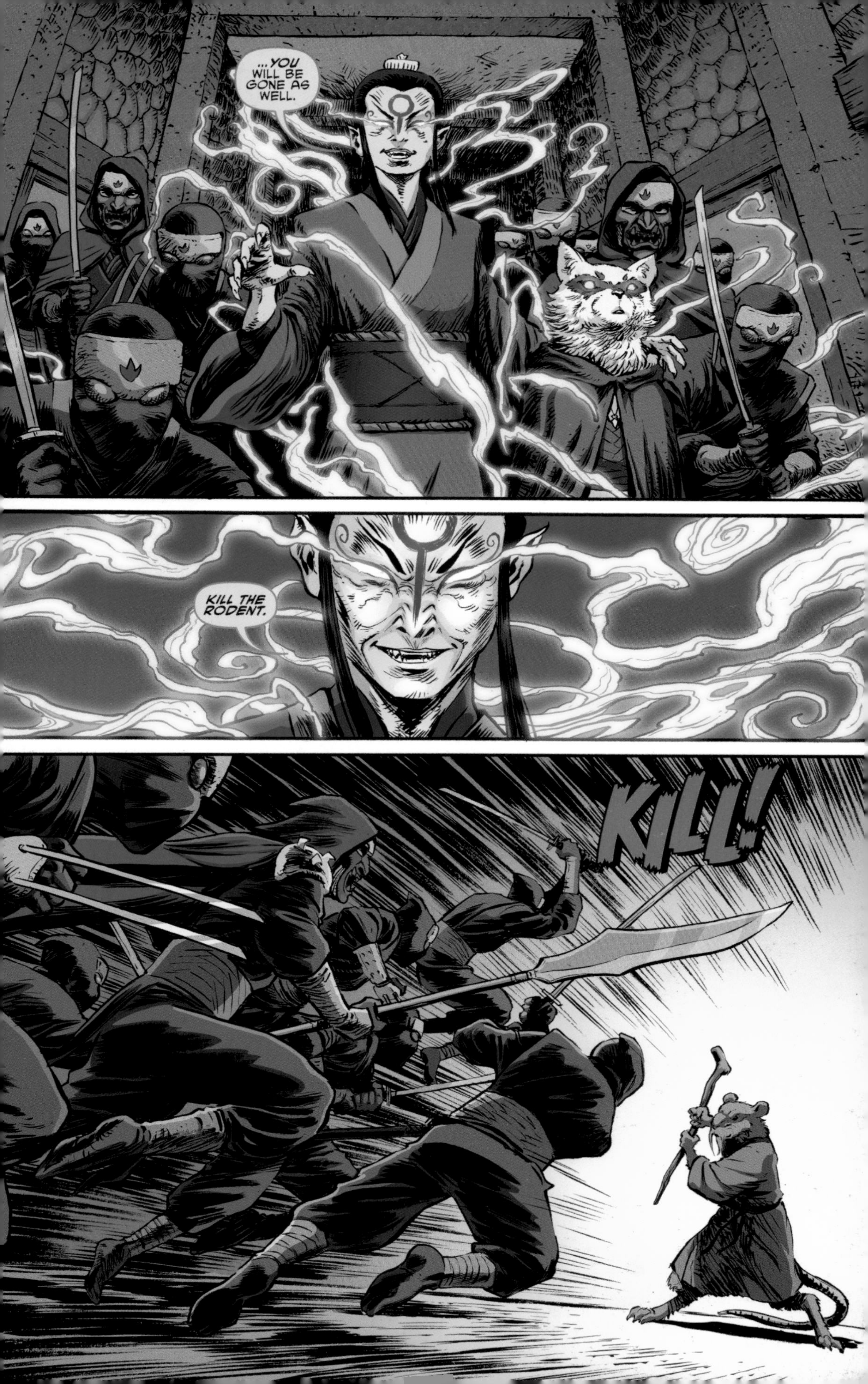
...YOU WILL BE GONE AS WELL.
KILL THE RODENT.
KILL!

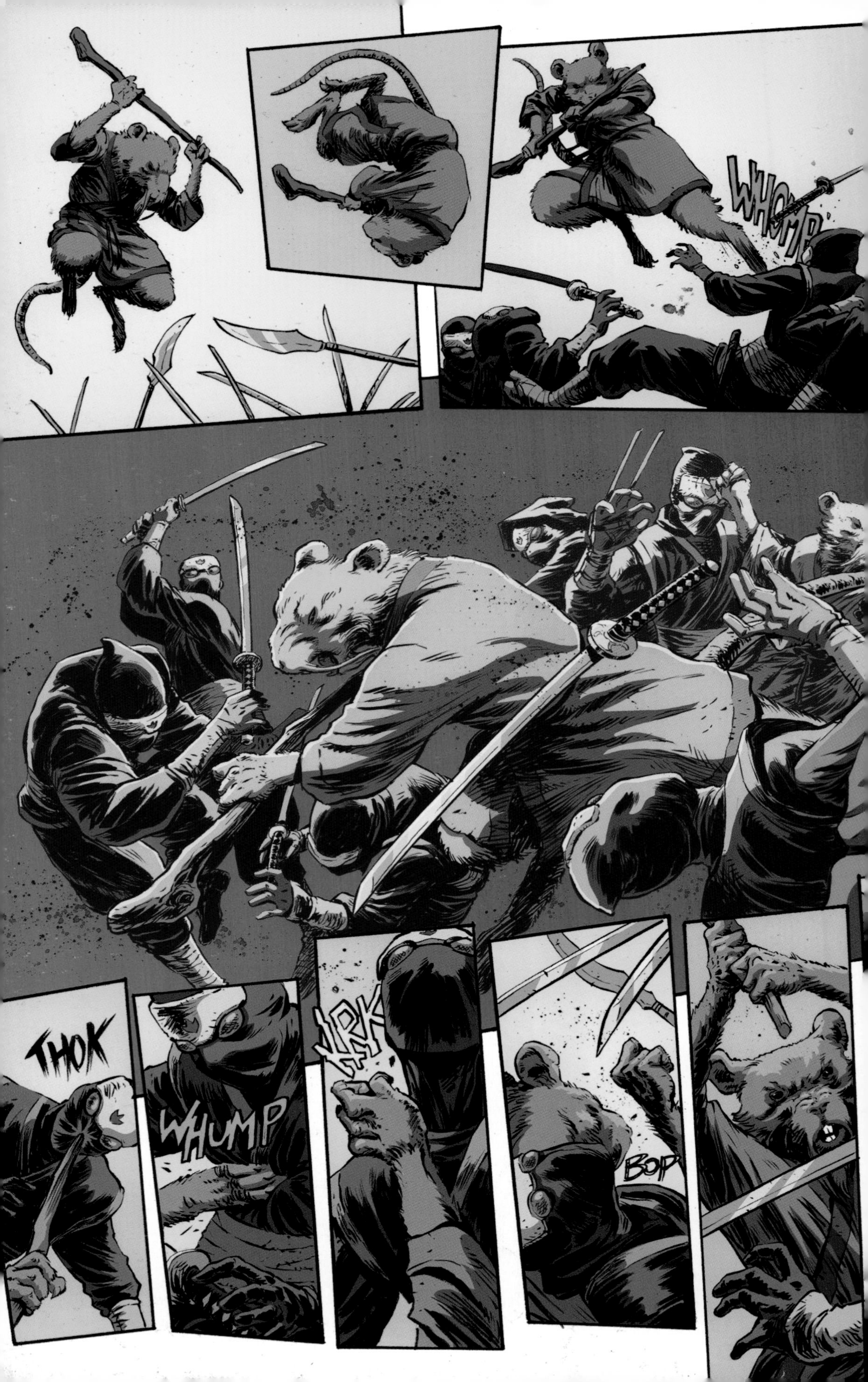
WHOMP
THOK
WHUMP
YRK
BOP

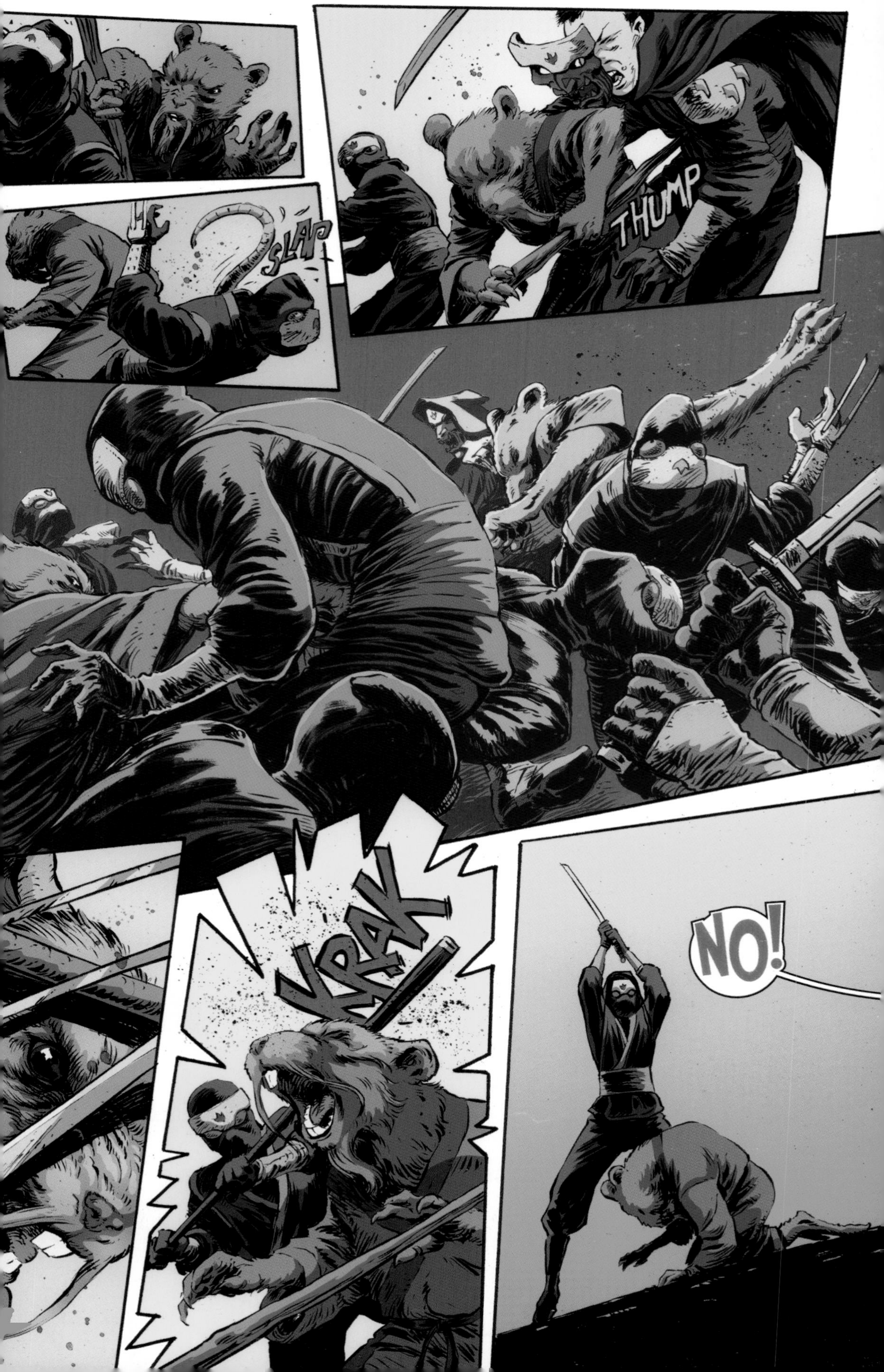
SLAP
THUMP
KRAK
NO!

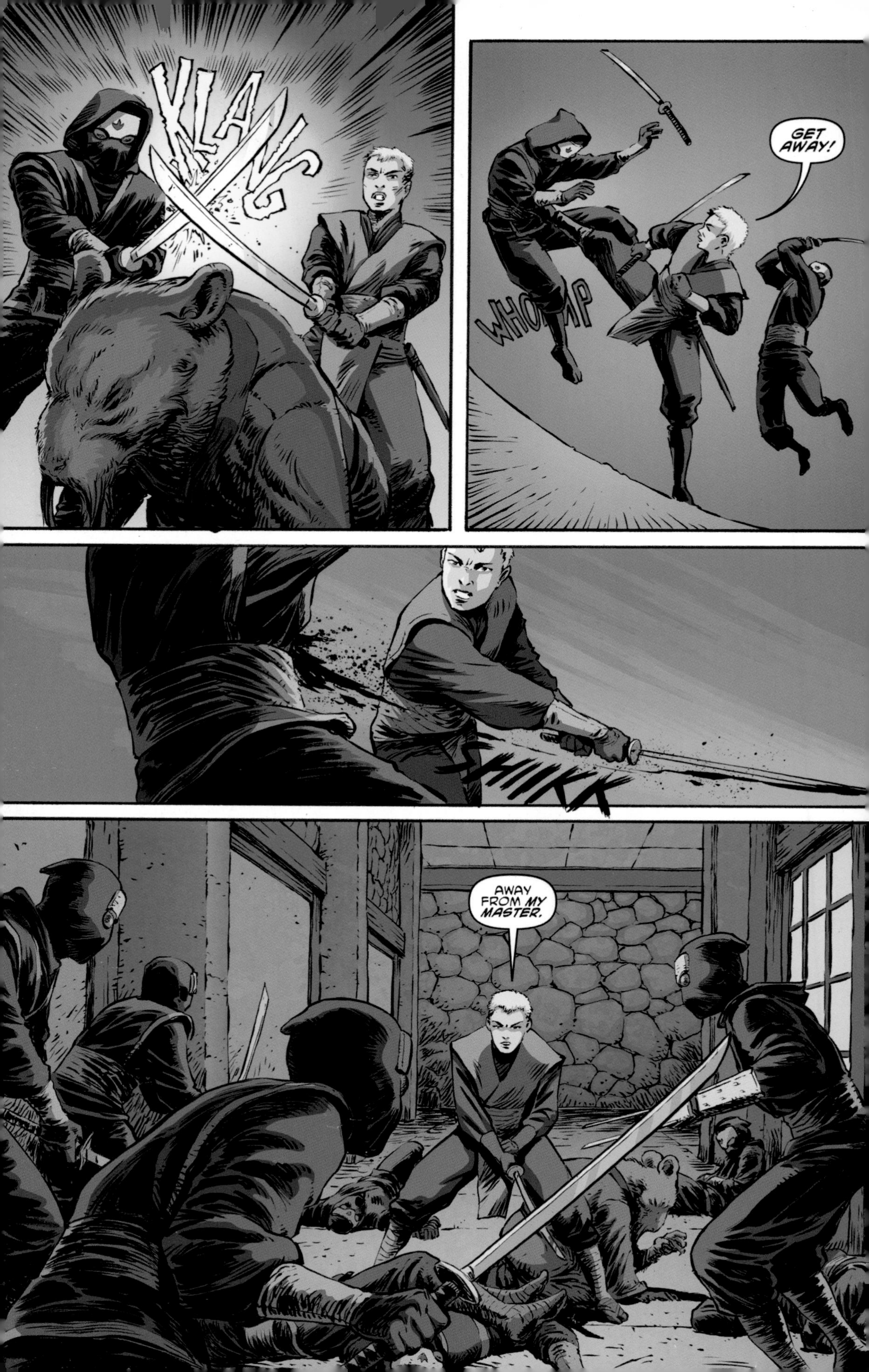
KLANG
GET AWAY!
WHOMP
SHIKK
AWAY FROM *MY MASTER.*

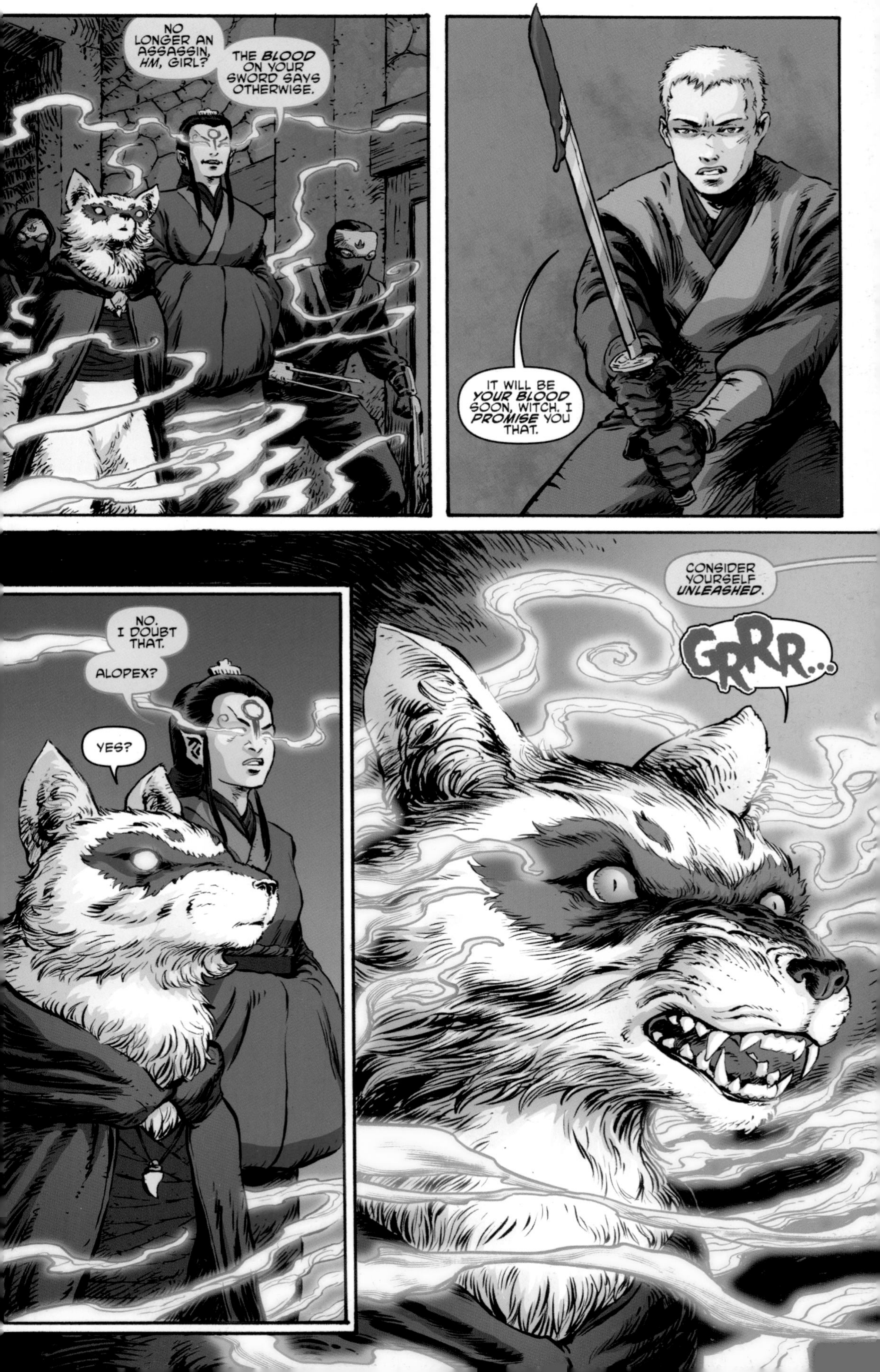
NO LONGER AN ASSASSIN, HM, GIRL?
THE BLOOD ON YOUR SWORD SAYS OTHERWISE.
IT WILL BE YOUR BLOOD SOON, WITCH. I PROMISE YOU THAT.
NO. I DOUBT THAT.
ALOPEX?
YES?
CONSIDER YOURSELF UNLEASHED.
GRRR...

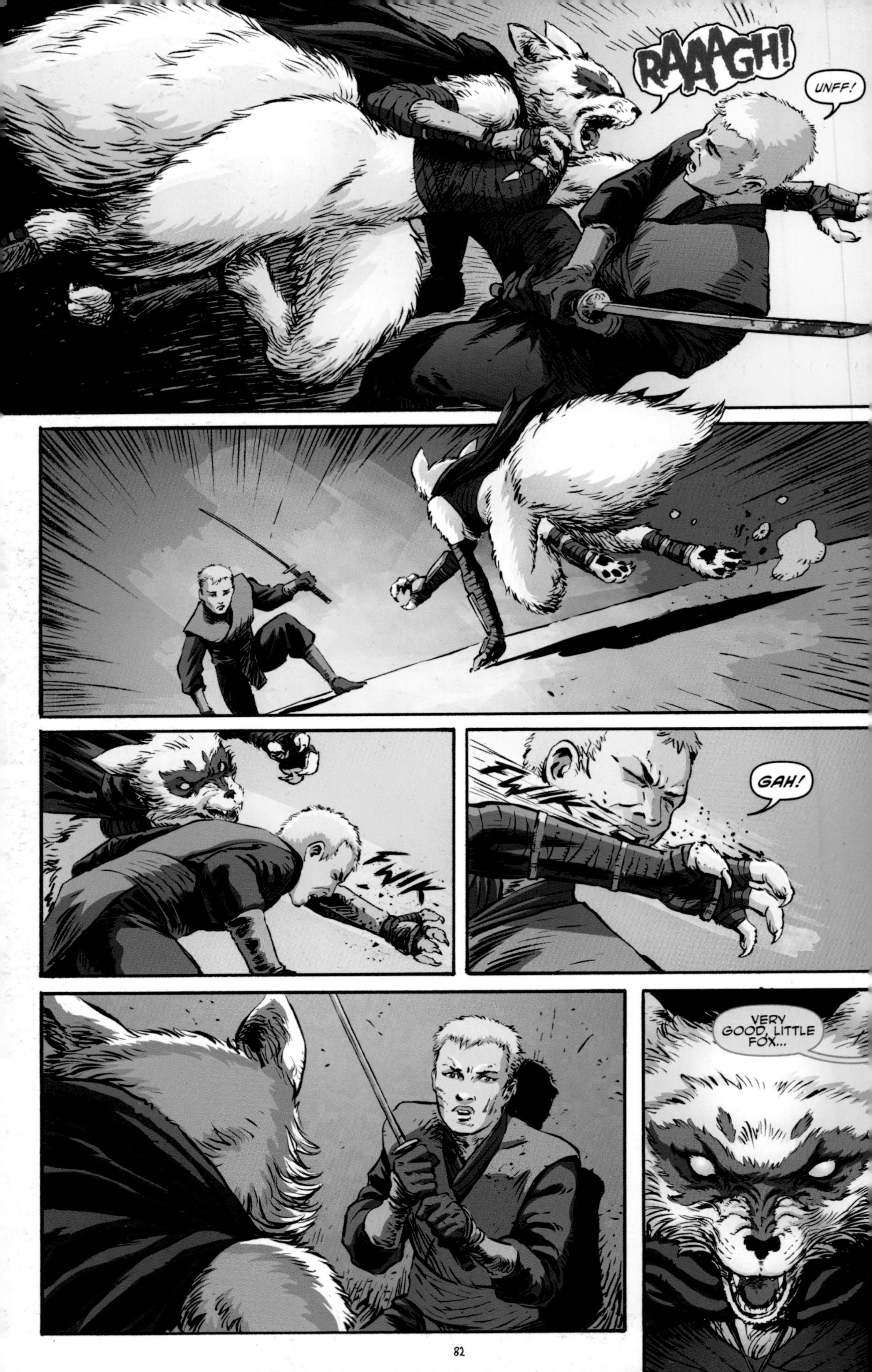
RAAAGH!
UNFF!
FWIK
FWIK
GAH!
VERY GOOD, LITTLE FOX...

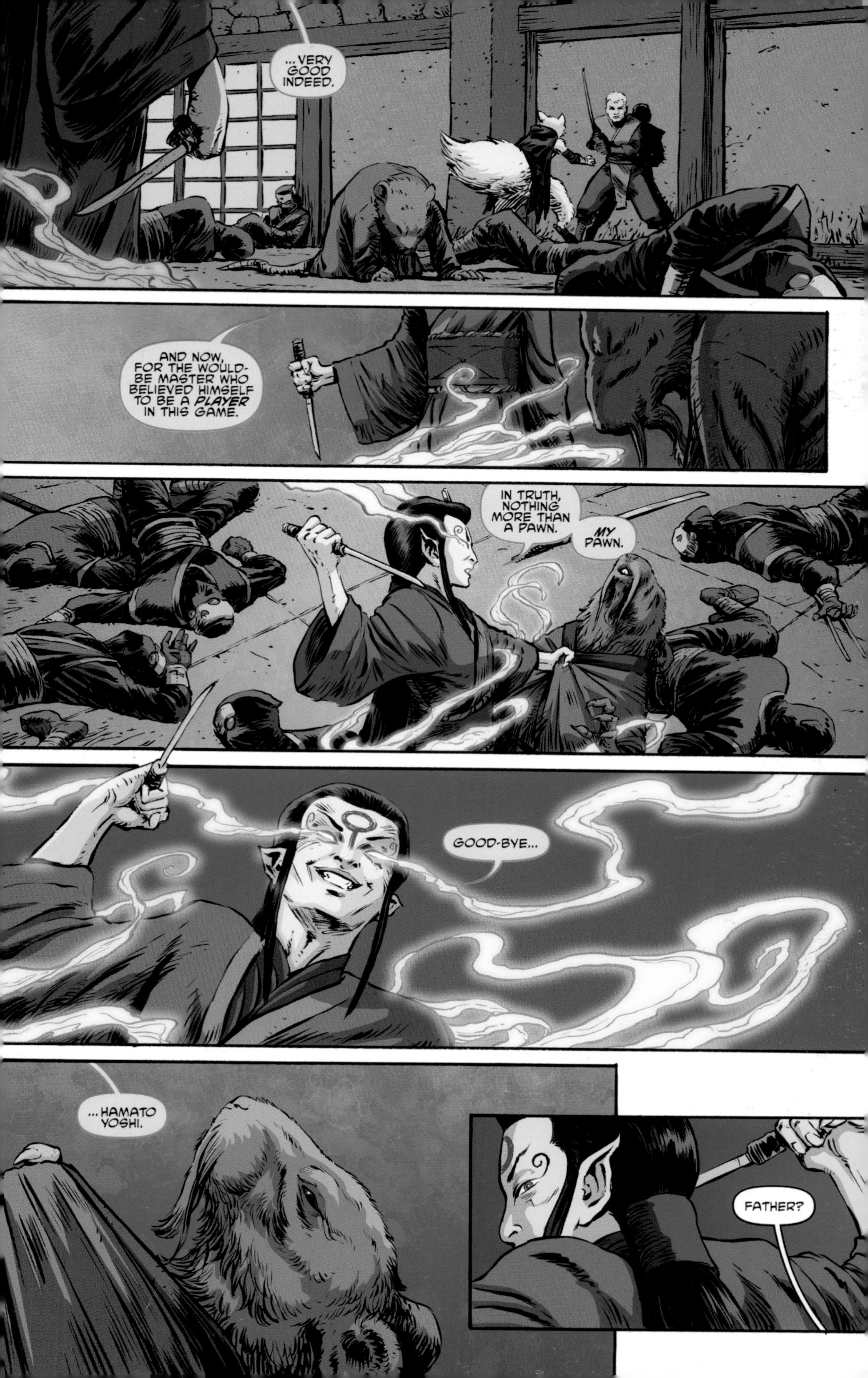
...VERY GOOD INDEED.
AND NOW, FOR THE WOULD-BE MASTER WHO BELIEVED HIMSELF TO BE A *PLAYER* IN THIS GAME.
IN TRUTH, NOTHING MORE THAN A PAWN.
MY PAWN.
GOOD-BYE...
...HAMATO YOSHI.
FATHER?

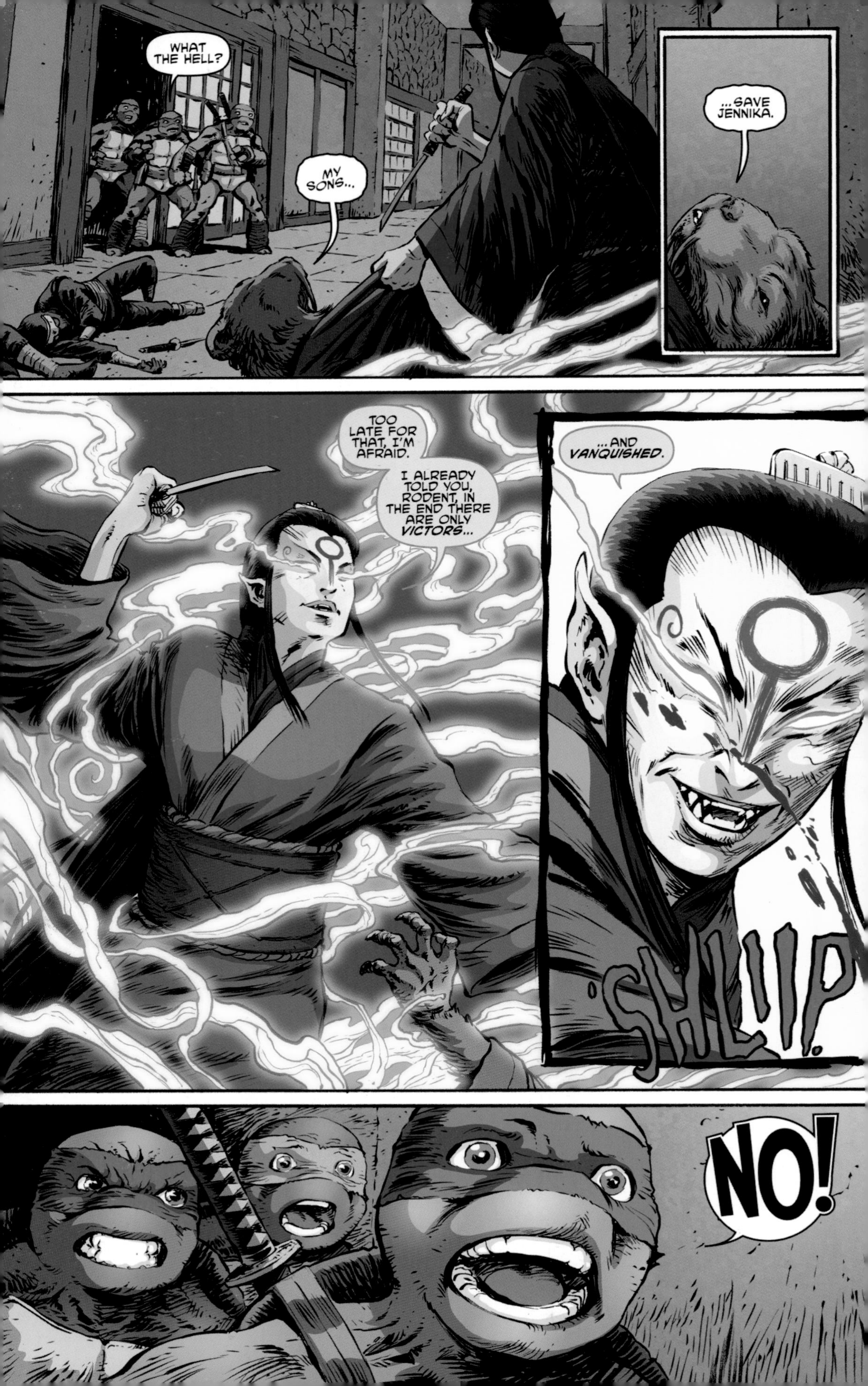
WHAT THE HELL?
MY SONS...
...SAVE JENNIKA.
TOO LATE FOR THAT, I'M AFRAID.
I ALREADY TOLD YOU, RODENT, IN THE END THERE ARE ONLY VICTORS...
...AND VANQUISHED.
SHLIIP.
NO!

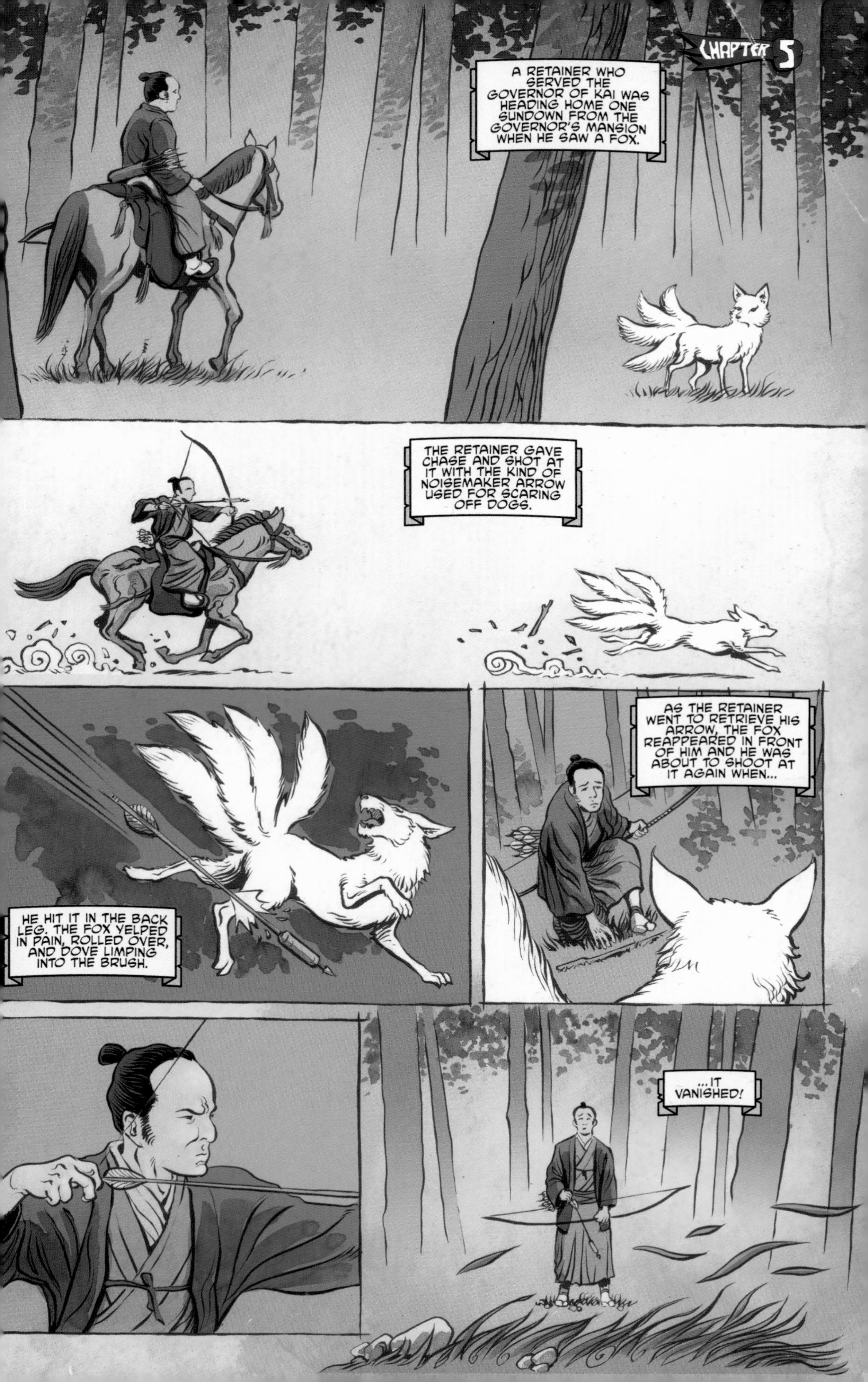
CHAPTER 5
A RETAINER WHO SERVED THE GOVERNOR OF KAI WAS HEADING HOME ONE SUNDOWN FROM THE GOVERNOR'S MANSION WHEN HE SAW A FOX.
THE RETAINER GAVE CHASE AND SHOT AT IT WITH THE KIND OF NOISEMAKER ARROW USED FOR SCARING OFF DOGS.
HE HIT IT IN THE BACK LEG. THE FOX YELPED IN PAIN, ROLLED OVER, AND DOVE LIMPING INTO THE BRUSH.
AS THE RETAINER WENT TO RETRIEVE HIS ARROW, THE FOX REAPPEARED IN FRONT OF HIM AND HE WAS ABOUT TO SHOOT AT IT AGAIN WHEN...
...IT VANISHED!

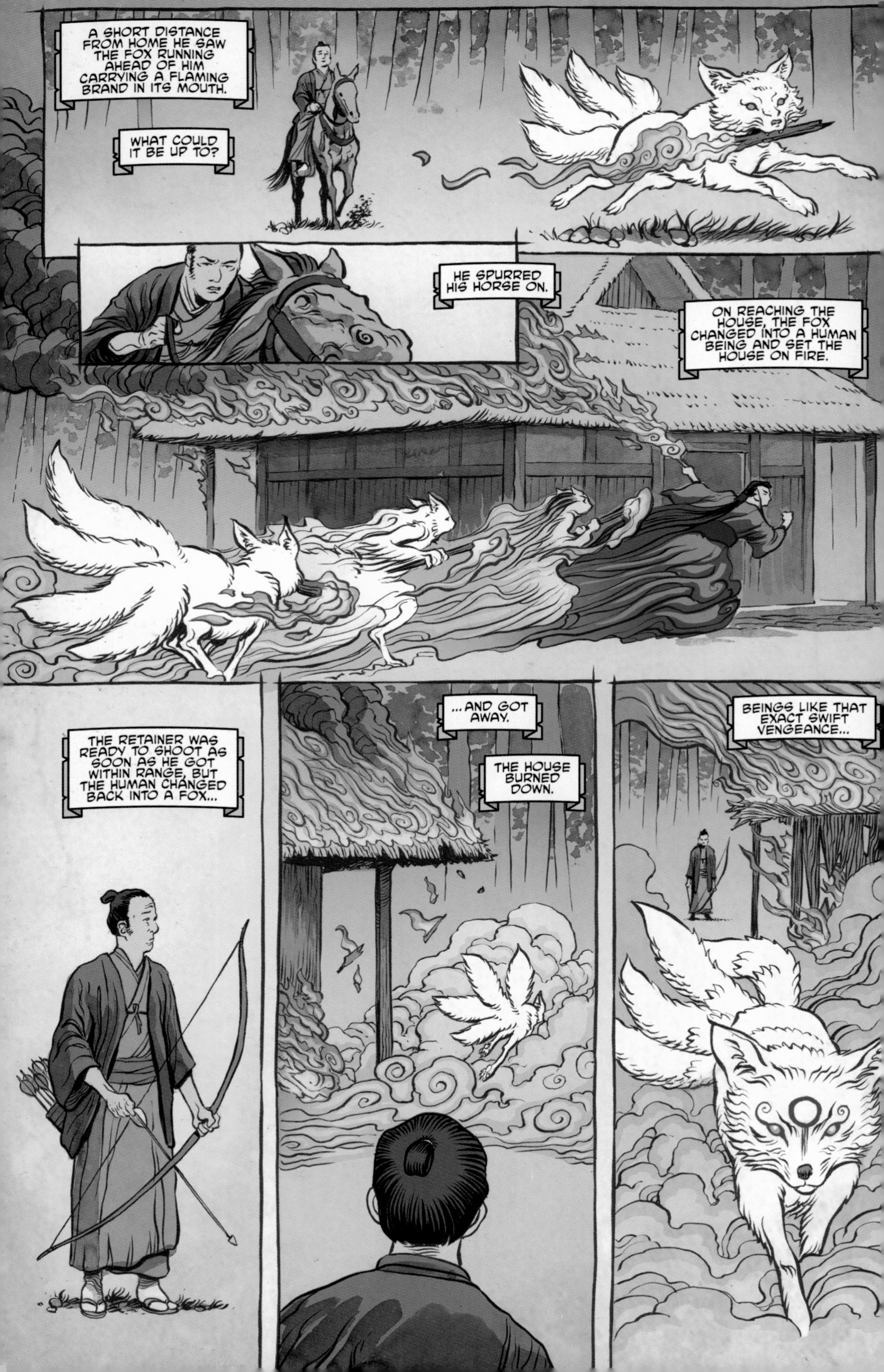
A SHORT DISTANCE FROM HOME HE SAW THE FOX RUNNING AHEAD OF HIM CARRYING A FLAMING BRAND IN ITS MOUTH.
WHAT COULD IT BE UP TO?
HE SPURRED HIS HORSE ON.
ON REACHING THE HOUSE, THE FOX CHANGED INTO A HUMAN BEING AND SET THE HOUSE ON FIRE.
THE RETAINER WAS READY TO SHOOT AS SOON AS HE GOT WITHIN RANGE, BUT THE HUMAN CHANGED BACK INTO A FOX...
...AND GOT AWAY.
THE HOUSE BURNED DOWN.
BEINGS LIKE THAT EXACT SWIFT VENGEANCE...

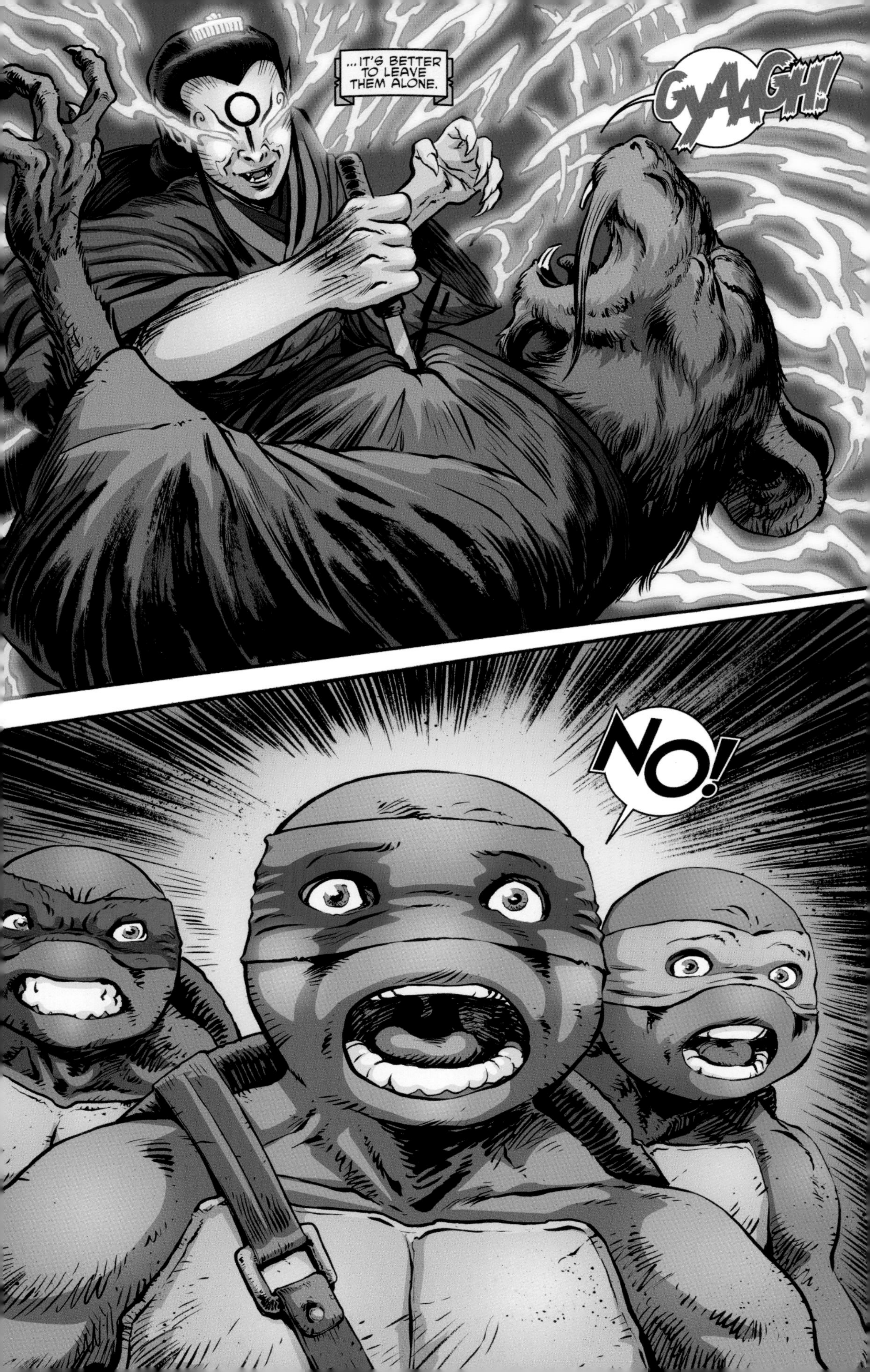
...IT'S BETTER TO LEAVE THEM ALONE.
GYAAGH!
NO!

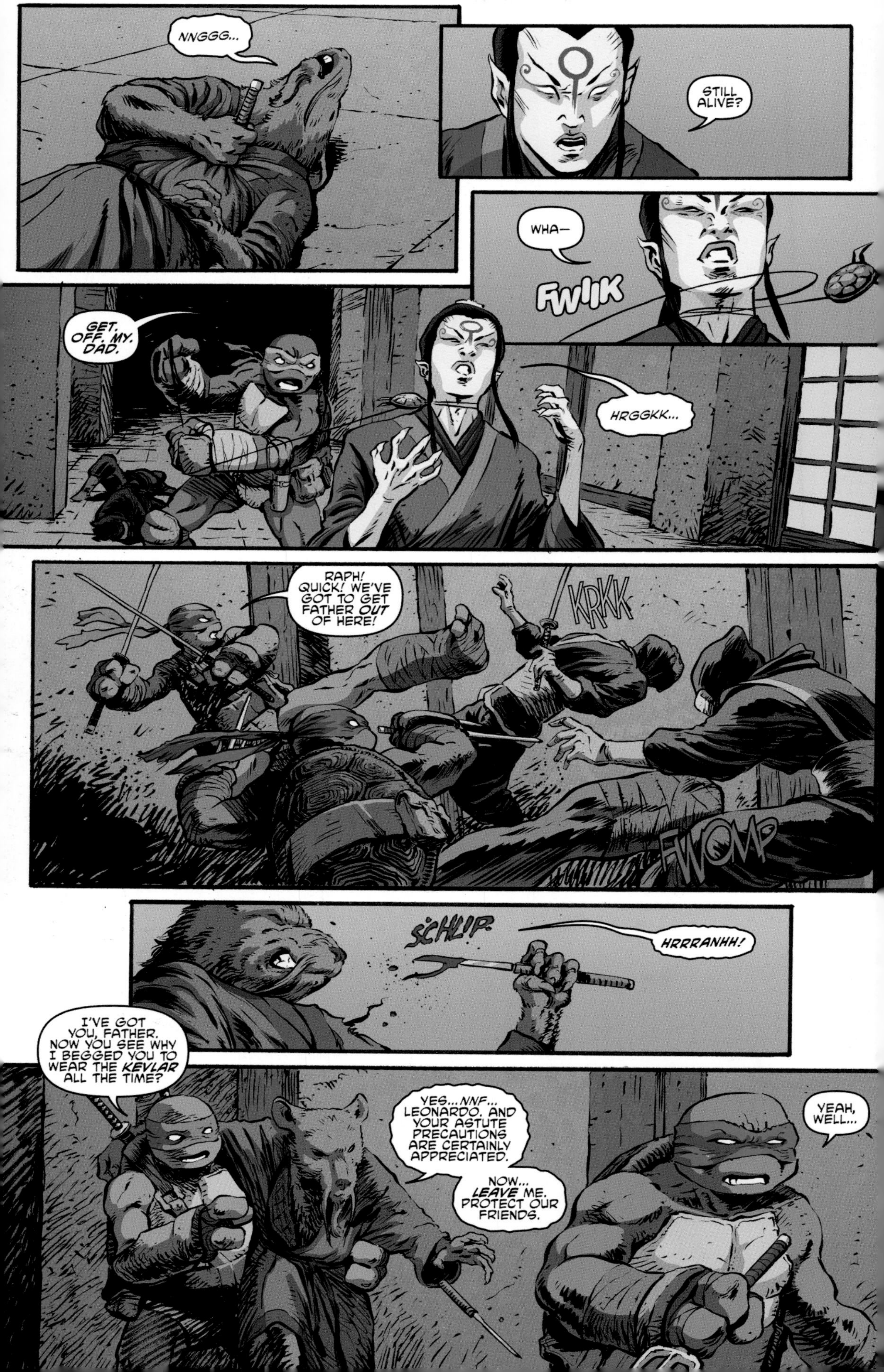
NNGGG...
STILL ALIVE?
WHA—
FWIIK
GET. OFF. MY. DAD.
HRGGKK...
RAPH! QUICK! WE'VE GOT TO GET FATHER *OUT* OF HERE!
KRKK
FWOMP
SCHLIP
HRRRANHH!
I'VE GOT YOU, FATHER. NOW YOU SEE WHY I BEGGED YOU TO WEAR THE *KEVLAR* ALL THE TIME?
YES... *NNF*... LEONARDO. AND YOUR ASTUTE PRECAUTIONS ARE CERTAINLY APPRECIATED.
NOW... *LEAVE* ME. PROTECT OUR FRIENDS.
YEAH, WELL...

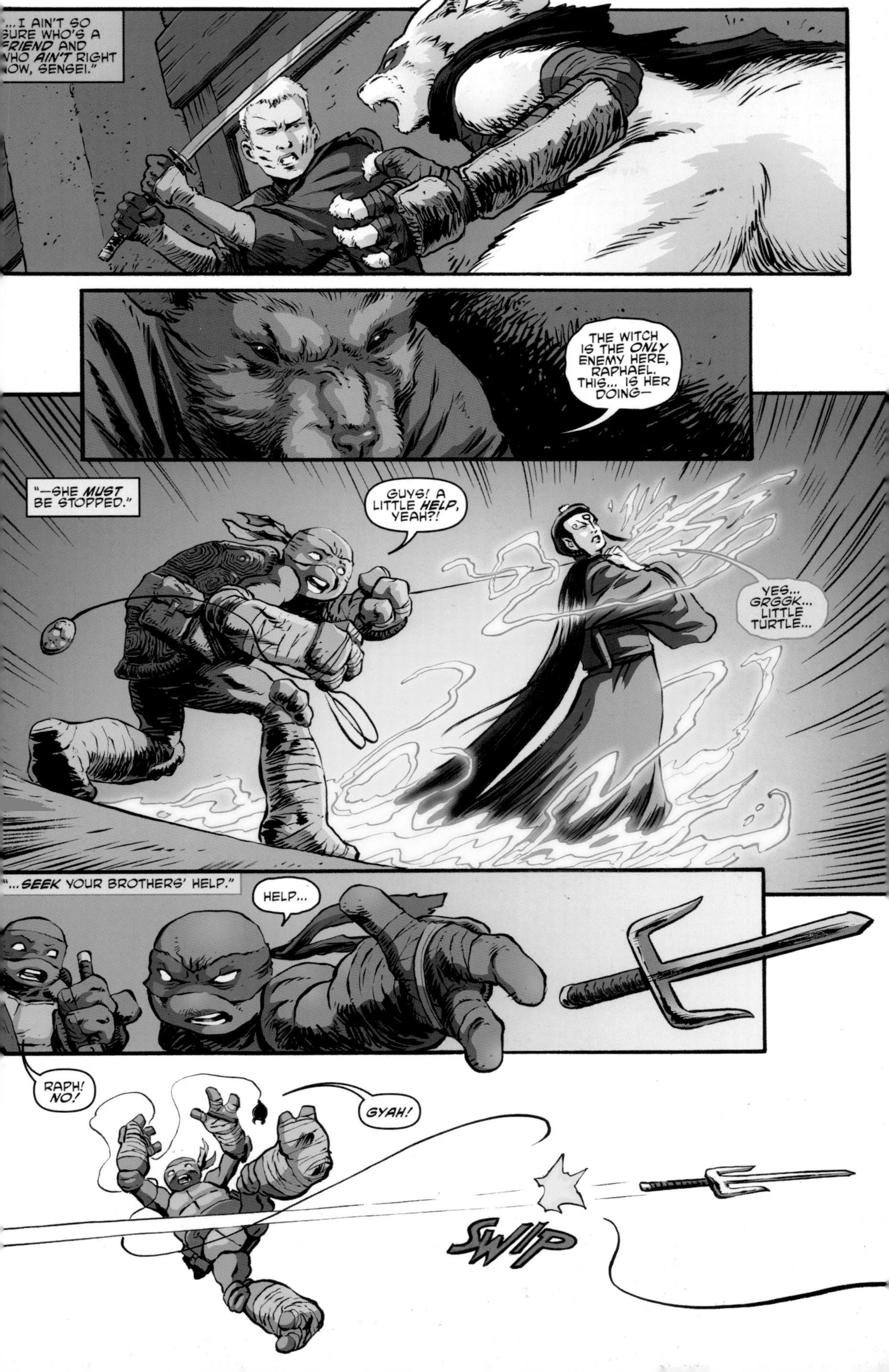
"...I AIN'T SO SURE WHO'S A FRIEND AND WHO AIN'T RIGHT NOW, SENSEI."
THE WITCH IS THE ONLY ENEMY HERE, RAPHAEL. THIS... IS HER DOING—
"—SHE MUST BE STOPPED."
GUYS! A LITTLE HELP, YEAH?!
YES... GRGGK... LITTLE TURTLE...
"...SEEK YOUR BROTHERS' HELP."
HELP...
RAPH! NO!
GYAH!
SWIP

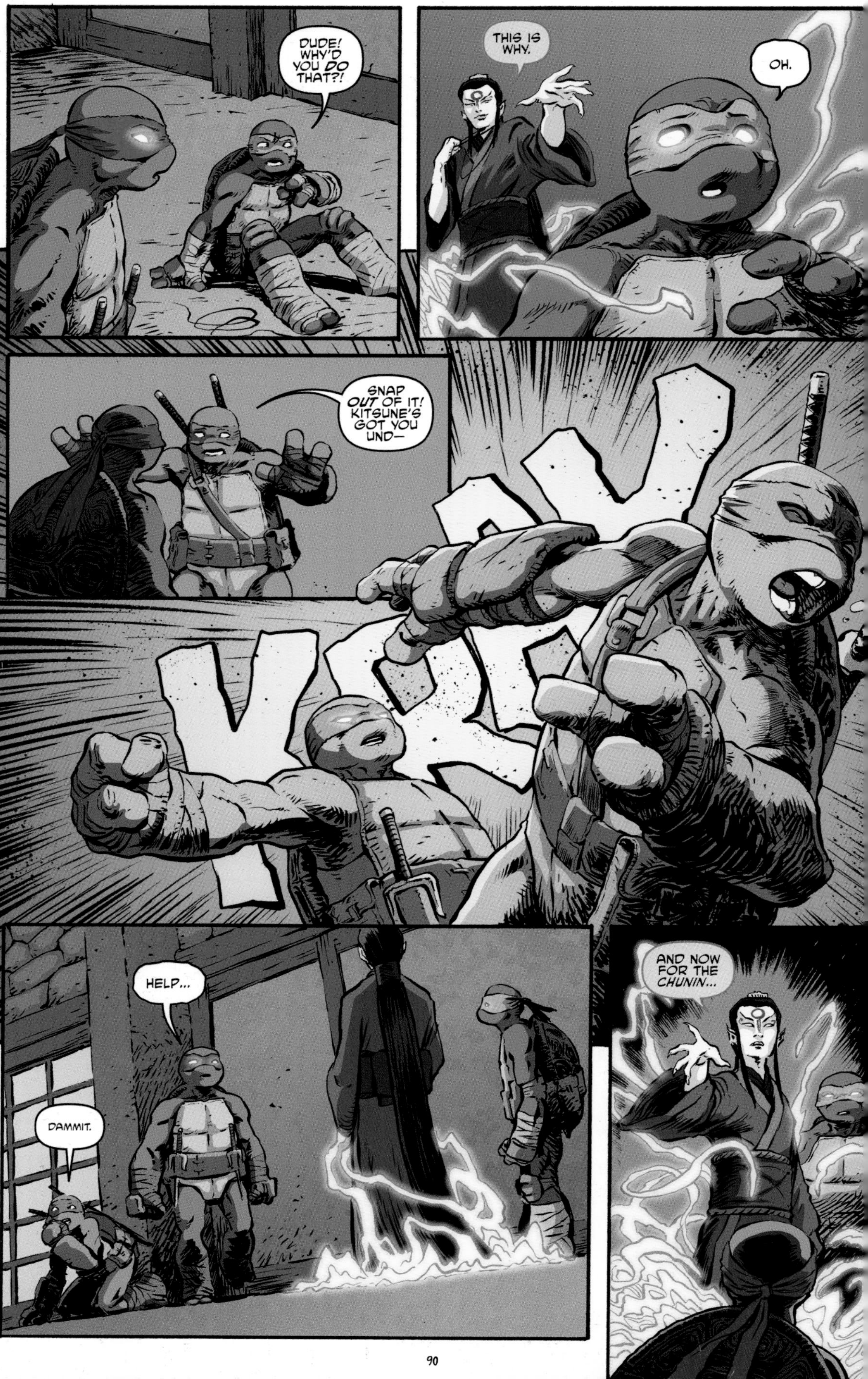
DUDE! WHY'D YOU DO THAT?!
THIS IS WHY.
OH.
SNAP OUT OF IT! KITSUNE'S GOT YOU UND—
HELP...
DAMMIT.
AND NOW FOR THE CHUNIN...

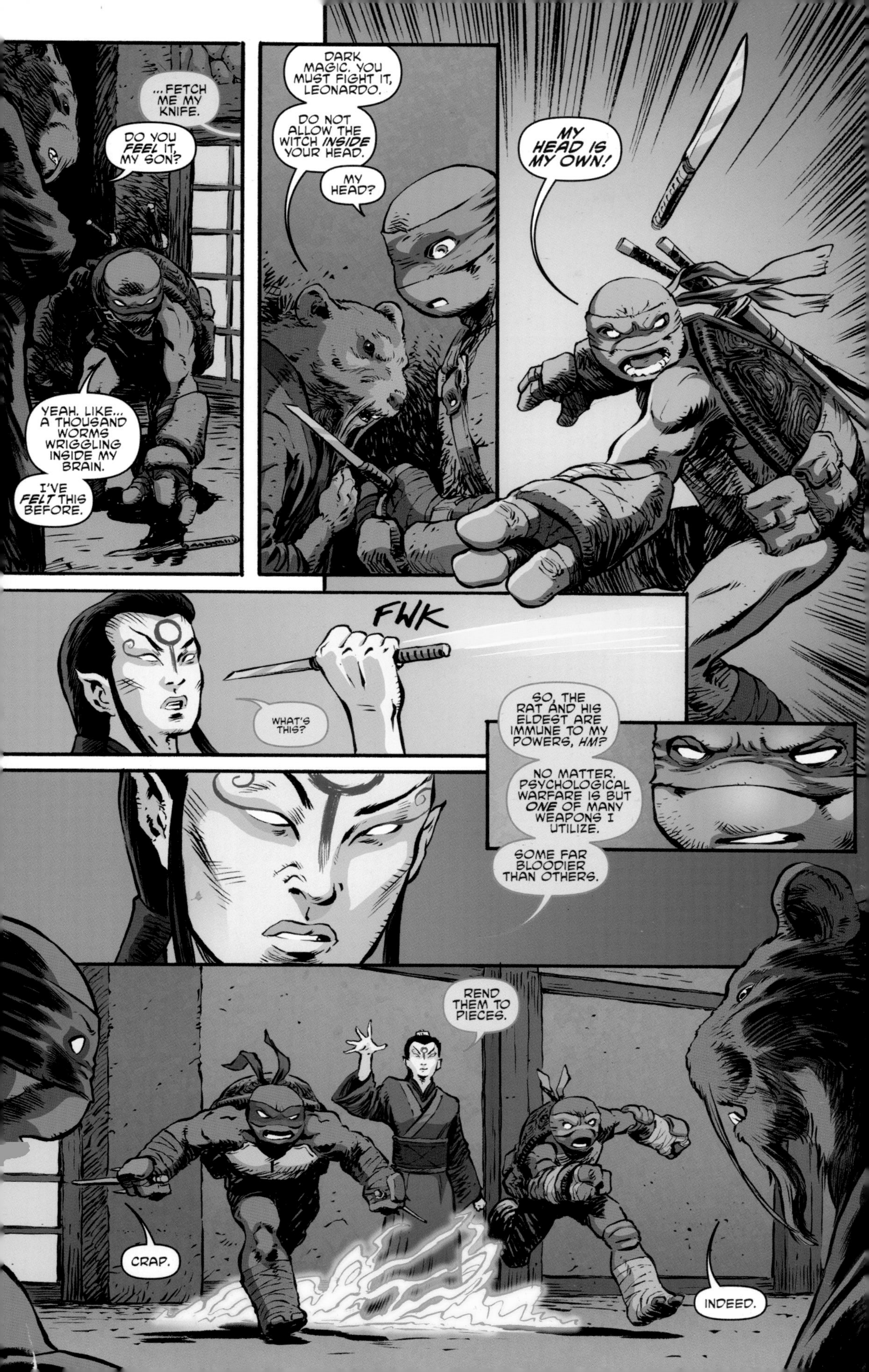
...FETCH ME MY KNIFE.
DO YOU FEEL IT, MY SON?
YEAH. LIKE... A THOUSAND WORMS WRIGGLING INSIDE MY BRAIN.
I'VE FELT THIS BEFORE.
DARK MAGIC. YOU MUST FIGHT IT, LEONARDO.
DO NOT ALLOW THE WITCH INSIDE YOUR HEAD.
MY HEAD?
MY HEAD IS MY OWN!
FWK
WHAT'S THIS?
SO, THE RAT AND HIS ELDEST ARE IMMUNE TO MY POWERS, HM?
NO MATTER. PSYCHOLOGICAL WARFARE IS BUT ONE OF MANY WEAPONS I UTILIZE.
SOME FAR BLOODIER THAN OTHERS.
REND THEM TO PIECES.
CRAP.
INDEED.

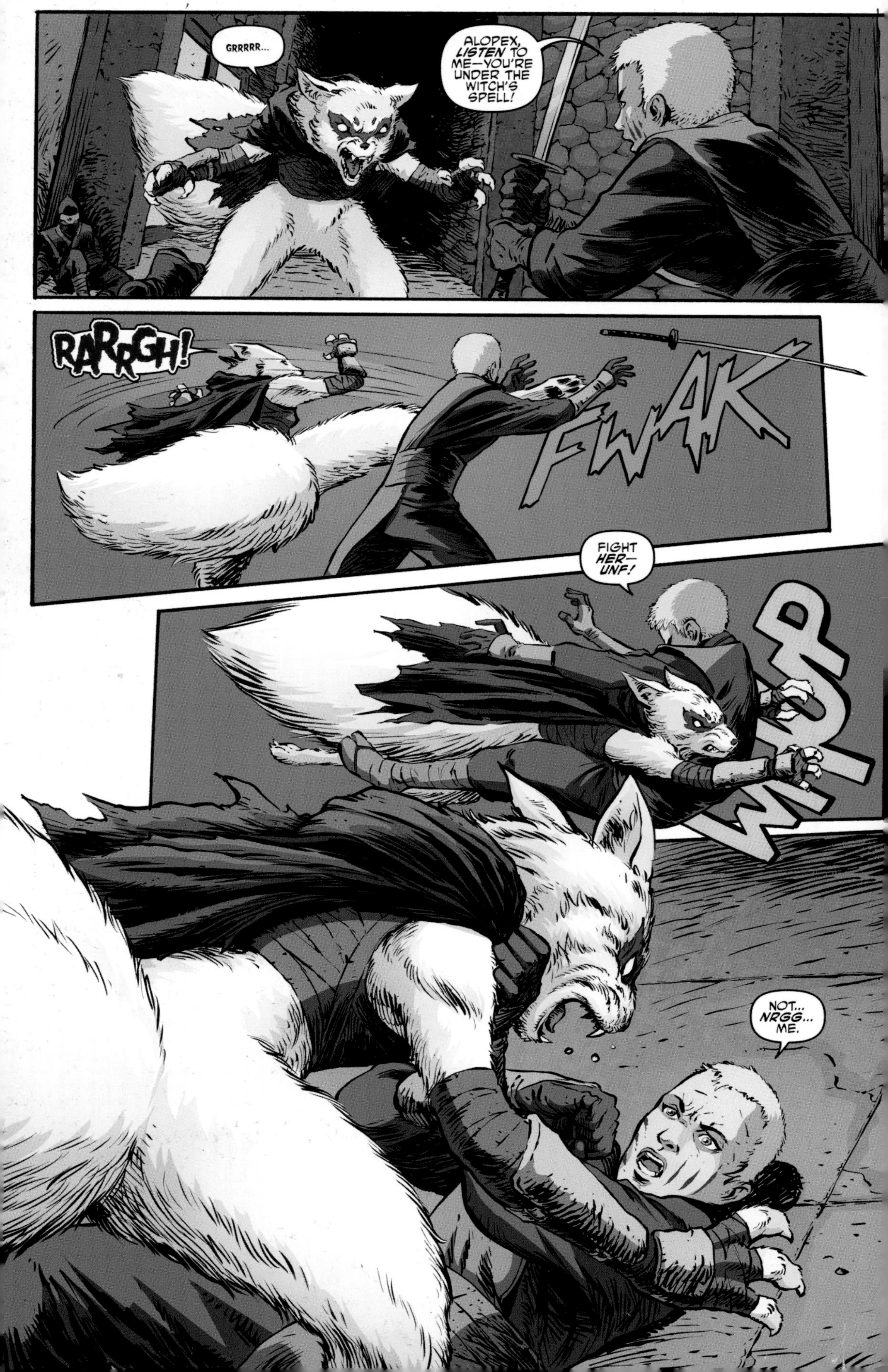
GRRRRR...
ALOPEX, LISTEN TO ME—YOU'RE UNDER THE WITCH'S SPELL!
RARRGH!
FWAK
FIGHT HER—UNF!
WHUP
NOT... NRGG... ME.

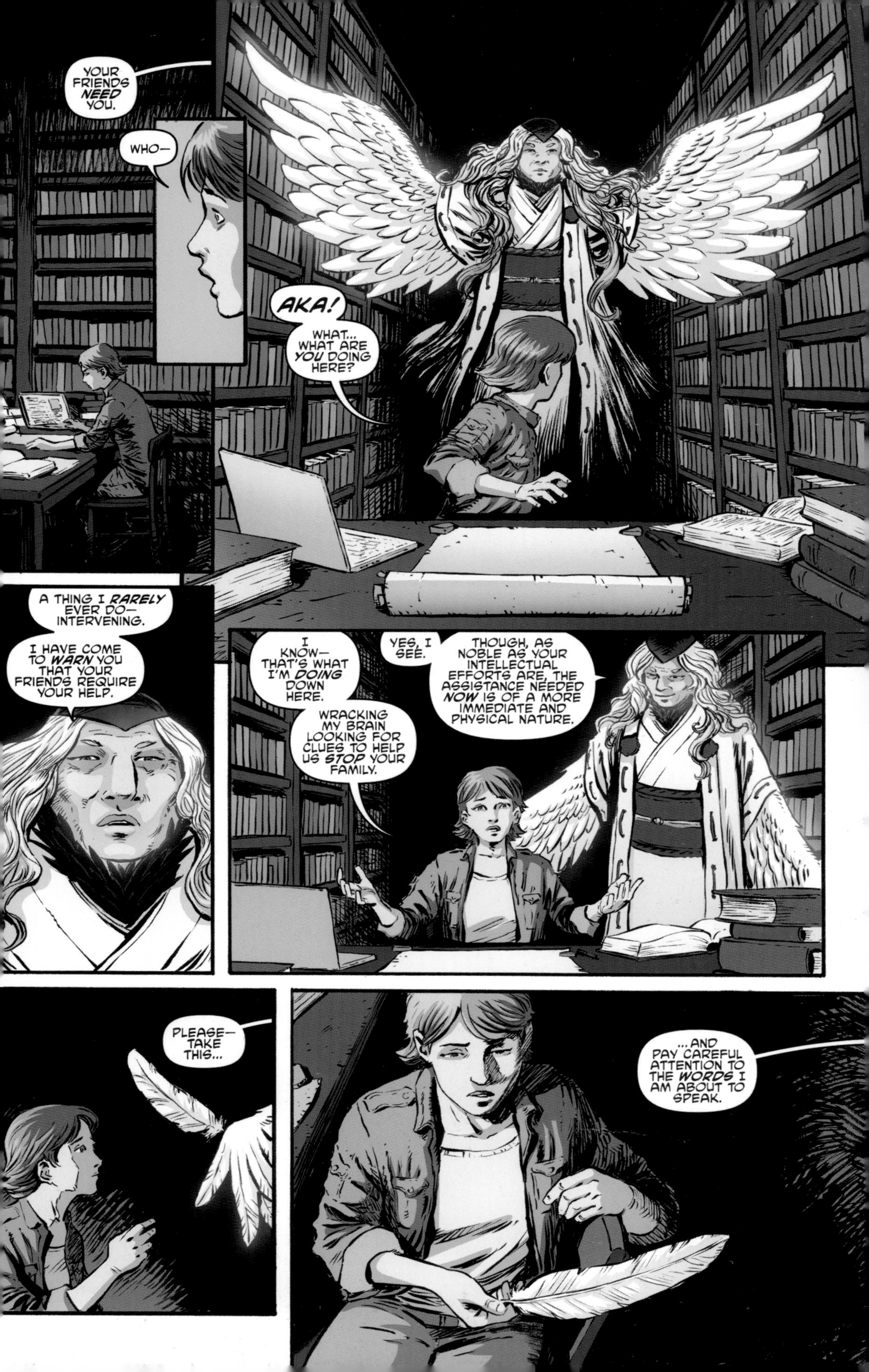

YOUR FRIENDS NEED YOU.
WHO—
AKA!
WHAT... WHAT ARE YOU DOING HERE?
A THING I RARELY EVER DO— INTERVENING.
I HAVE COME TO WARN YOU THAT YOUR FRIENDS REQUIRE YOUR HELP.
I KNOW— THAT'S WHAT I'M DOING DOWN HERE.
WRACKING MY BRAIN LOOKING FOR CLUES TO HELP US STOP YOUR FAMILY.
YES, I SEE.
THOUGH, AS NOBLE AS YOUR INTELLECTUAL EFFORTS ARE, THE ASSISTANCE NEEDED NOW IS OF A MORE IMMEDIATE AND PHYSICAL NATURE.
PLEASE— TAKE THIS...
...AND PAY CAREFUL ATTENTION TO THE WORDS I AM ABOUT TO SPEAK.

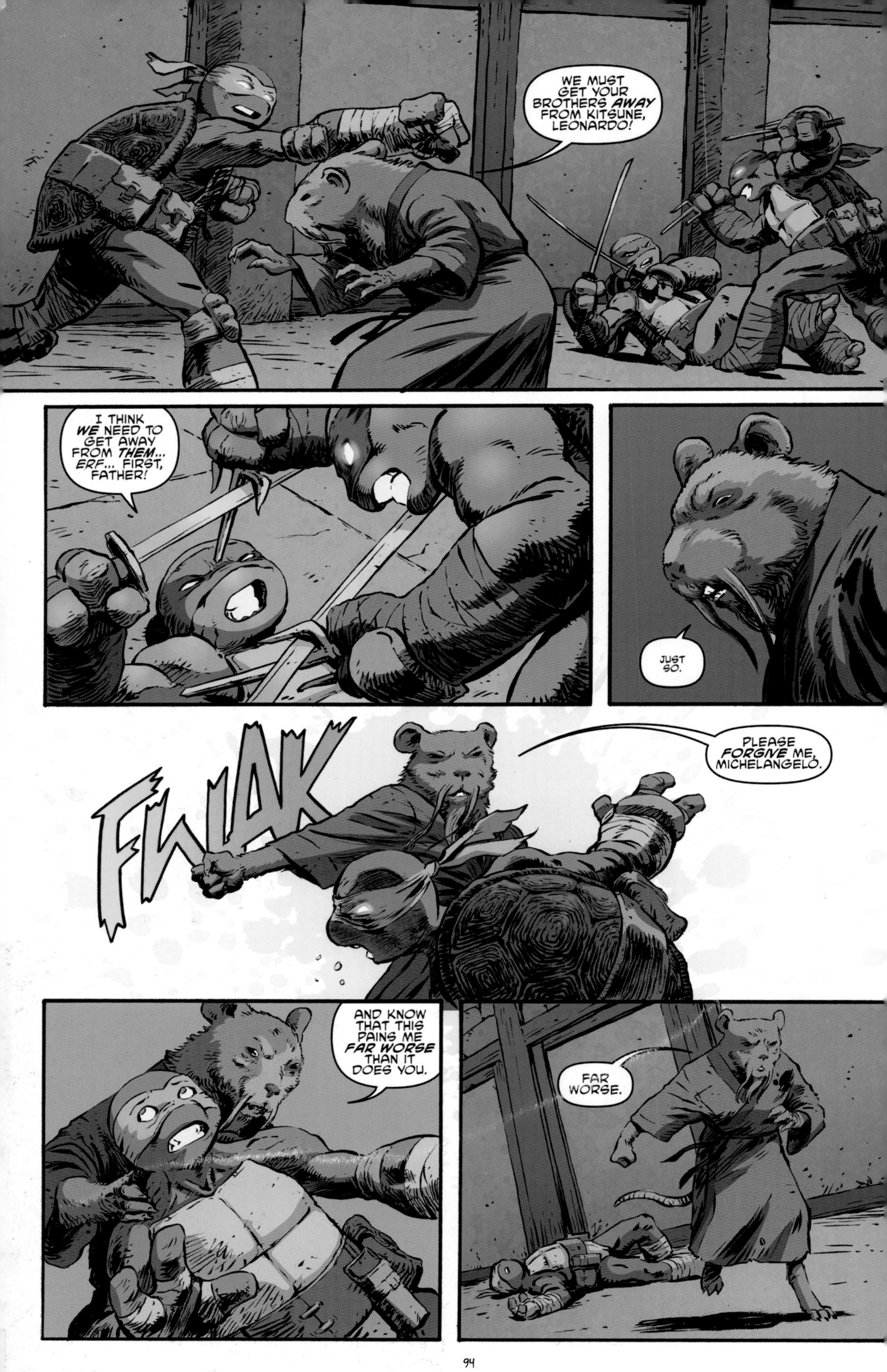
WE MUST GET YOUR BROTHERS AWAY FROM KITSUNE, LEONARDO!
I THINK WE NEED TO GET AWAY FROM THEM... ERF... FIRST, FATHER!
JUST SO.
FWAK
PLEASE FORGIVE ME, MICHELANGELO.
AND KNOW THAT THIS PAINS ME FAR WORSE THAN IT DOES YOU.
FAR WORSE.

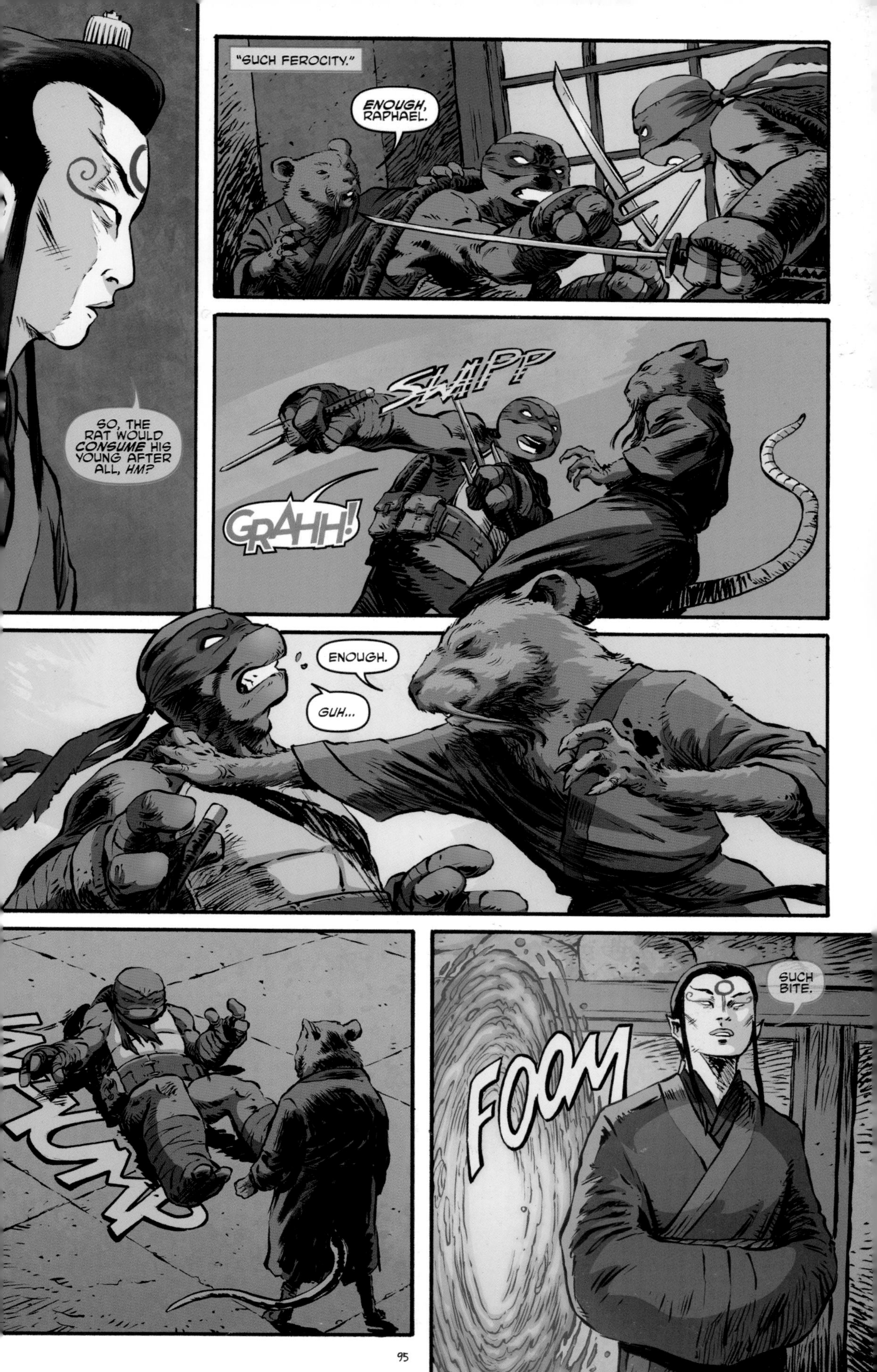
"SUCH FEROCITY."
ENOUGH, RAPHAEL.
SO, THE RAT WOULD CONSUME HIS YOUNG AFTER ALL, HM?
SWAPP
GRAHH!
ENOUGH.
GUH...
WHUMP
FOOM
SUCH BITE.

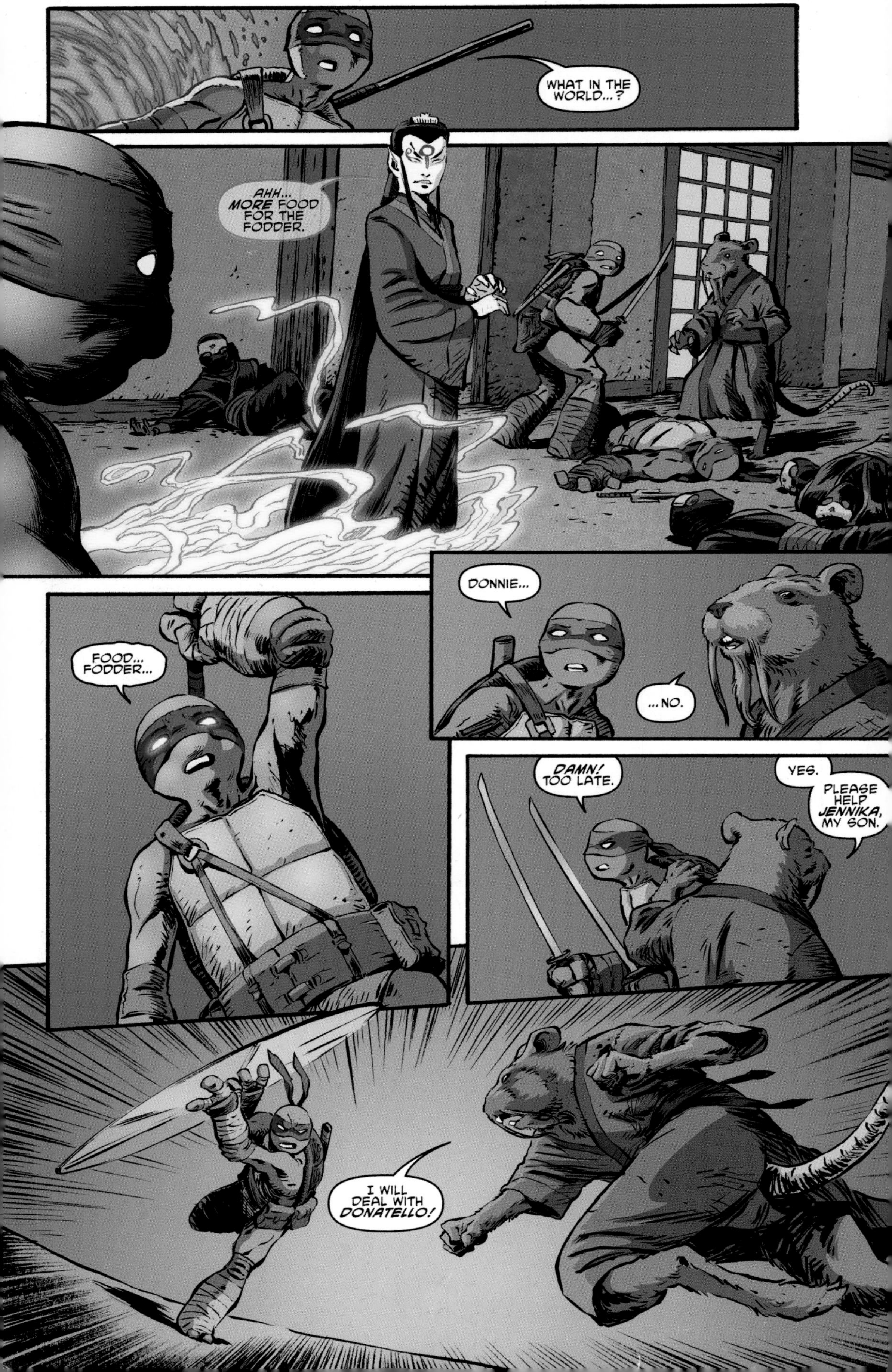
WHAT IN THE WORLD...?
AHH... MORE FOOD FOR THE FODDER.
DONNIE...
...NO.
FOOD... FODDER...
DAMN! TOO LATE.
YES. PLEASE HELP JENNIKA, MY SON.
I WILL DEAL WITH DONATELLO!

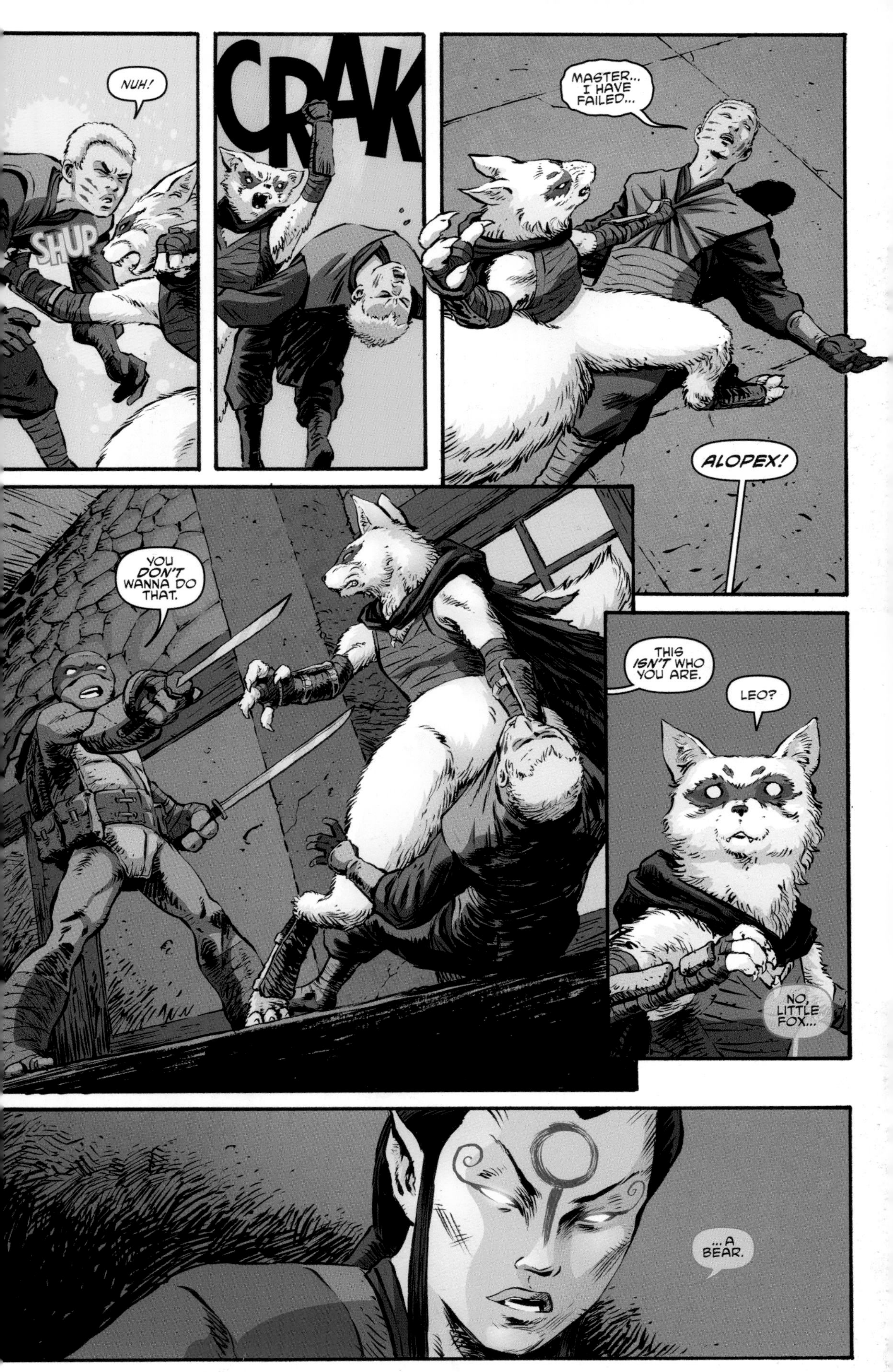
NUH!
SHUP
CRAK
MASTER... I HAVE FAILED...
ALOPEX!
YOU DON'T WANNA DO THAT.
THIS ISN'T WHO YOU ARE.
LEO?
NO, LITTLE FOX...
...A BEAR.

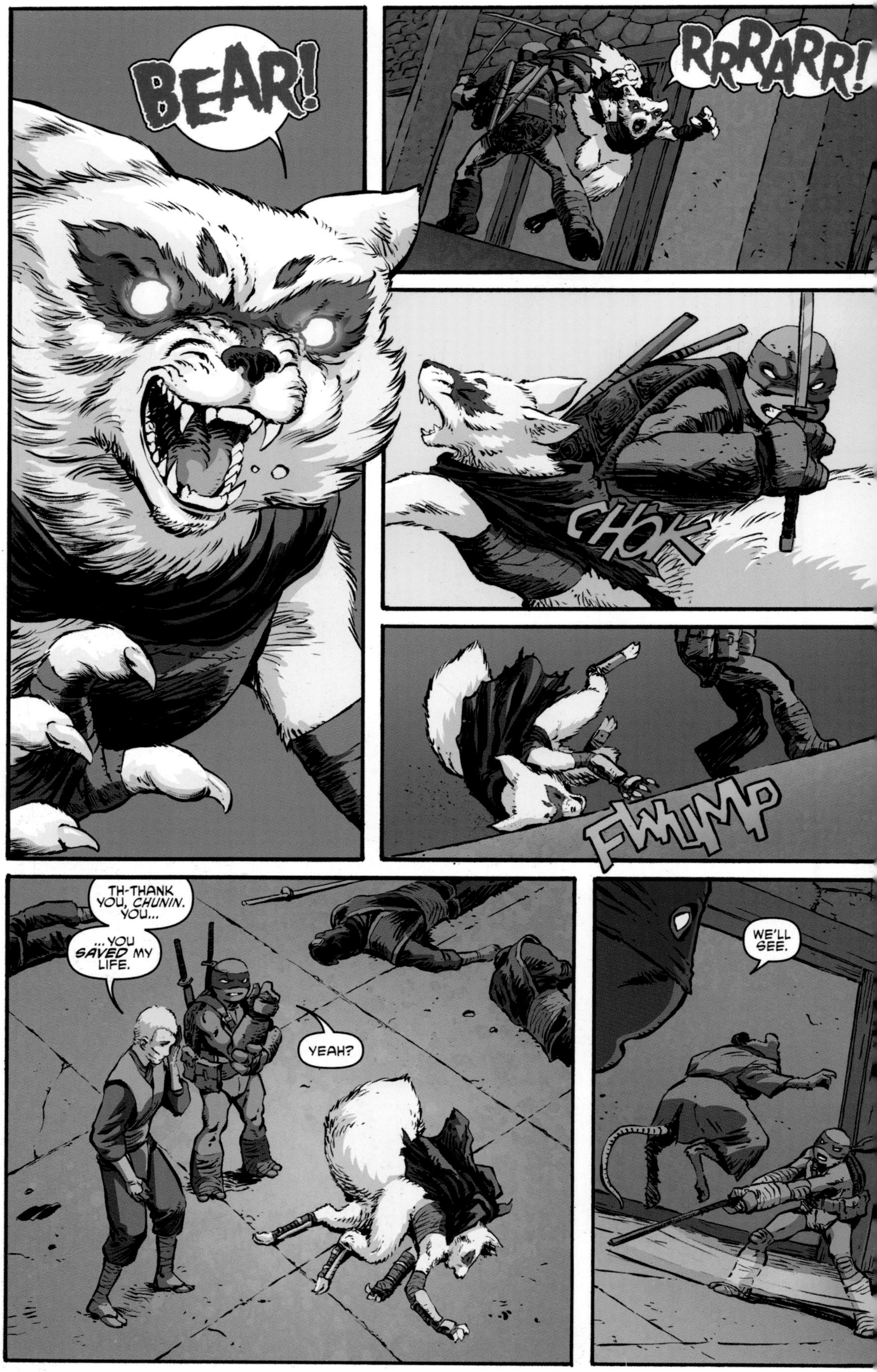
BEAR!
RRRARR!
CHOK
FWUMP
TH-THANK YOU, CHUNIN. YOU...
...YOU SAVED MY LIFE.
YEAH?
WE'LL SEE.

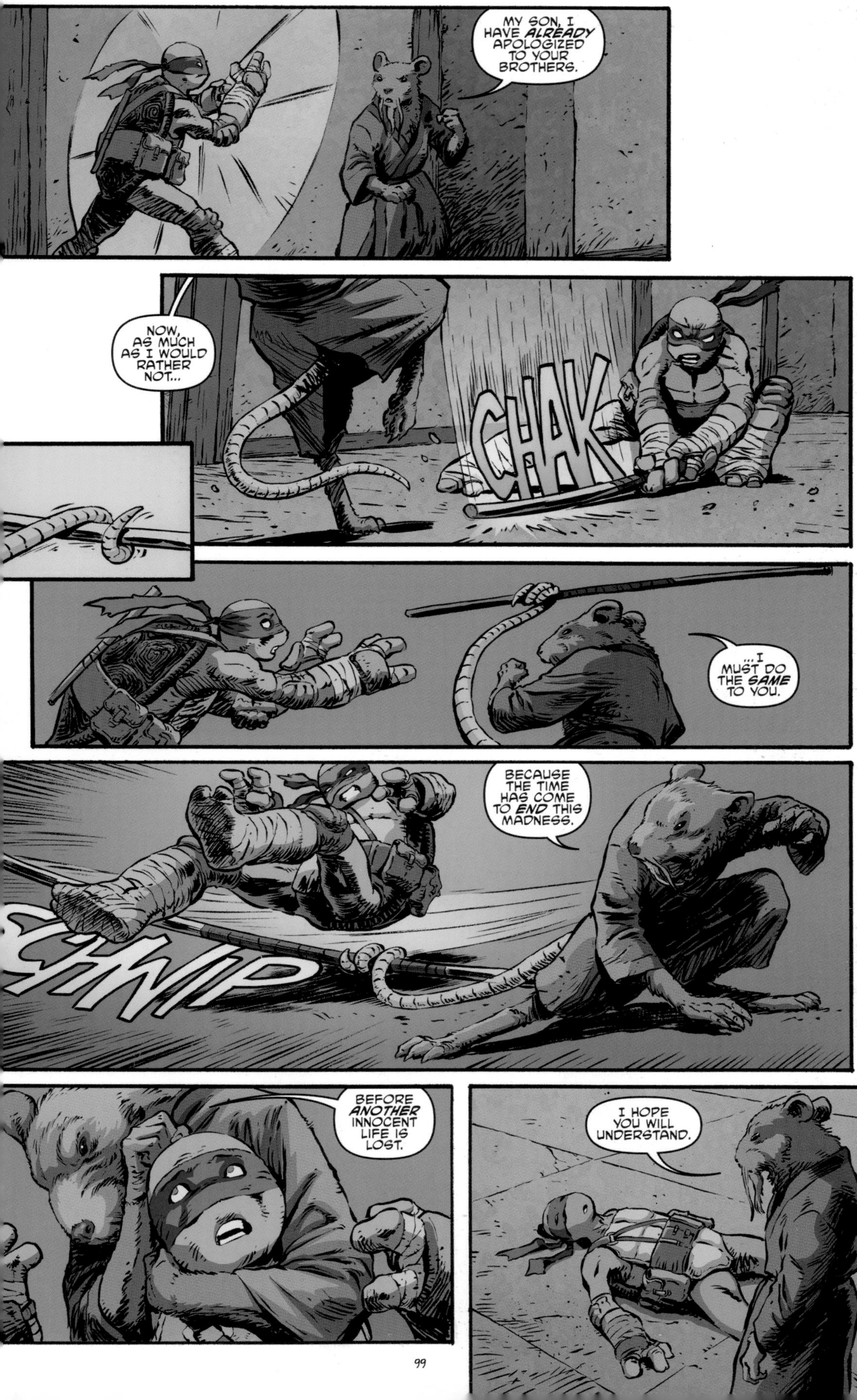
MY SON, I HAVE ALREADY APOLOGIZED TO YOUR BROTHERS.
NOW, AS MUCH AS I WOULD RATHER NOT...
CHAK
...I MUST DO THE SAME TO YOU.
BECAUSE THE TIME HAS COME TO END THIS MADNESS.
BEFORE ANOTHER INNOCENT LIFE IS LOST.
I HOPE YOU WILL UNDERSTAND.

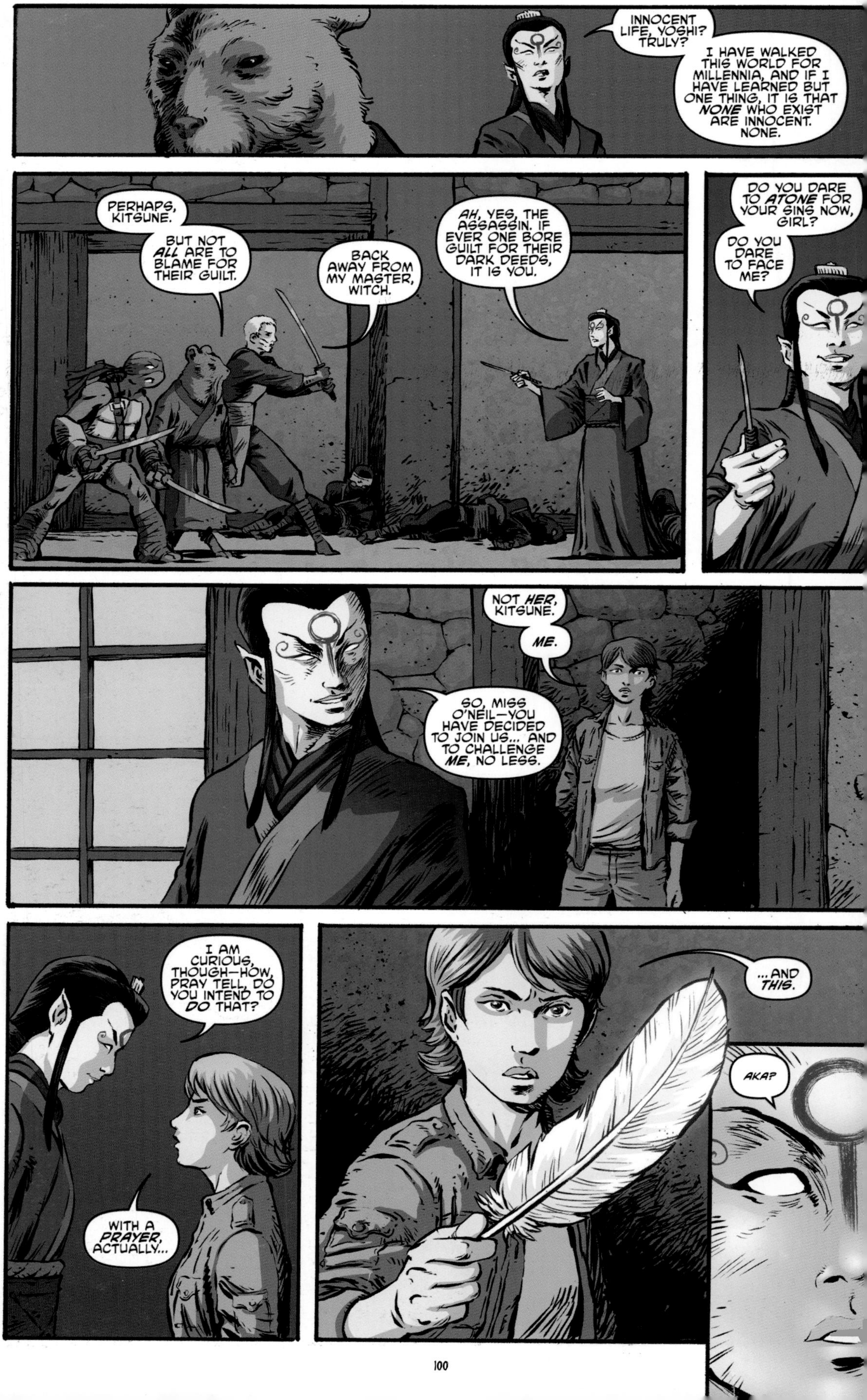
INNOCENT LIFE, YOSHI? TRULY?
I HAVE WALKED THIS WORLD FOR MILLENNIA, AND IF I HAVE LEARNED BUT ONE THING, IT IS THAT *NONE* WHO EXIST ARE INNOCENT. NONE.
PERHAPS, KITSUNE.
BUT NOT *ALL* ARE TO BLAME FOR THEIR GUILT.
BACK AWAY FROM MY MASTER, WITCH.
AH, YES, THE ASSASSIN. IF EVER ONE BORE GUILT FOR THEIR DARK DEEDS, IT IS YOU.
DO YOU DARE TO *ATONE* FOR YOUR SINS NOW, GIRL?
DO YOU DARE TO FACE ME?
NOT *HER*, KITSUNE.
ME.
SO, MISS O'NEIL—YOU HAVE DECIDED TO JOIN US... AND TO CHALLENGE *ME*, NO LESS.
I AM CURIOUS, THOUGH—HOW, PRAY TELL, DO YOU INTEND TO *DO* THAT?
WITH A *PRAYER*, ACTUALLY...
...AND *THIS*.
AKA?

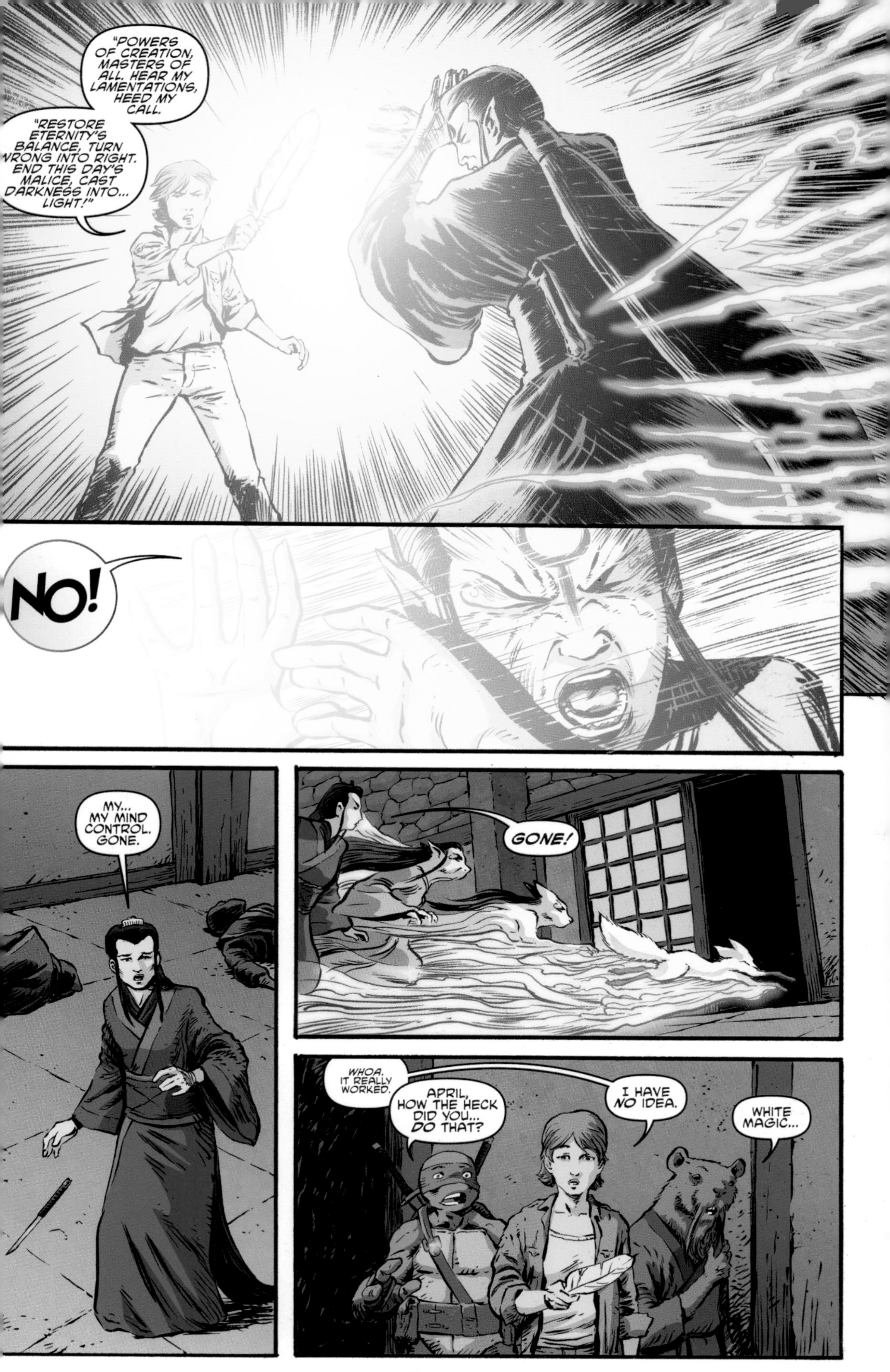
"POWERS OF CREATION, MASTERS OF ALL. HEAR MY LAMENTATIONS, HEED MY CALL.
"RESTORE ETERNITY'S BALANCE, TURN WRONG INTO RIGHT. END THIS DAY'S MALICE, CAST DARKNESS INTO... LIGHT!"
NO!
MY... MY MIND CONTROL. GONE.
GONE!
WHOA. IT REALLY WORKED.
APRIL, HOW THE HECK DID YOU... DO THAT?
I HAVE NO IDEA.
WHITE MAGIC...

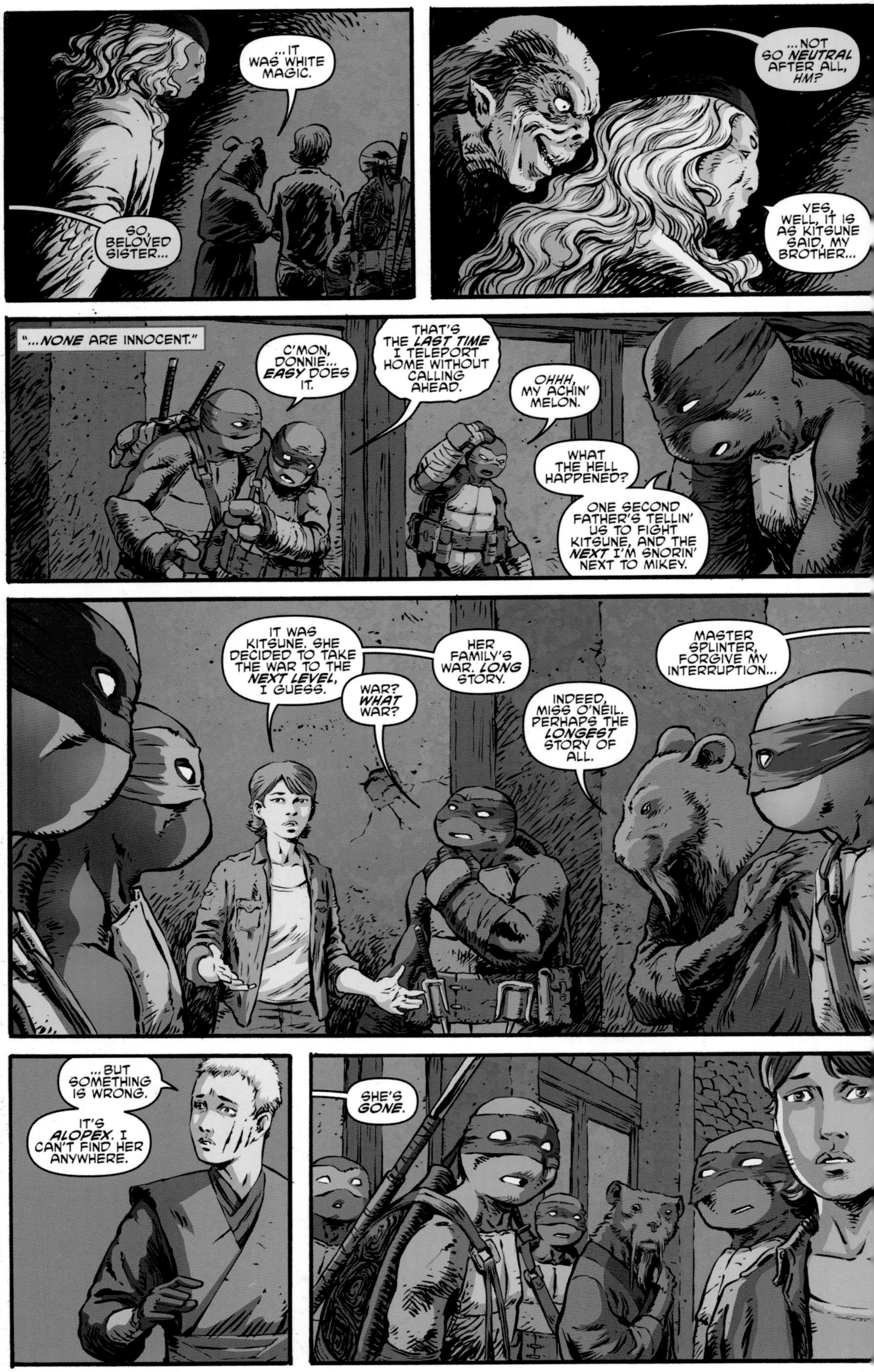
...IT WAS WHITE MAGIC.
SO, BELOVED SISTER...
...NOT SO NEUTRAL AFTER ALL, HM?
YES, WELL, IT IS AS KITSUNE SAID, MY BROTHER...
"...NONE ARE INNOCENT."
C'MON, DONNIE... EASY DOES IT.
THAT'S THE LAST TIME I TELEPORT HOME WITHOUT CALLING AHEAD.
OHHH, MY ACHIN' MELON.
WHAT THE HELL HAPPENED?
ONE SECOND FATHER'S TELLIN' US TO FIGHT KITSUNE, AND THE NEXT I'M SNORIN' NEXT TO MIKEY.
IT WAS KITSUNE. SHE DECIDED TO TAKE THE WAR TO THE NEXT LEVEL, I GUESS.
WAR? WHAT WAR?
HER FAMILY'S WAR. LONG STORY.
INDEED, MISS O'NEIL. PERHAPS THE LONGEST STORY OF ALL.
MASTER SPLINTER, FORGIVE MY INTERRUPTION...
...BUT SOMETHING IS WRONG.
IT'S ALOPEX. I CAN'T FIND HER ANYWHERE.
SHE'S GONE.

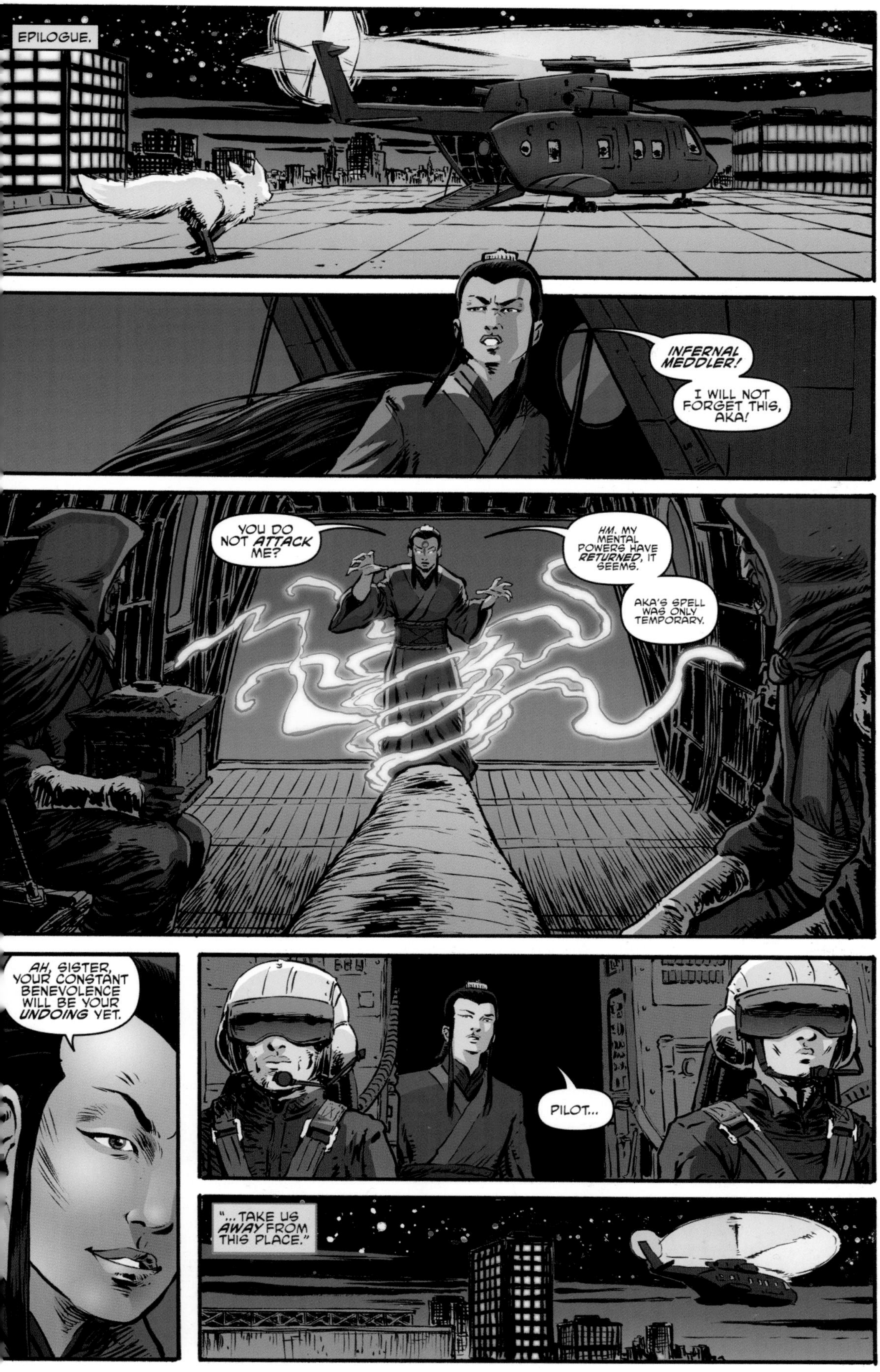

EPILOGUE.
INFERNAL MEDDLER!
I WILL NOT FORGET THIS, AKA!
YOU DO NOT ATTACK ME?
HM. MY MENTAL POWERS HAVE RETURNED, IT SEEMS.
AKA'S SPELL WAS ONLY TEMPORARY.
AH, SISTER, YOUR CONSTANT BENEVOLENCE WILL BE YOUR UNDOING YET.
PILOT...
"...TAKE US AWAY FROM THIS PLACE."

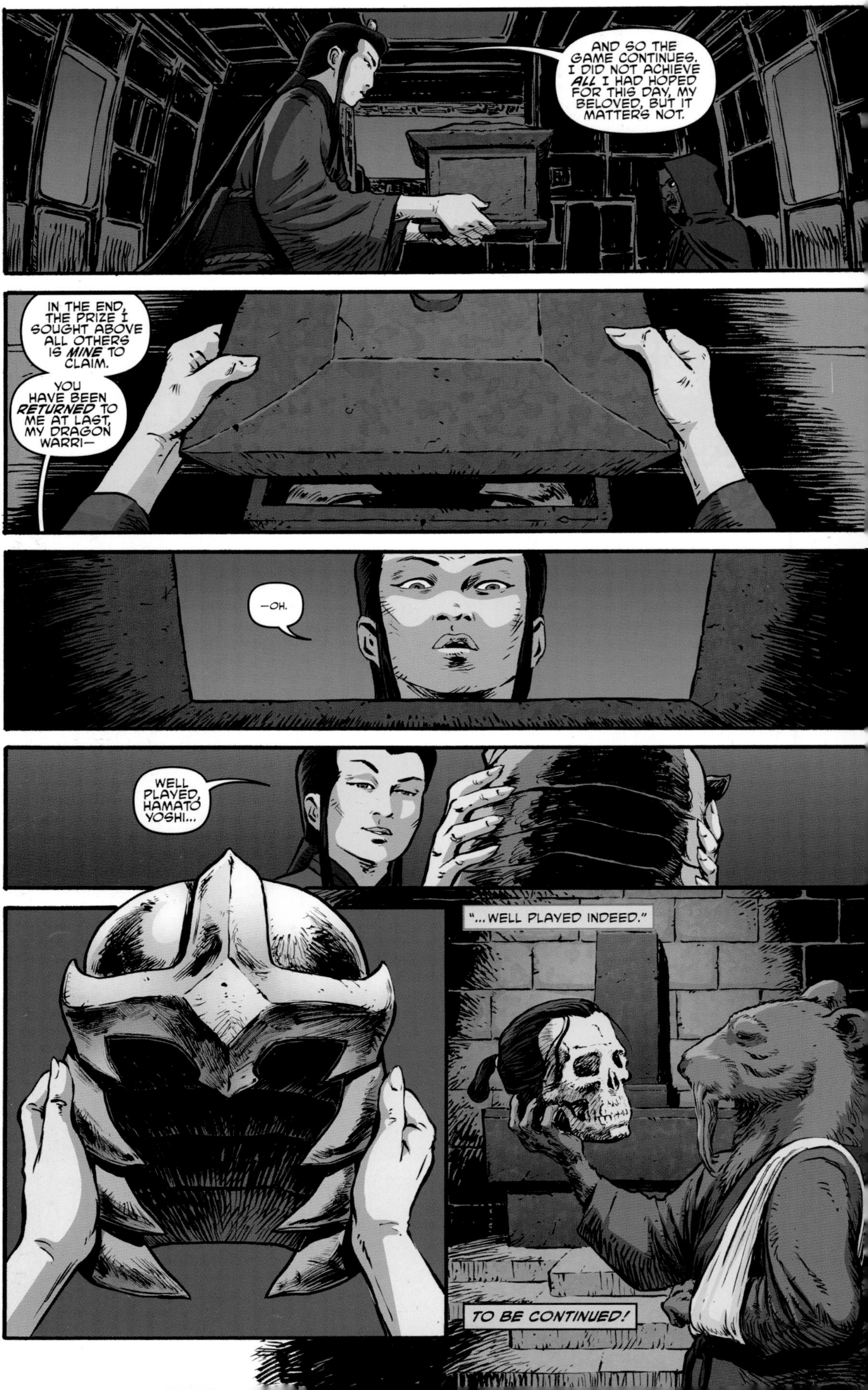
AND SO THE GAME CONTINUES. I DID NOT ACHIEVE ALL I HAD HOPED FOR THIS DAY, MY BELOVED, BUT IT MATTERS NOT.
IN THE END, THE PRIZE I SOUGHT ABOVE ALL OTHERS IS MINE TO CLAIM.
YOU HAVE BEEN RETURNED TO ME AT LAST, MY DRAGON WARRI—
—OH.
WELL PLAYED, HAMATO YOSHI...
"...WELL PLAYED INDEED."
TO BE CONTINUED!

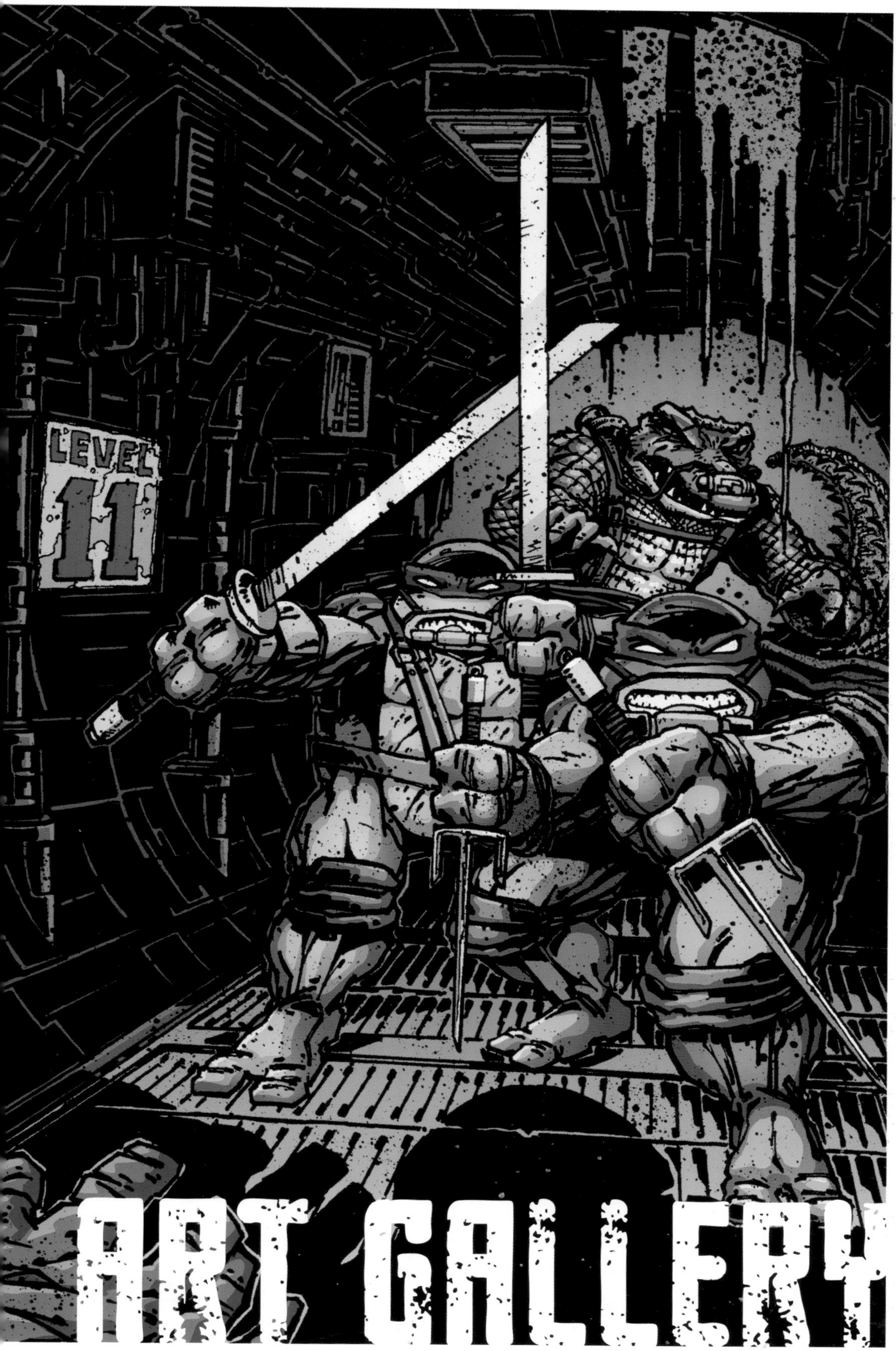
LEVEL
11

ART GALLERY

ART BY KEVIN EASTMAN

COLORS BY RONDA PATTISON

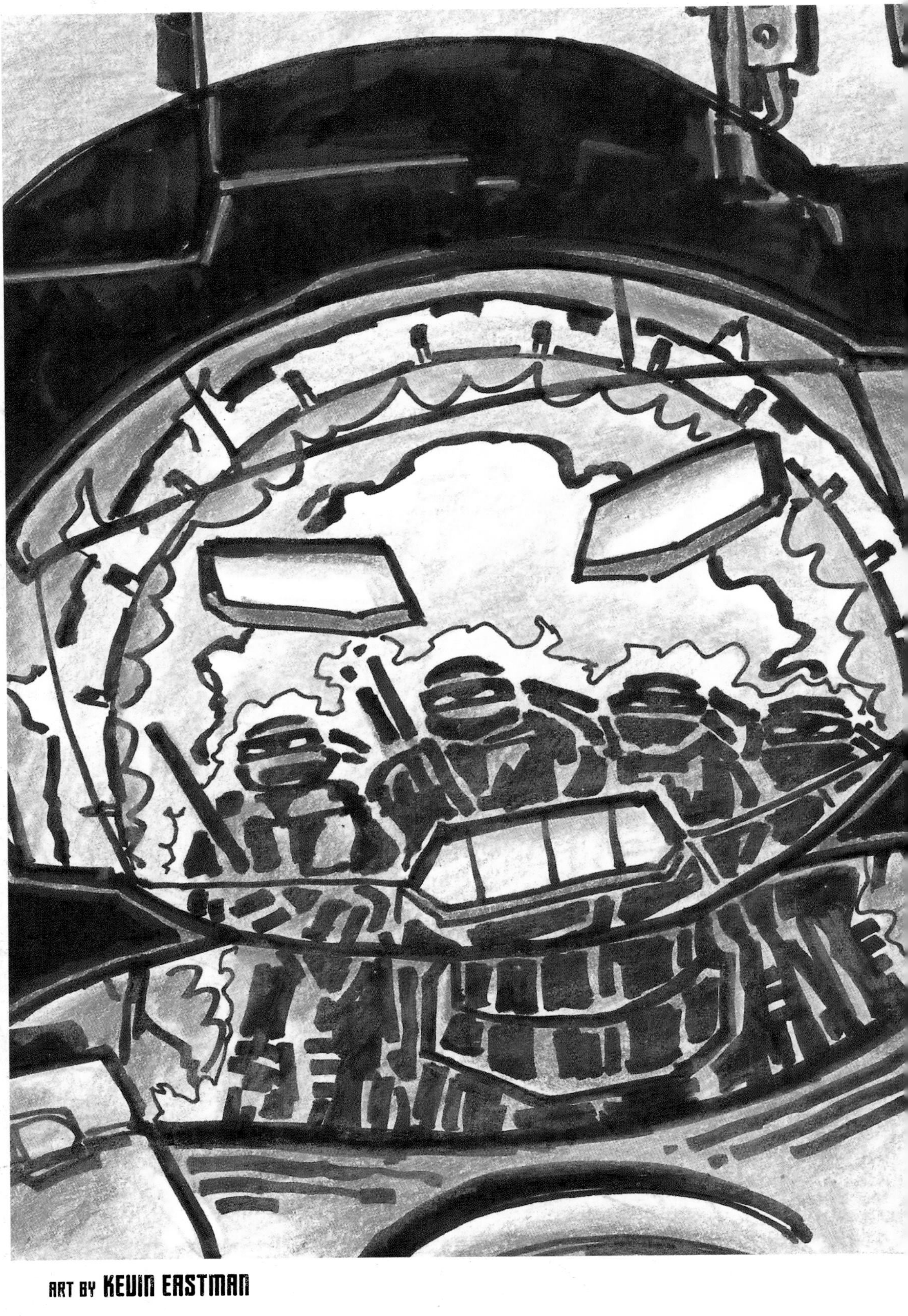

ART BY KEVIN EASTMAN

OPPOSITE PAGE: ART BY PABLO TUNICA

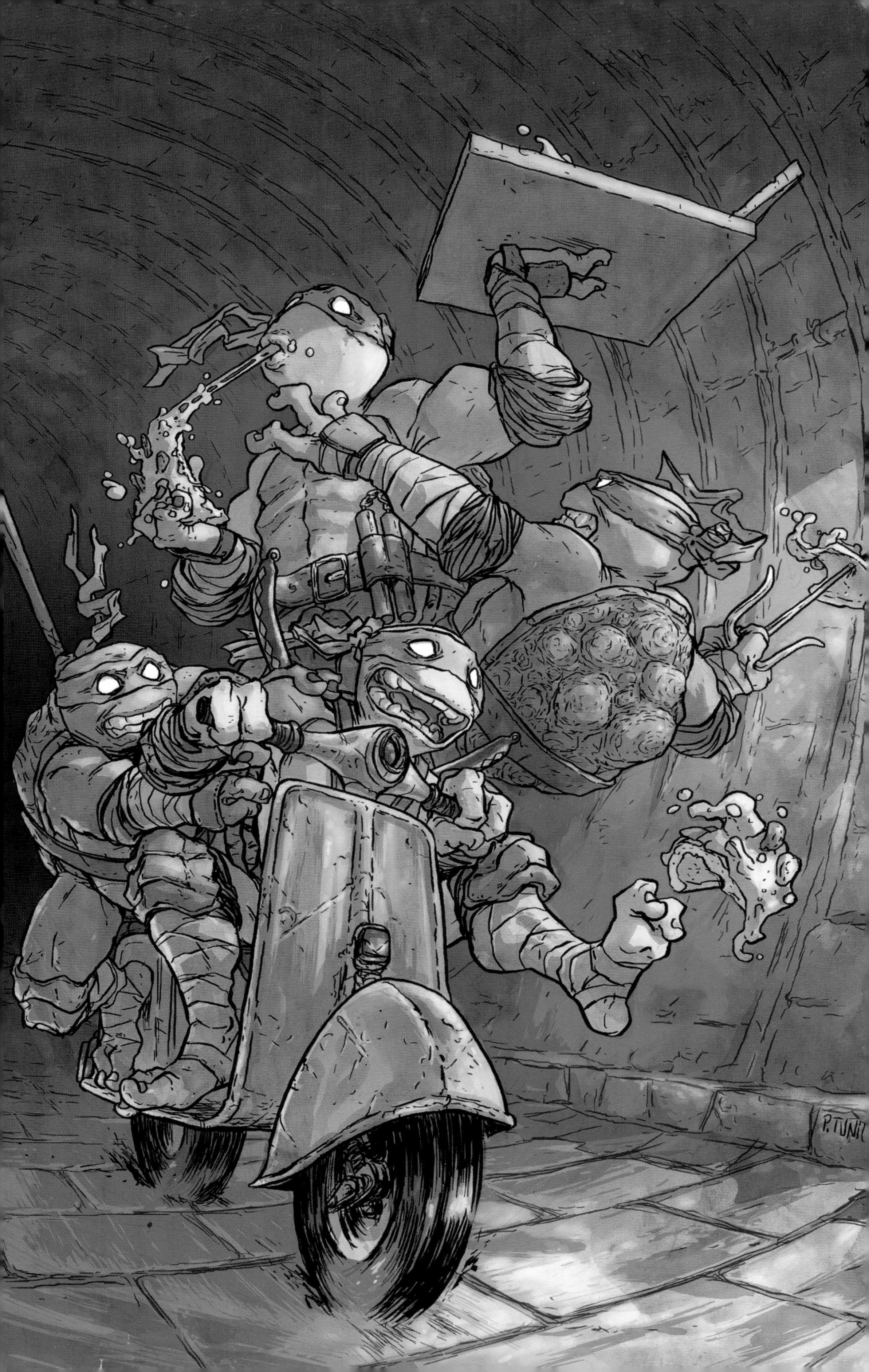
P. TUNR

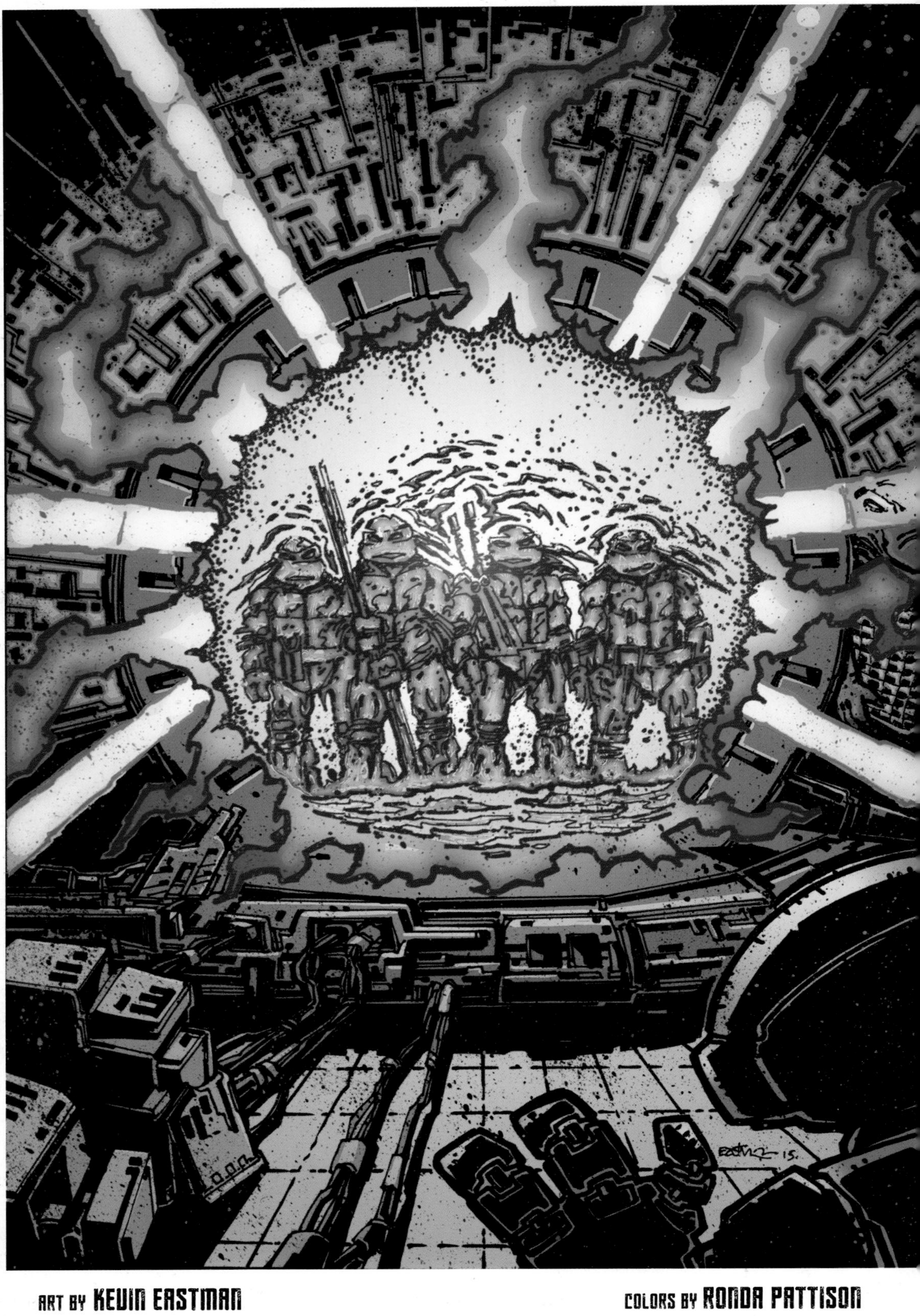

ART BY KEVIN EASTMAN

COLORS BY RONDA PATTISON

OPPOSITE PAGE: ART BY MATEUS SANTOLOUCO

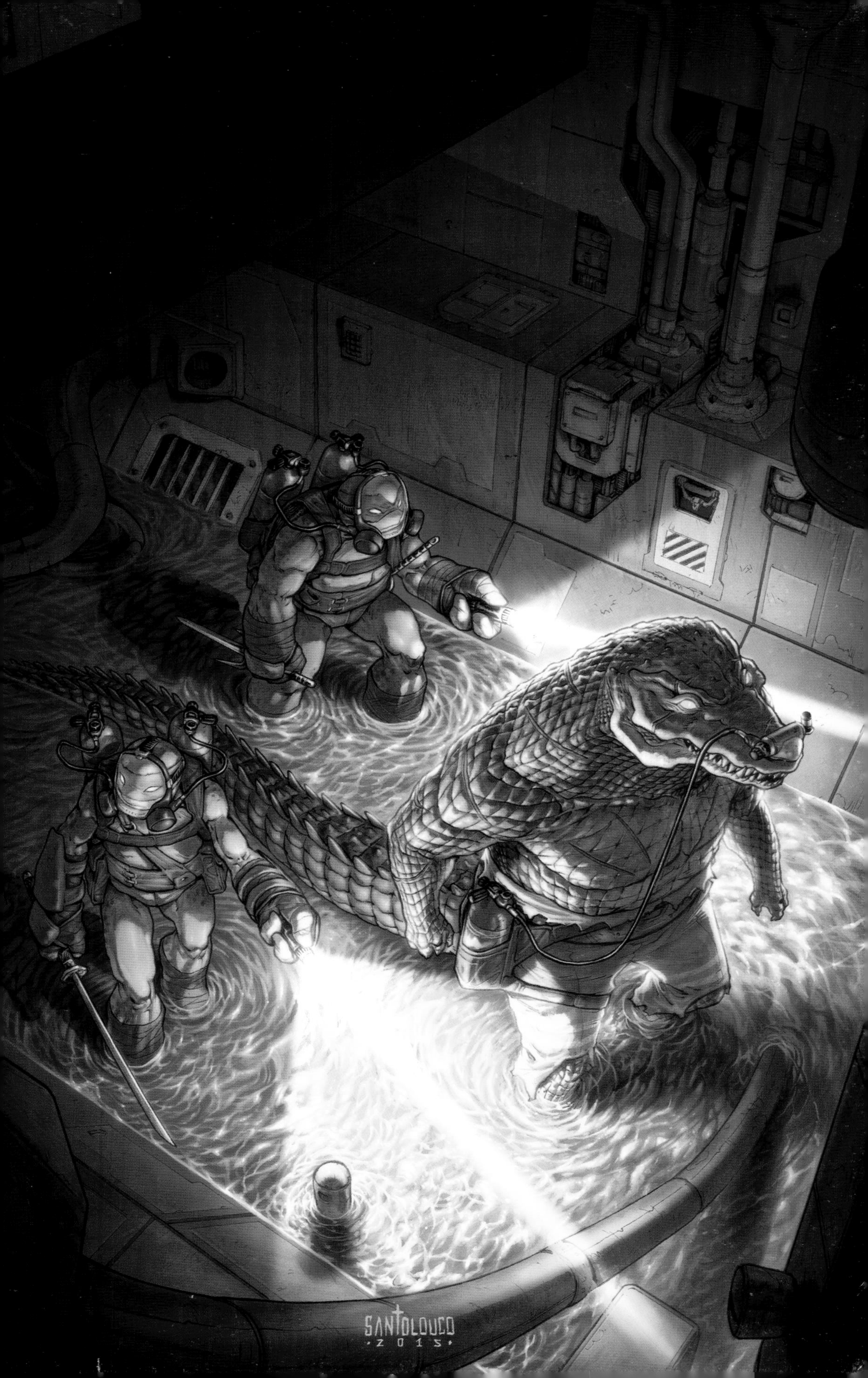
SANTOLOUCO
2015

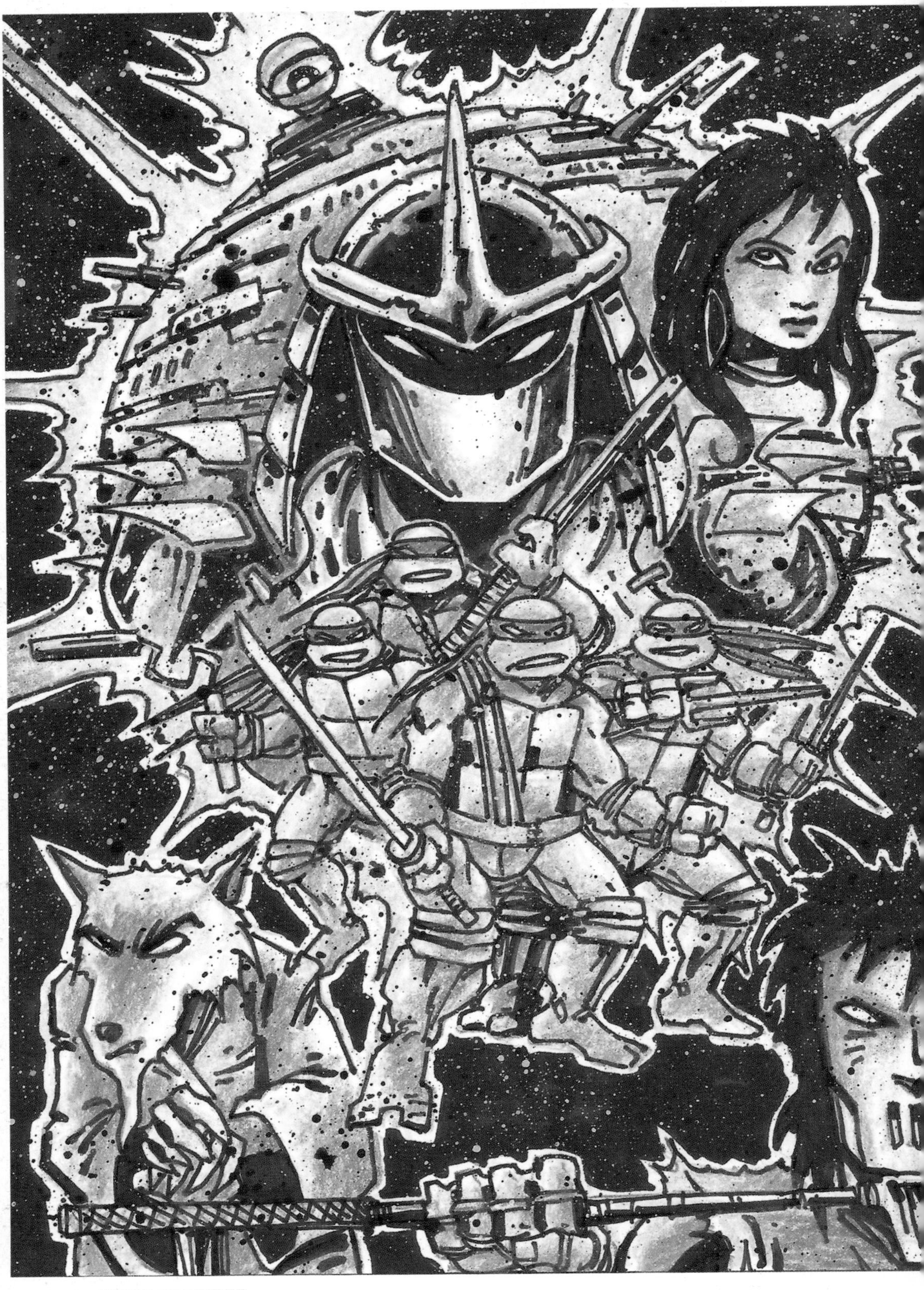

ART BY KEVIN EASTMAN

OPPOSITE PAGE: ART BY KEVIN EASTMAN

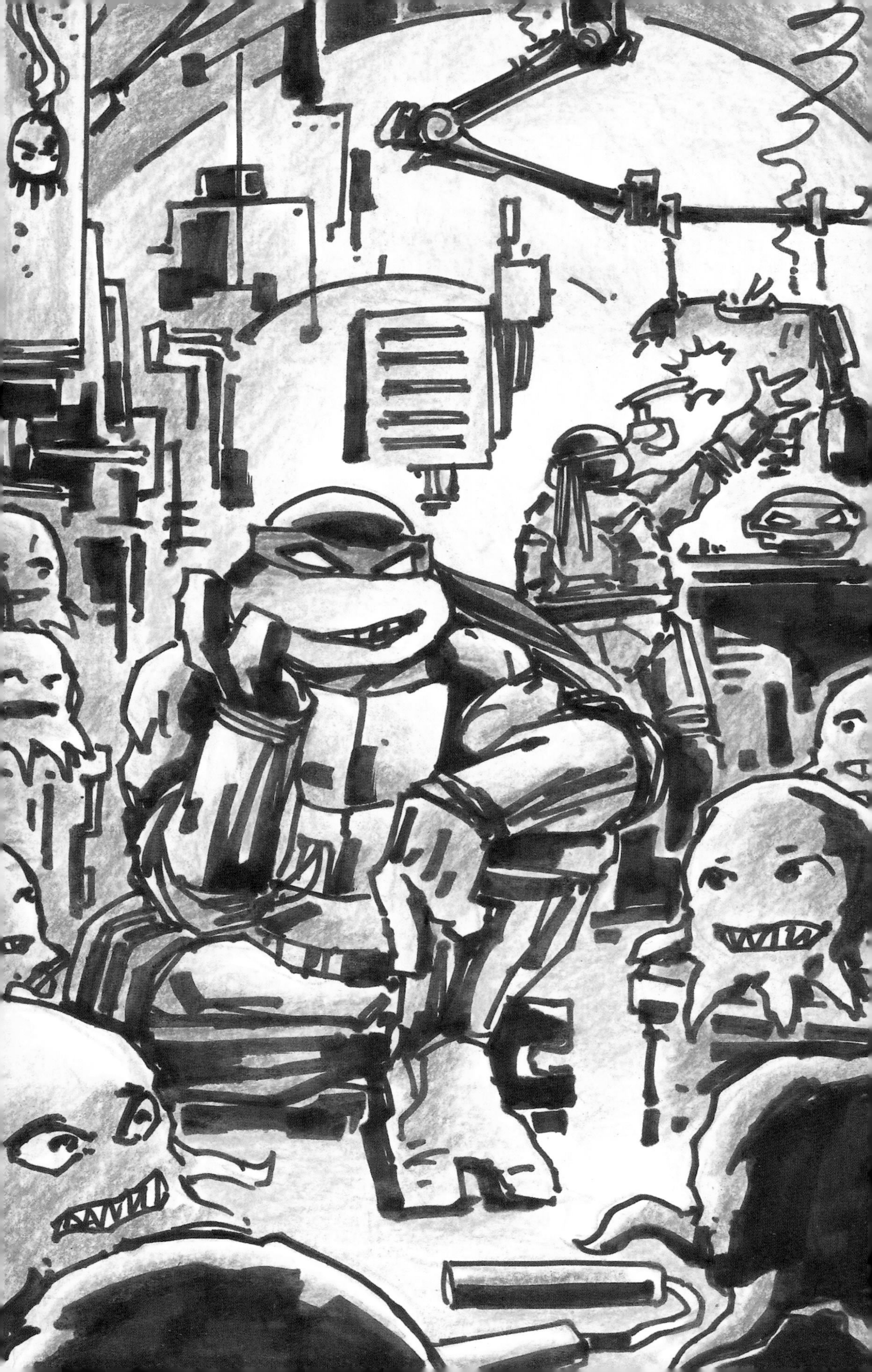

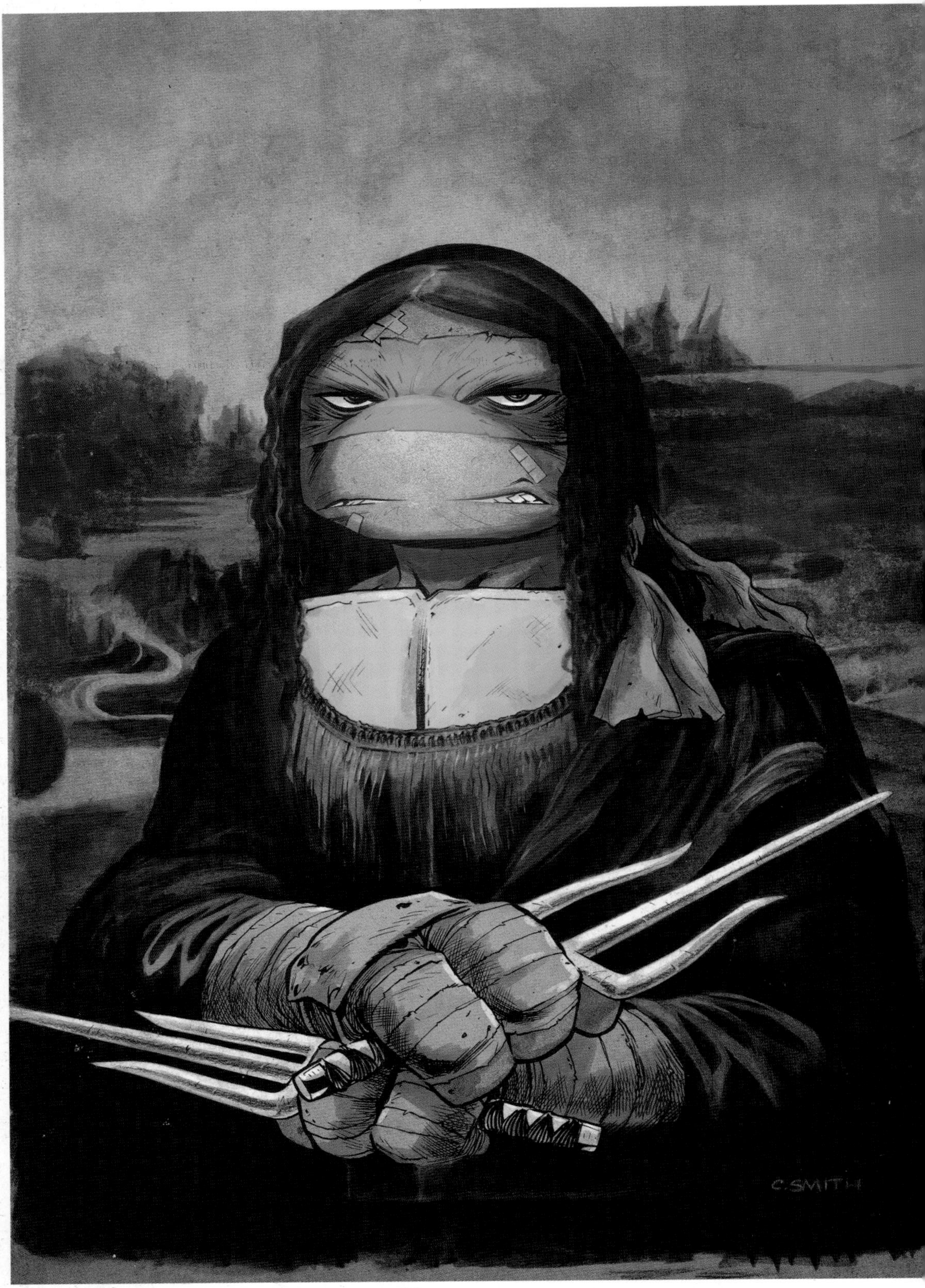
C.SMITH

ART BY CORY SMITH AFTER LEONARDO DAVINCI

OPPOSITE PAGE: ART BY MATEUS SANTOLOUCO

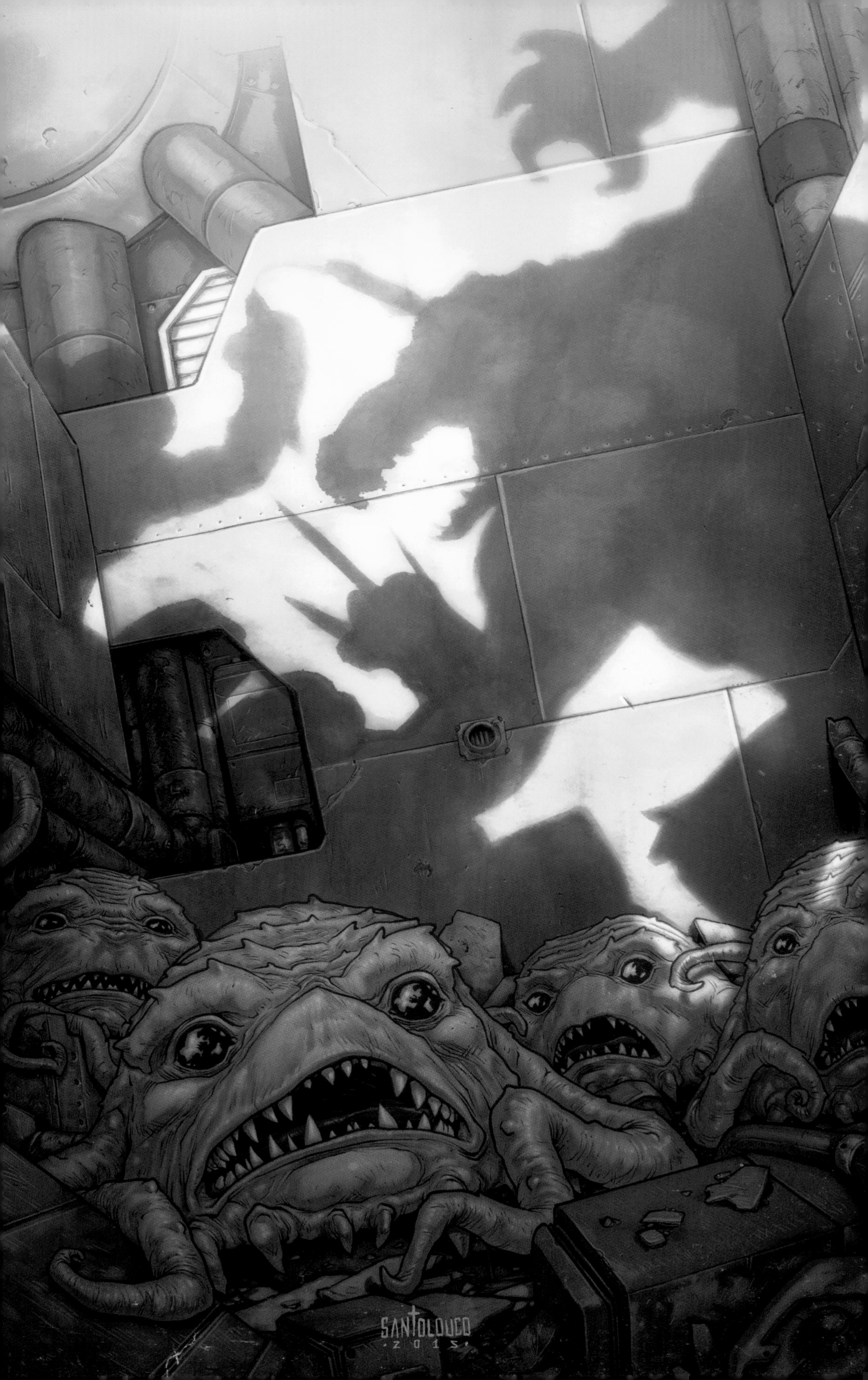
SANTOLOUCO
2015

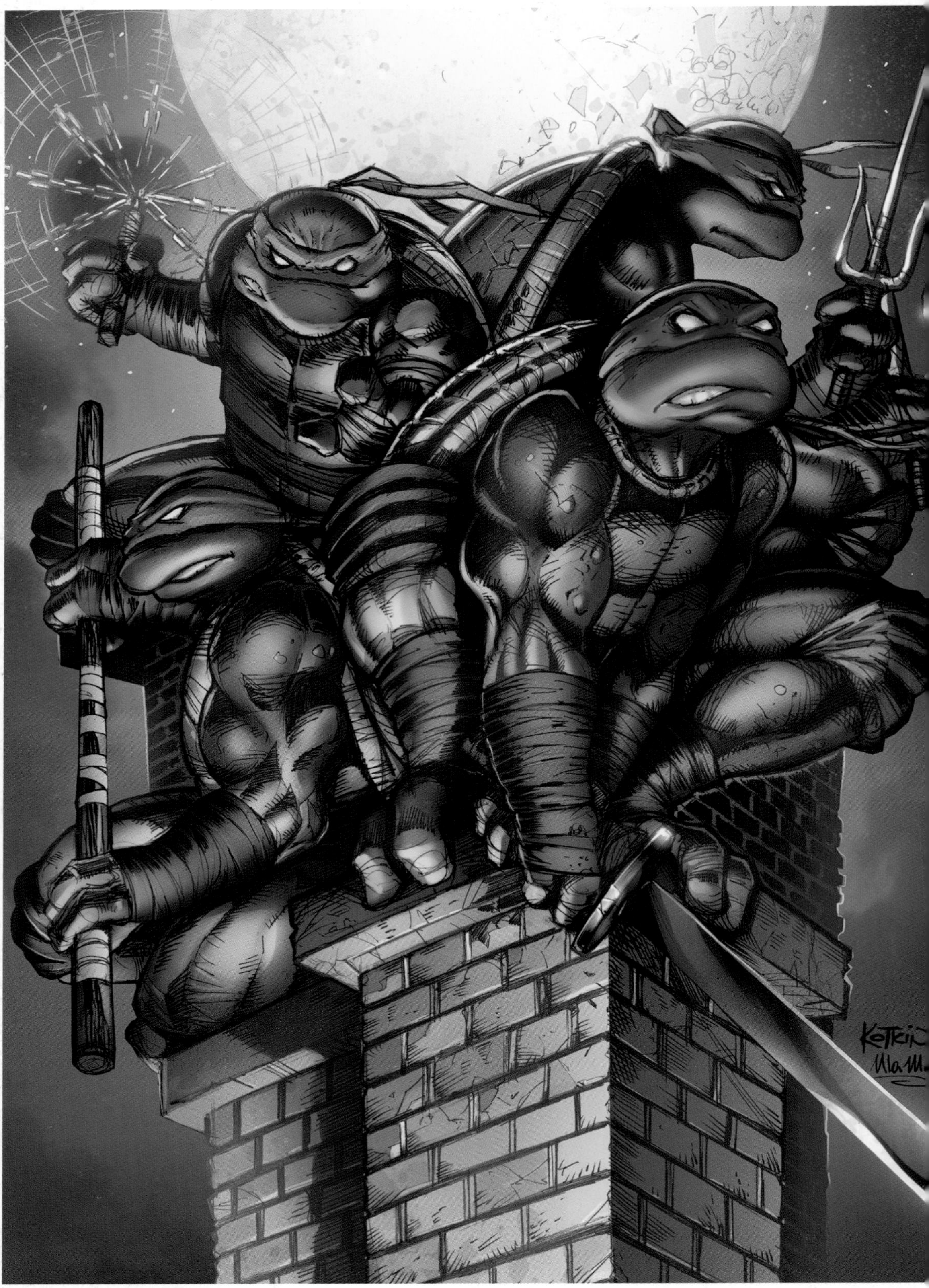
Kotkin
Ula M.

ART BY ALEX KOTKIN

COLORS BY ULA MOS

OPPOSITE PAGE: ART BY KEVIN EASTMAN

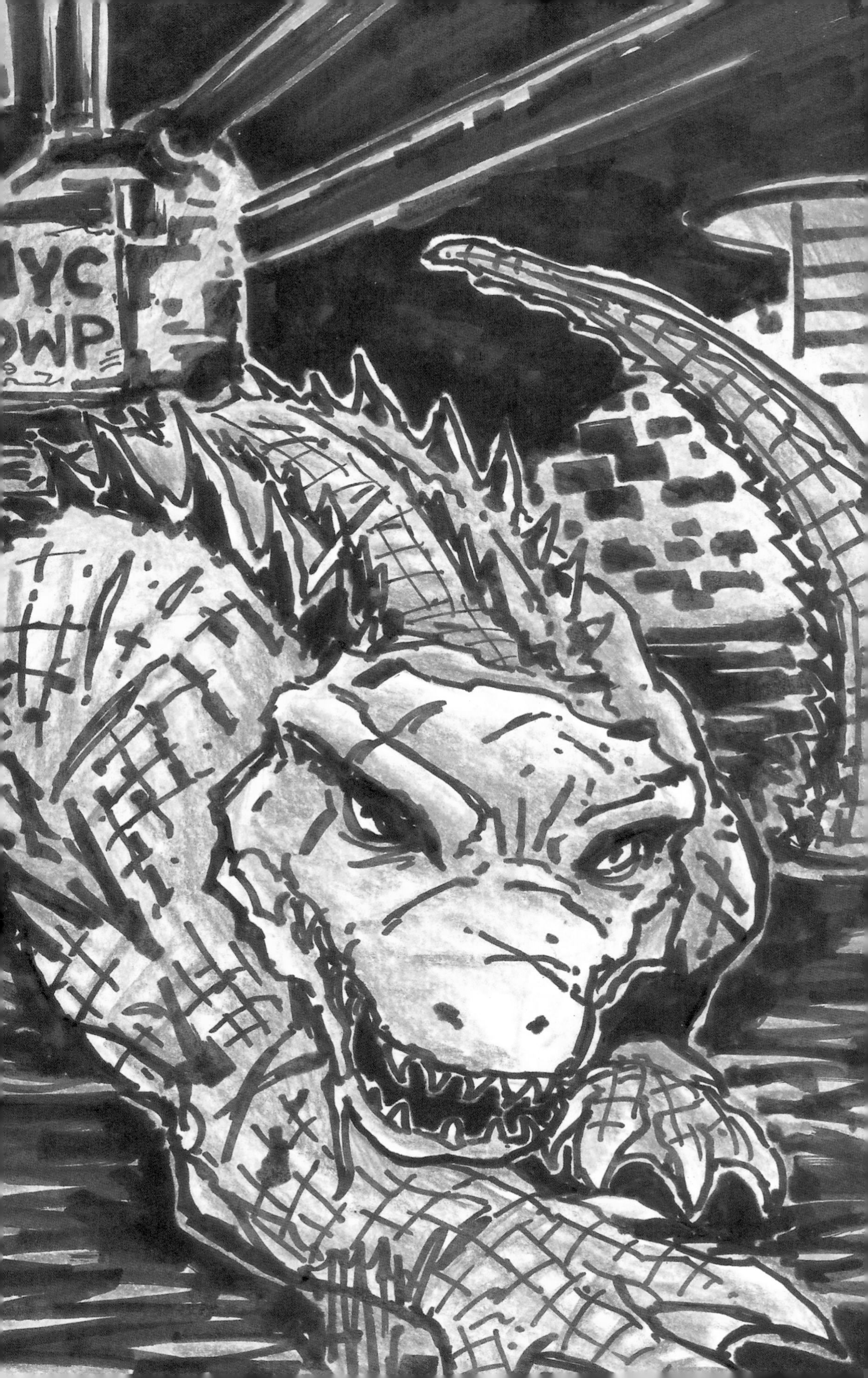
YC
WP

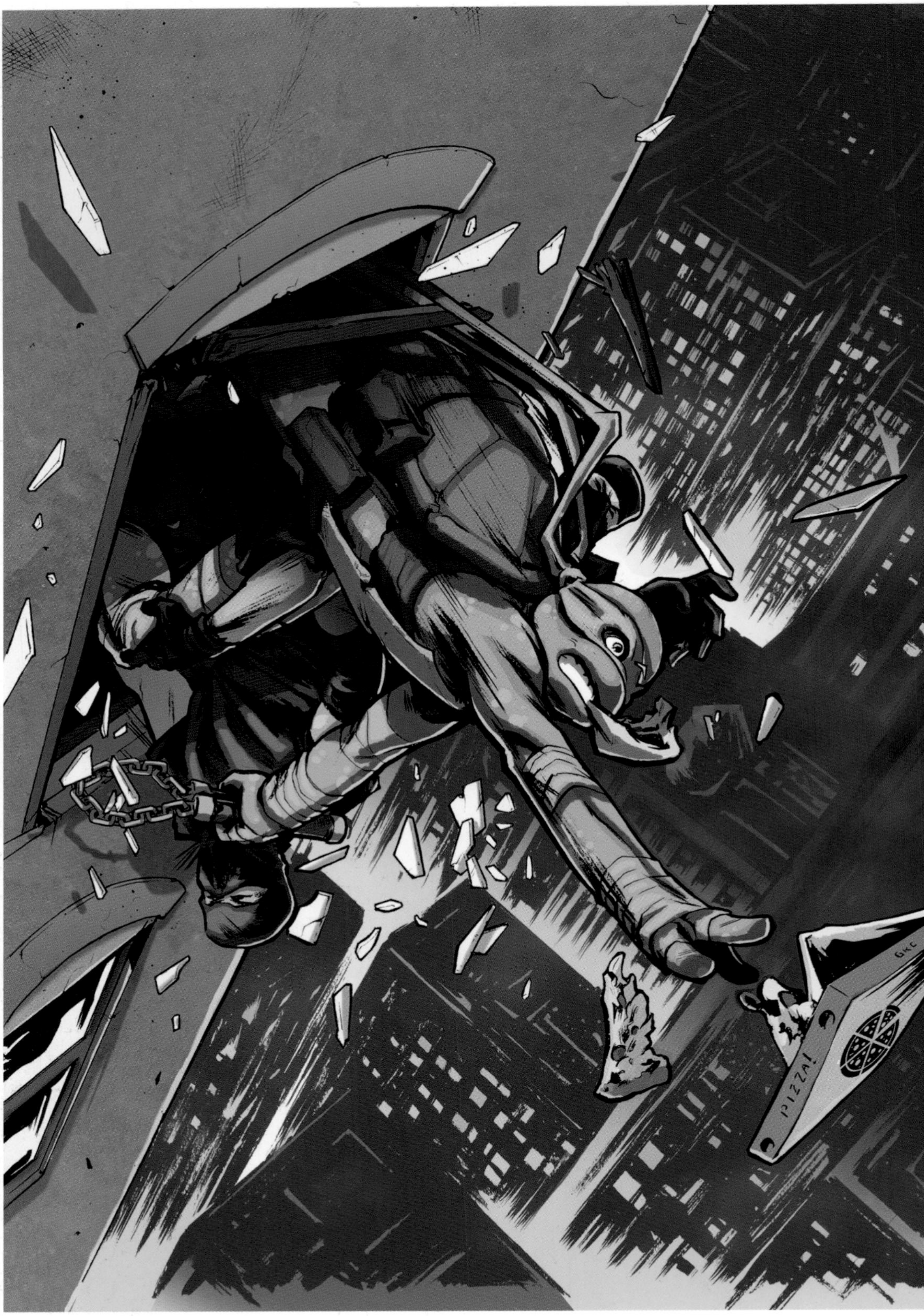
PIZZA!

ART BY PAOLO VILLANELLI

OPPOSITE PAGE: ART BY KEVIN EASTMAN
COLORS BY TOMI VARGA

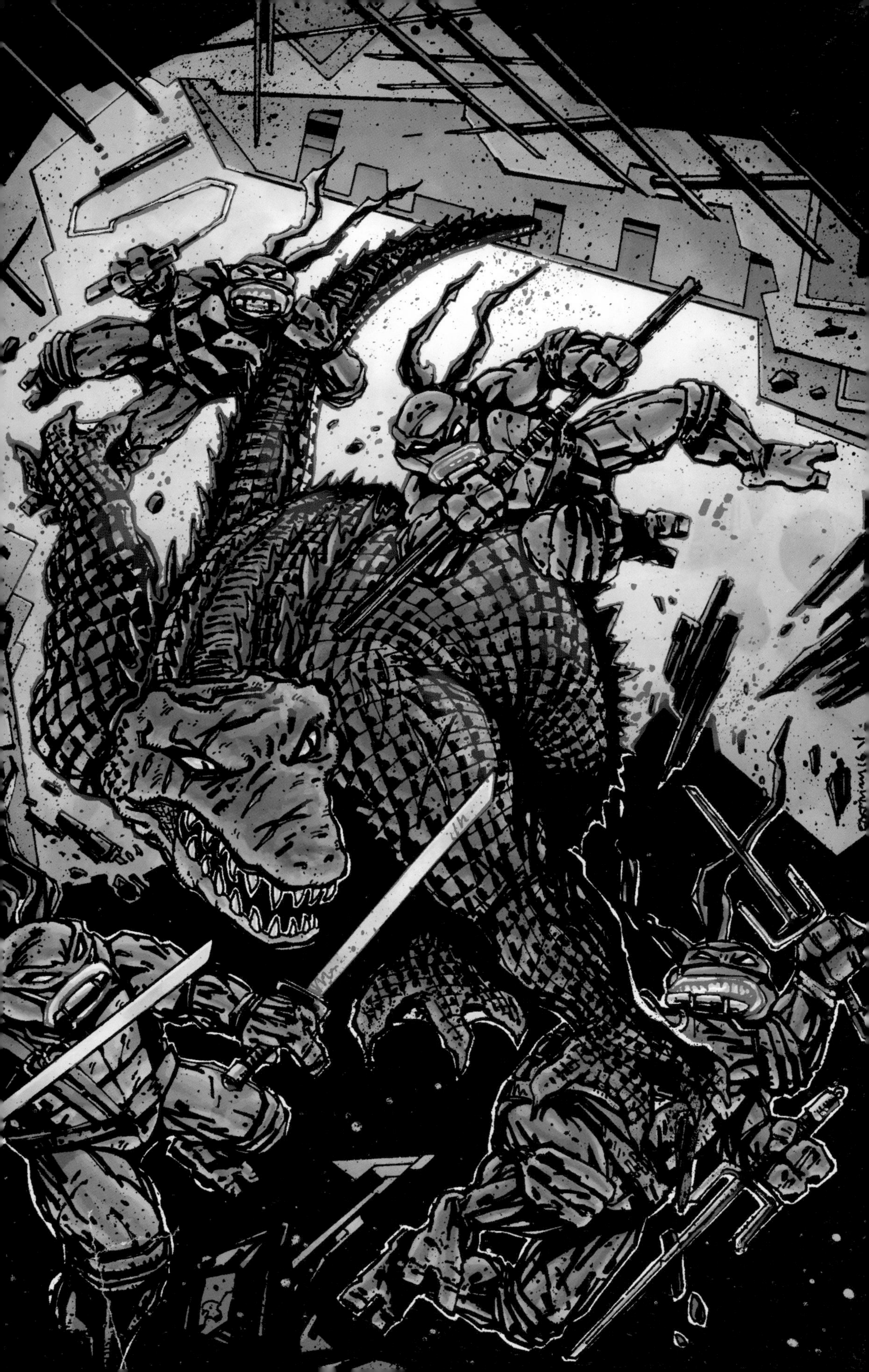

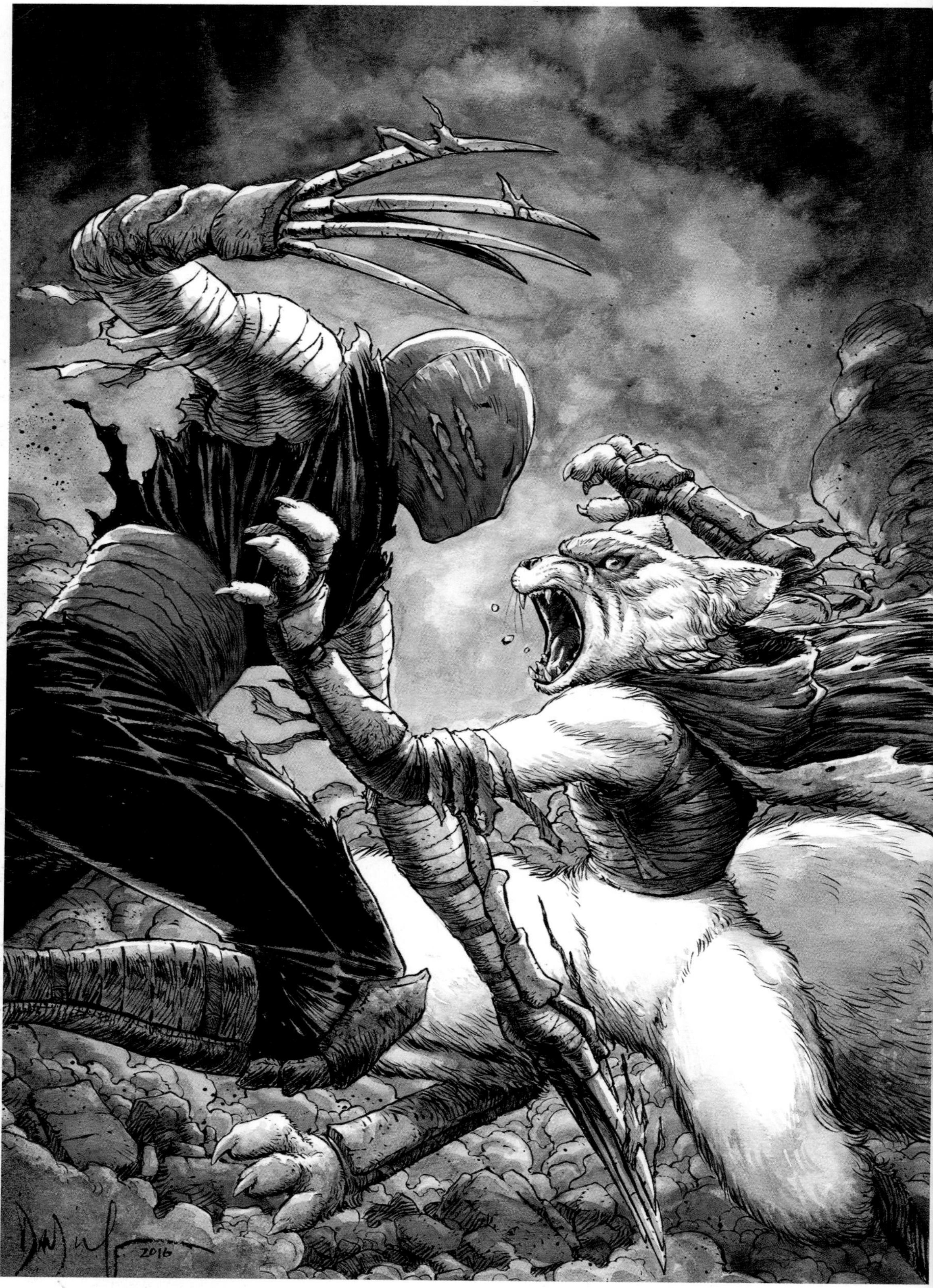

ART BY DAVE WACHTER

*OPPOSITE PAGE: ART BY KEVIN EASTMAN

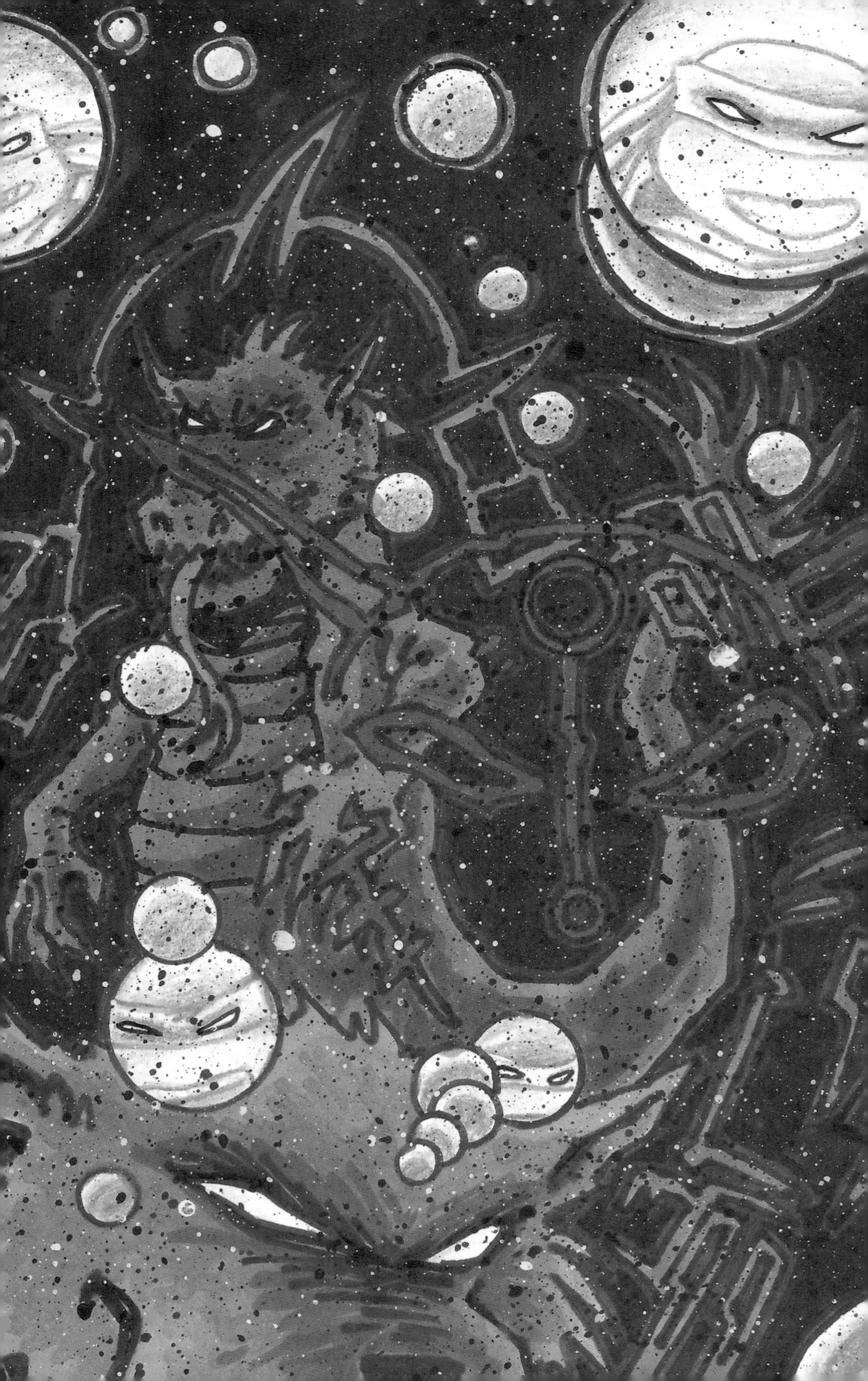

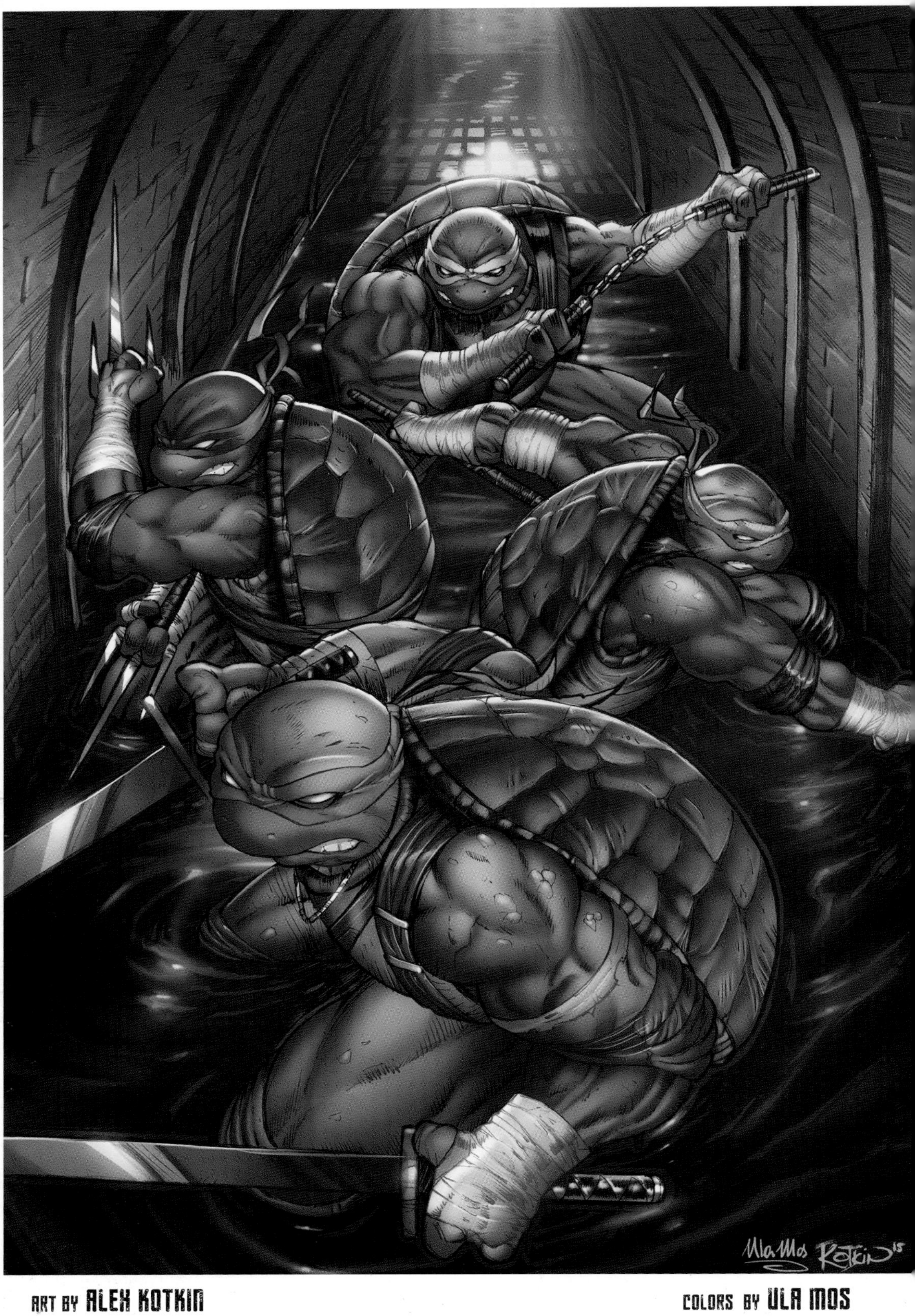

ART BY ALEX KOTKIN

COLORS BY ULA MOS

OPPOSITE PAGE: ART BY MICHAEL WALSH

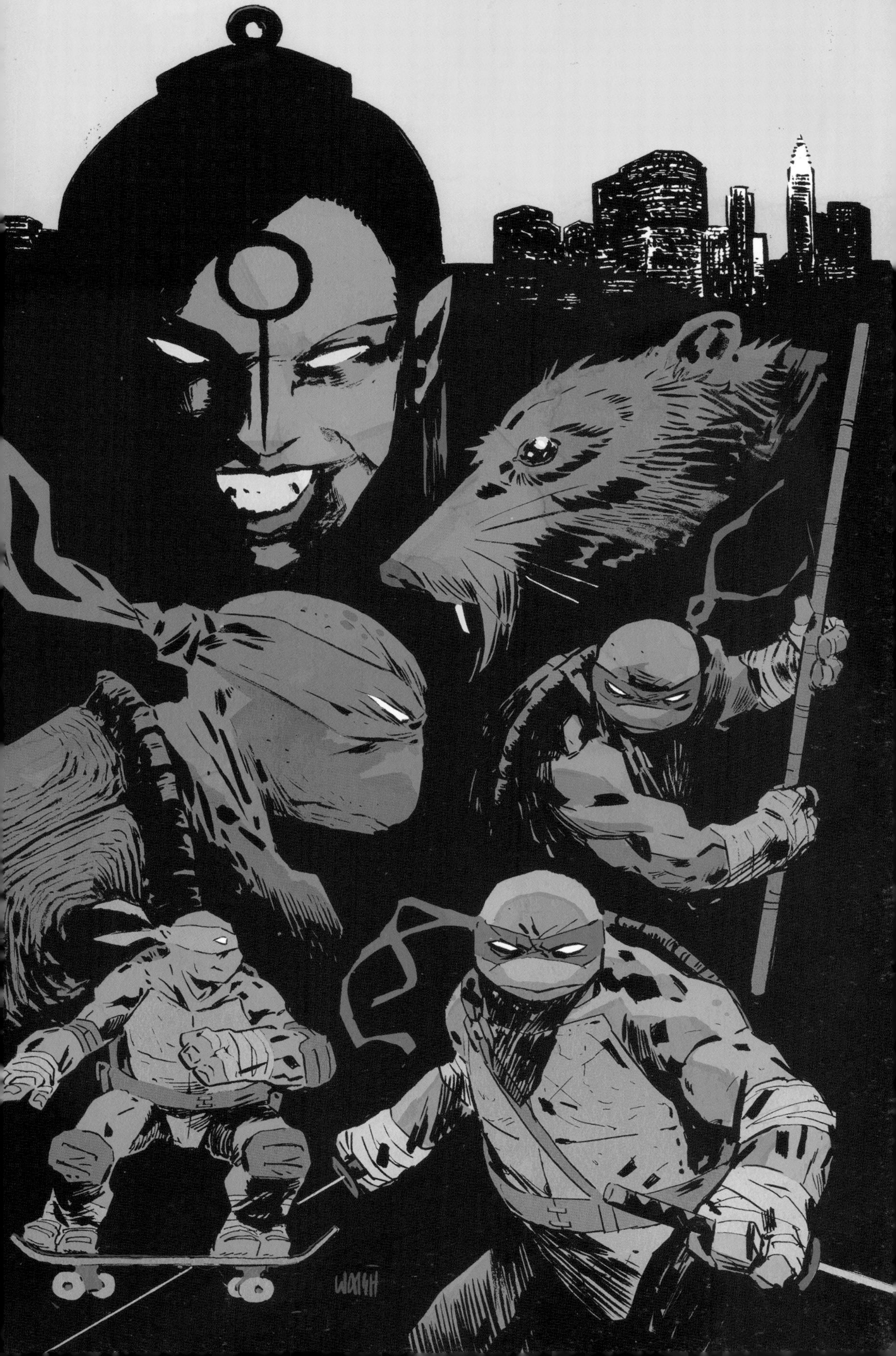
WALSH

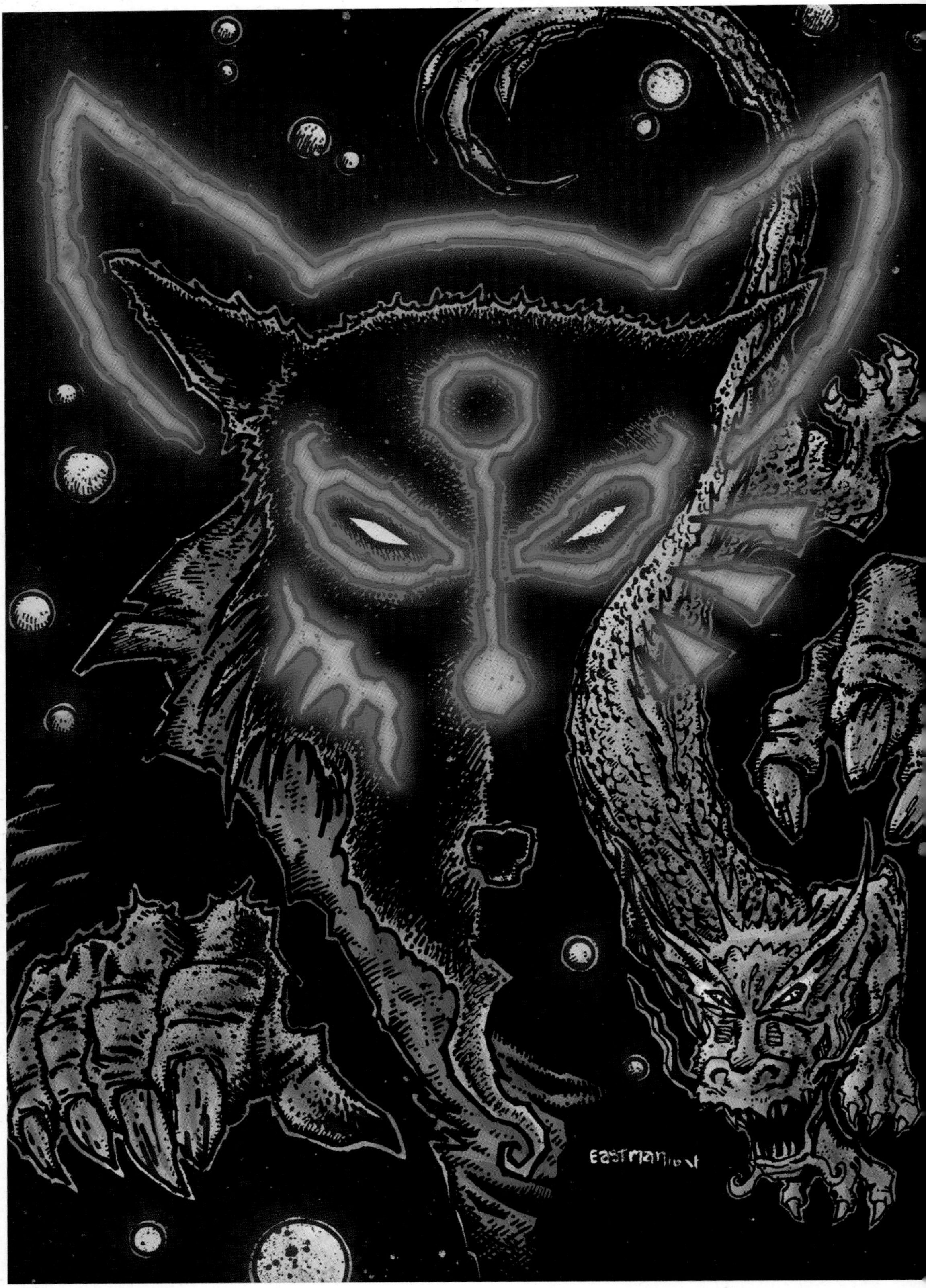
EASTMAN

ART BY KEVIN EASTMAN

COLORS BY TOMI VARGA

OPPOSITE PAGE: ART BY DAVE WACHTER

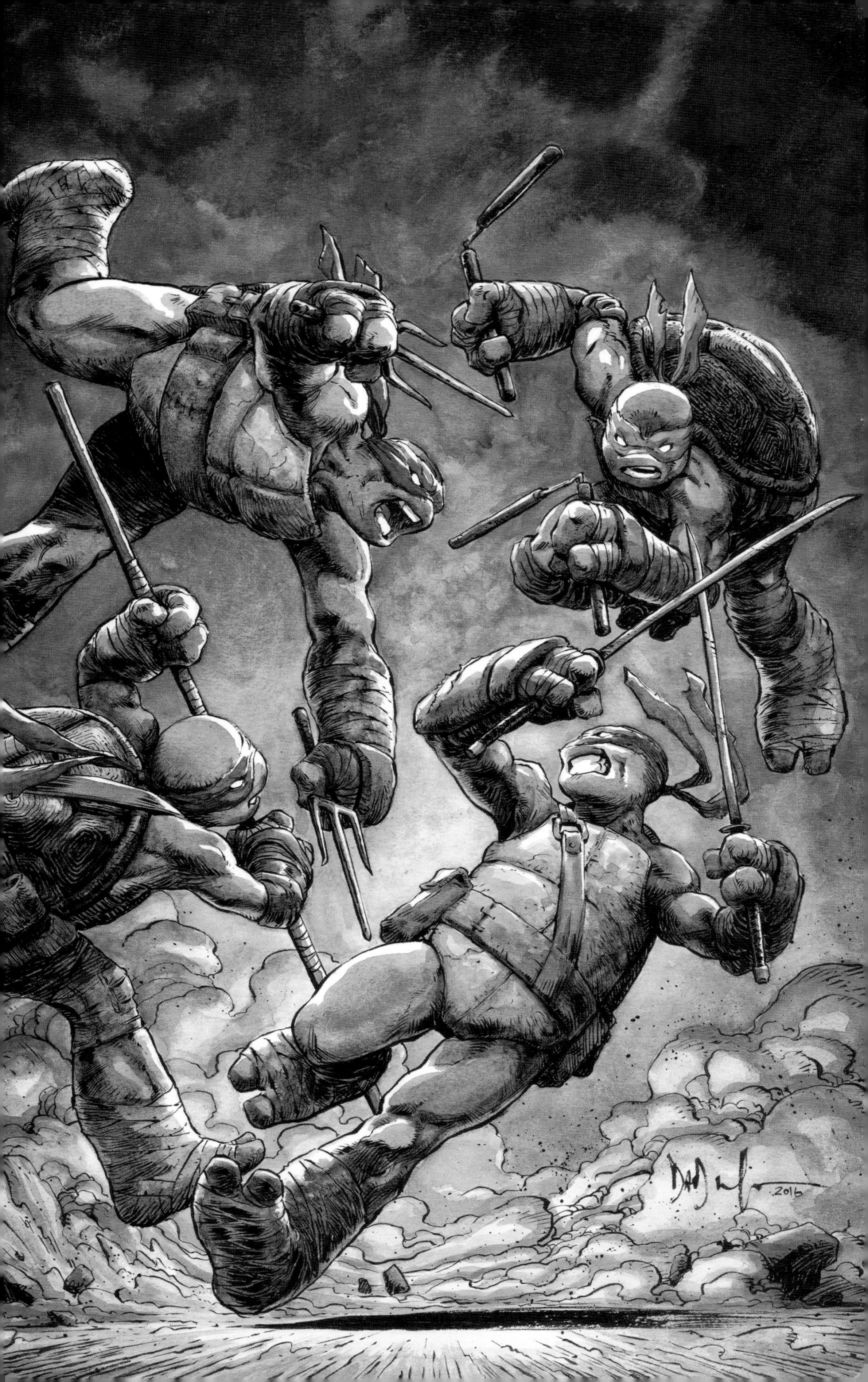

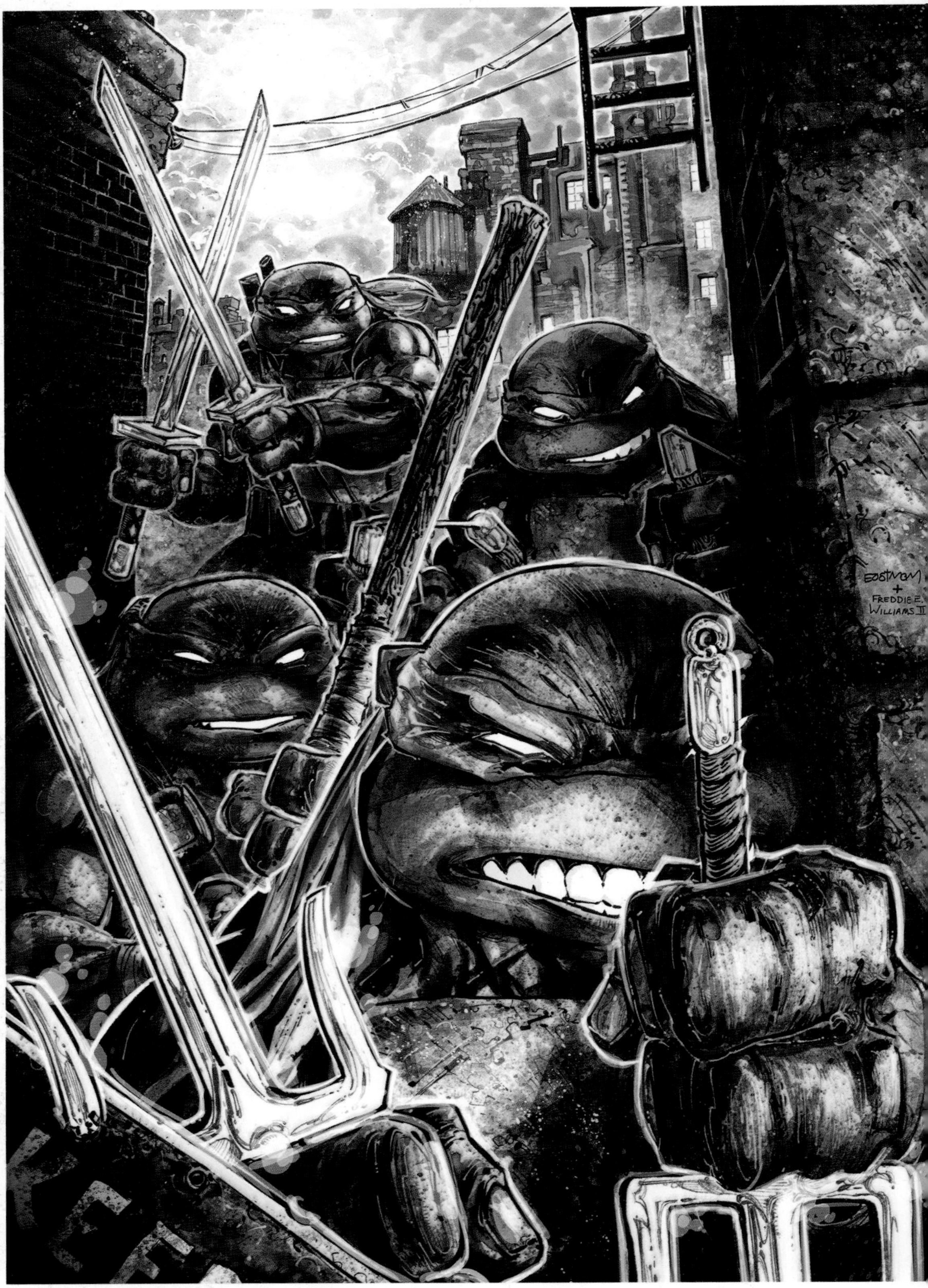
EASTMAN
+
FREDDIE E. WILLIAMS II

ART BY KEVIN EASTMAN AND FREDDIE WILLIAMS II

OPPOSITE PAGE: ART BY KEVIN EASTMAN
AND TOMI VARGA

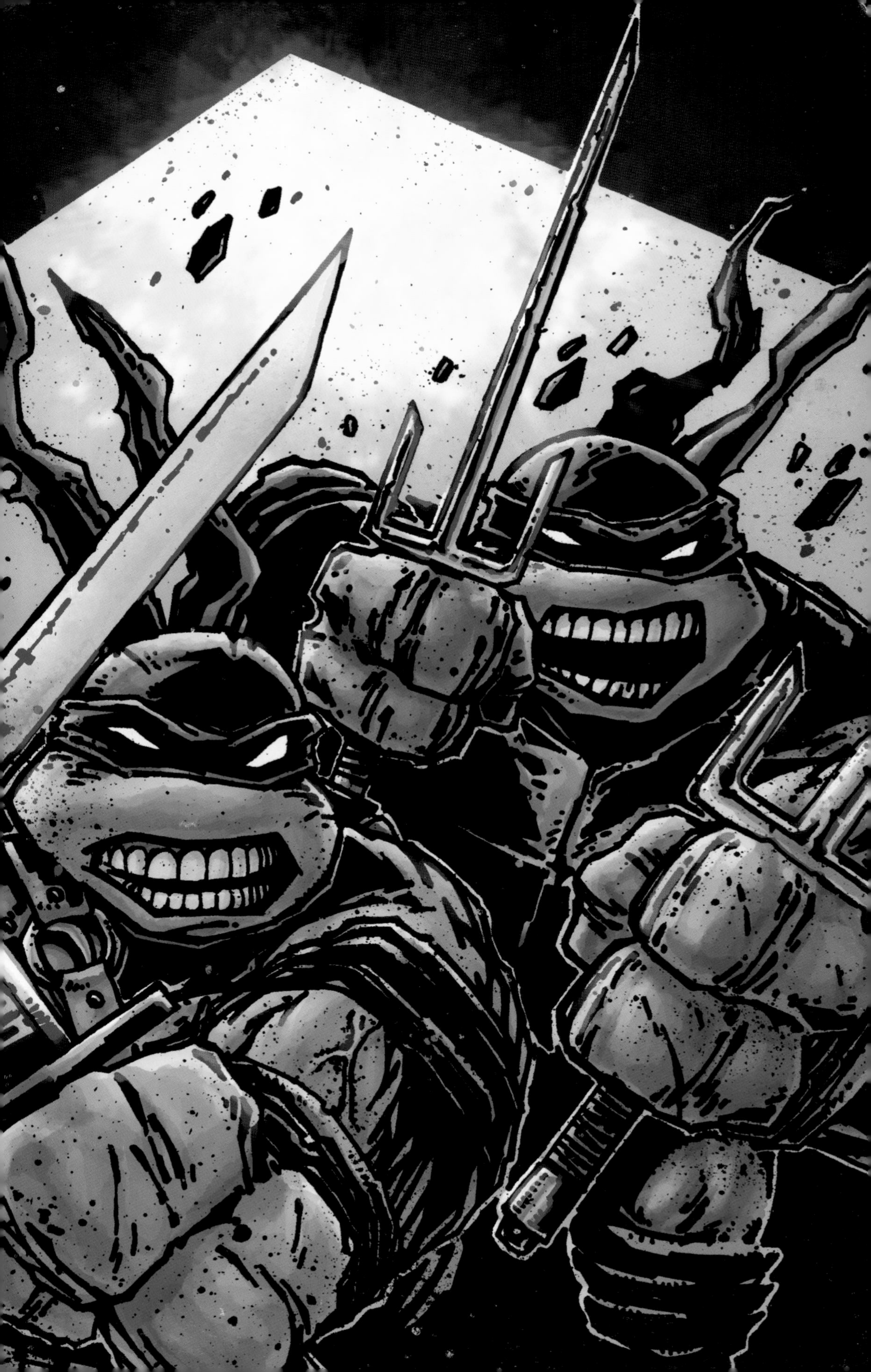

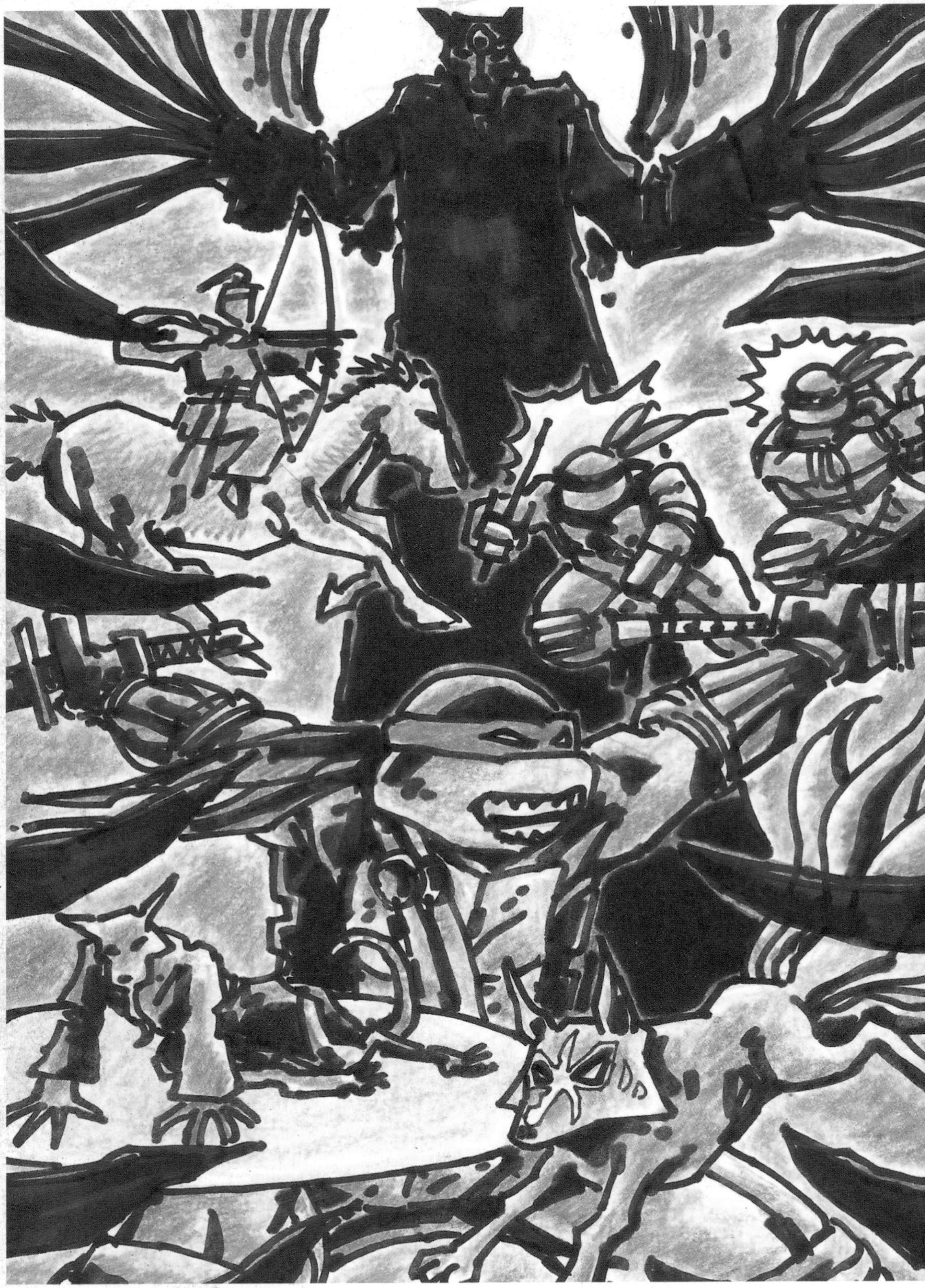

ART BY KEVIN EASTMAN

OPPOSITE PAGE: ART BY DAMIEN COUCEIRO

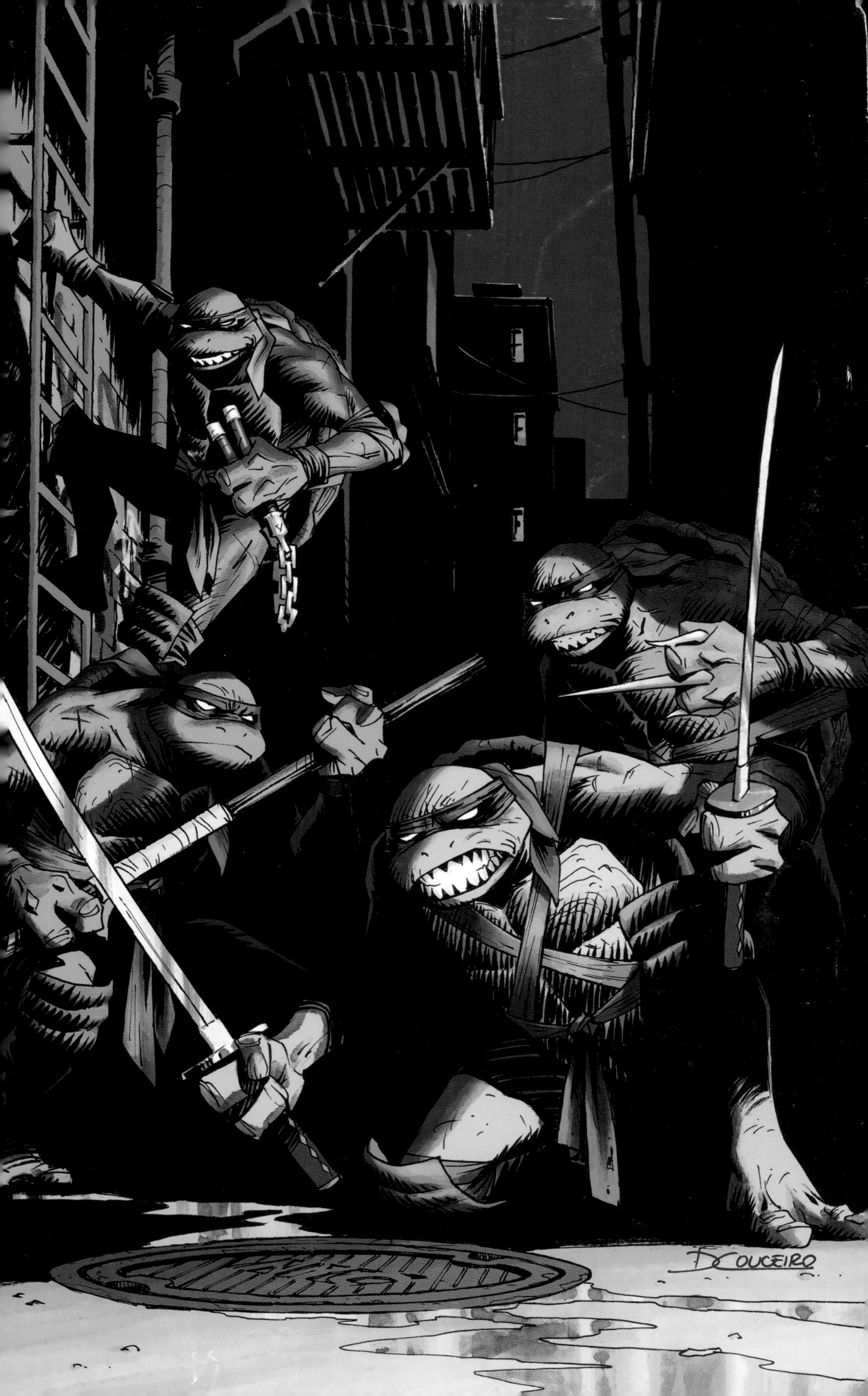

DCOUCEIRO

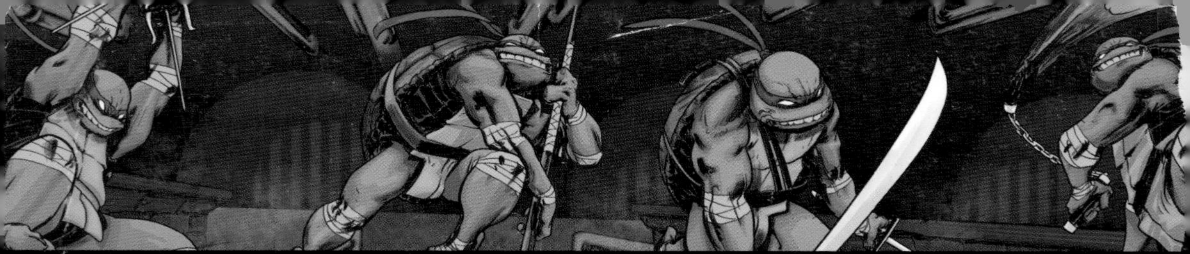

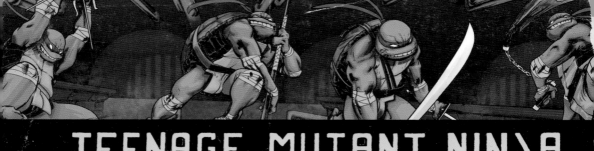

TEENAGE MUTANT NINJA TURTLES

MORE TURTLE ACTION!

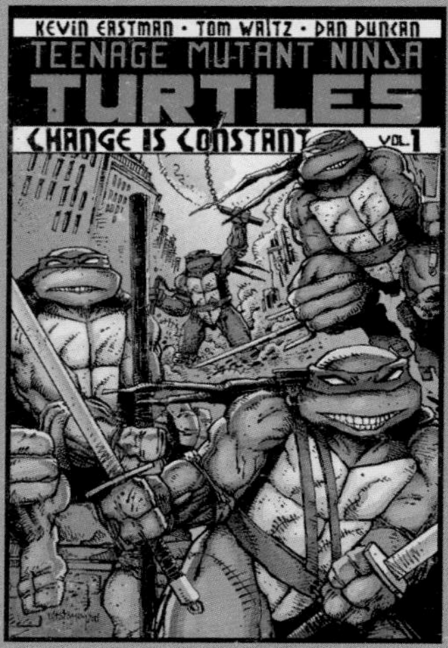

KEVIN EASTMAN · TOM WALTZ · DAN DUNCAN
TEENAGE MUTANT NINJA TURTLES
CHANGE IS CONSTANT VOL. 1

Teenage Mutant Ninja Turtles, Vol. 1:
Change is Constant
ISBN: 978-1-61377-139-6

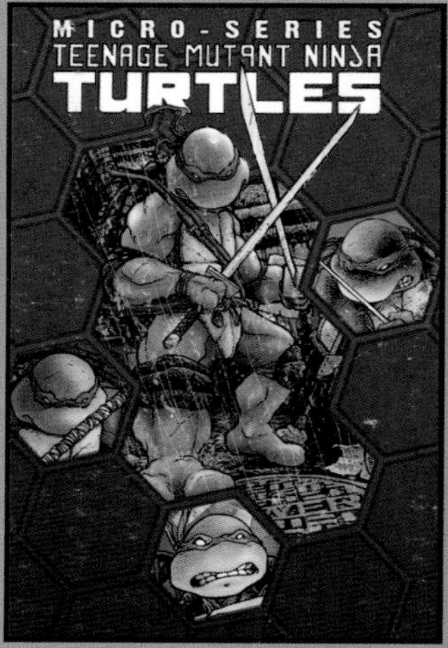

MICRO-SERIES
TEENAGE MUTANT NINJA TURTLES

Teenage Mutant Ninja Turtles:
Micro-Series, Vol. 1
ISBN: 978-1-61377-232-4

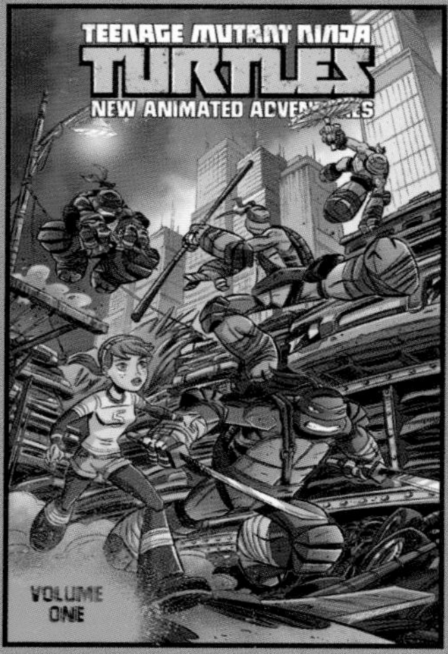

TEENAGE MUTANT NINJA TURTLES
VOLUME ONE

Teenage Mutant Ninja Turtles:
New Animated Adventures, Vol. 1
ISBN: 978-1-61377-856-2

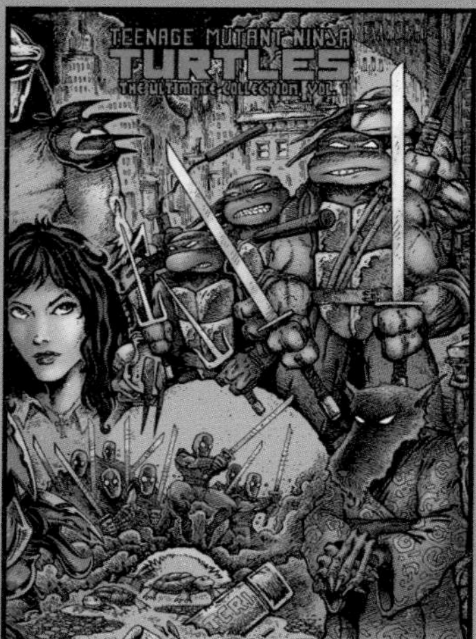

TEENAGE MUTANT NINJA TURTLES
THE ULTIMATE COLLECTION VOL. 1

Teenage Mutant Ninja Turtles
Ultimate Collection, Vol. 1
ISBN: 978-1-61377-007-8

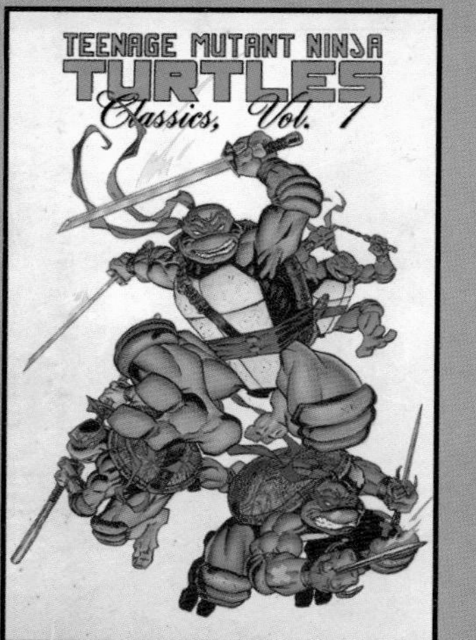

TEENAGE MUTANT NINJA TURTLES
Classics, Vol. 1

Teenage Mutant Ninja Turtles:
Classics, Vol. 1
ISBN: 978-1-61377-234-8

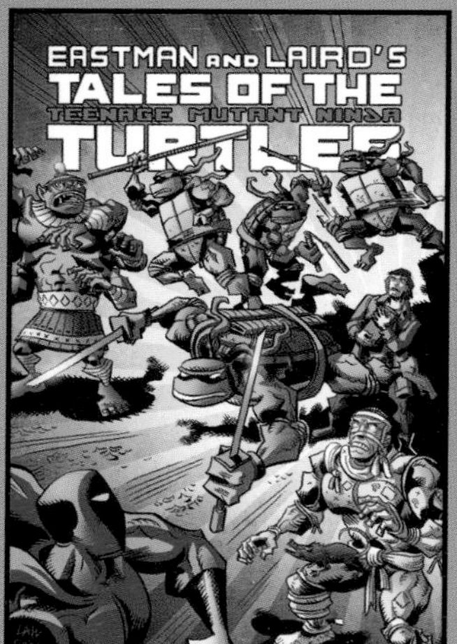

EASTMAN AND LAIRD'S
TALES OF THE
TEENAGE MUTANT NINJA
TURTLES

Tales of the Teenage
Mutant Ninja Turtles, Vol. 1
ISBN: 978-1-61377-416-8